Smelling t

Smelling the Breezes

A Journey through the High Lebanon

RALPH AND MOLLY IZZARD

ELAND
London

First published by Hodder & Stoughton in 1959
This new edition published by Eland Publishing Ltd
61 Exmouth Market, London EC1R 4QL in 2022

ISBN 978 1 78060 198 4

Cover image: *The Izzard family on the road*

Text set in Great Britain by James Morris
Printed in England by Clays Ltd, Elcograf S.p.A

Contents

Author's Note

THE JOURNEY DESCRIBED IN THIS BOOK was made in the summer of 1957 prior to the uprising and disorders of the early part of 1958. Much of the territory we walked through then has now slipped back into the lawlessness common to the country in the last century, and it will be some time before a foreigner can venture with any confidence into the wild mountain regions of the northern Lebanon. The same applies to a great deal of the Beka'a, and the Druze country of the southern Lebanon.

Haphazard and improvised though our journey was, we could not have started without a certain amount of planning and forethought, and advice from the Lebanese Government Tourist Bureau. We should like to thank M Michel Touma, Director of Tourism, for his most useful letter of introduction, and our friend Sami Kerkabi, also of the Bureau of Tourism, for his assistance with maps, itineraries and practical advice.

We should also like to thank our friends Captain and Mrs Peter Norton, RN, of the British Embassy, Beirut, who provided an invaluable backstop in Beirut, and Gerry Stewart and Anthony Daniels, all of whom on separate occasions took the trouble to make long and arduous excursions into the mountains to meet us and bring us stores, money and news from our old life.

Finally, it would be impossible not to acknowledge our great debt to The Hon. Edward Gathorne-Hardy, recently of the British Embassy, Beirut. He it was who first taught us how to enjoy the Lebanon, and many of the places described in this book were first visited by us in his company or on his advice. It is also to him that we owe the acquisition of the invaluable Elias.

Preface

LEBANON IS A SMALL COUNTRY on the Asiatic coast of the Eastern Mediterranean. It has an area of approximately 3,977 square miles, and is surrounded on two sides by Syria, in whose lap it lies, and on the third side by Israel. The actual length of its coastline is approximately 135 miles. Its dominant physical characteristic is a high and abrupt mountain range rising steeply from a narrow coastal plain. This mountain range is the Lebanon, which gives its name to the country. It is a limestone rock in its upper and lower strata, with a layer of sandstone between. The rock is porous, and the snow and the rain seep down into immense underground cisterns. The range is deeply scored by the gorges and chasms of the rivers carving their way through the soft rock to the sea, and it is these rivers, gushing from their caverns in the flanks of the mountains, that give identity and life to the different sections of the mountains. Behind the Lebanon lies a third factor in the composition of the modern Republic of Lebanon. This is the plain of the Beka'a, a long, level rift between the range of the Lebanon and its one-time component, the Anti-Lebanon. The Beka'a is about 110 miles in length, six to ten miles in width, and is 2,500 feet above sea level. The range of mountains known as the Anti-Lebanon is smaller, more arid and less inhabited than the Lebanon itself, and along its crest runs the frontier of Lebanon with Syria.

The coastal plain of Lebanon is of astonishing richness, and its narrow width is crowded with orange and banana groves, with olives and umbrella pines marking the first gentle swell of the foothills. The width of the plain varies. In the north, near Tripoli, it is four miles wide; lower down, near the bay of Jounieh, it is a mile wide. At several places the mountain itself comes right down to the sea, and the coastal road has to edge its way around or through towering cliffs.

The alternations of plain and mountain, valley and mountain, run roughly north to south. The mountain mass itself has two natural delimitations – in the north the River El Kebir, the Eleutherus of antiquity, carves its way through gorges to the sea, and provides a natural frontier for the state; in the south it is the River Litani which, running down the centre of the Beka'a, turns suddenly right-handed through the Lebanon, and enters the sea between Sidon and Tyre. The modern frontier, however, extends further southwards, beyond Tyre, and runs across the rolling upland of what was once Palestine, culminating in the frowning headland of the Ras Nakoura.

Lebanon has no desert, and no indigenous nomads. Its people are farmers and herders, growing citrus fruit and grain on the plains, fruit, vines and olives on the terraced slopes of the hills, and grazing their flocks of goats and sheep on the crests of the high mountain. The characteristic feature of the country is the Lebanon range, and it is this great mass of mountain, split and seamed by its rivers, and cutting off the inhabitants of the coastal strip from the steppe-lands of Syria, that has conditioned the temper of its people.

The long walk we took through the high Lebanon in the summer of 1957 was inspired by no other motive than pleasure. We had lived in Beirut since the autumn of 1954, and had formed the habit of walking about and exploring the countryside whenever we could. It is a very beautiful country, filled with objects of cultural and architectural interest, from the flint chipping of pre-historic man to the Corbusier-inspired constructions of modern architects. Few periods of history are unrepresented, and the reliefs carved on the rocks of the Dog River, where it runs into the sea, commemorate the passing of armies from the Egyptians of the thirteenth century BC warring against the Hittites, through Assyrians, Babylonians, Romans, Ottomans, to the last movement of French Mandatory troops leaving the country in 1946.

The people who inhabit the country are Arab-speaking, but are not Arabs of the pure Semitic strain. The physical structure of the country, with its alternations of plain and mountain, accounts in some measure for this. The mountains for many hundreds of years have served as a refuge for political and religious dissidents from the surrounding areas. Secure in the high, hidden valleys, people have lived their lives in their own way, separate communities existing in close proximity to each other, yet each retaining its own individual characteristics. The people of the plains, however, have been exposed to every influence which conquest and commerce can bring with them. The inland plain of the Beka'a has been a major trade route from time immemorial, linking the civilisations of Mesopotamia with the Nile basin. The coastal plain has been the commercial seaboard of the entire area, and its inhabitants today retain to a remarkable degree the trading instinct and energy which made their Phoenician ancestors the great middlemen of the ancient world. They are commercial adventurers in the purest sense of the word, adepts at trimming their sails to the winds of political change, shrewd, industrious, enterprising, ready to do business anywhere, and seeing all in terms of profit and loss.

The old life of the mountains is dying away, unable to withstand the expanding material prosperity of the towns and the pressures of modern political and social developments. Yet the old virtues of hardihood and independence still remain, the generosity, the unstinting acceptance of, and kindness towards, the stranger. To the people of the Mountain – the *ahl el Jebel*, as the Lebanese call themselves – their name is no empty distinction. It is a way of life that is still valid, and we were absorbed into it for the last summer of our time in the Lebanon.

PART ONE

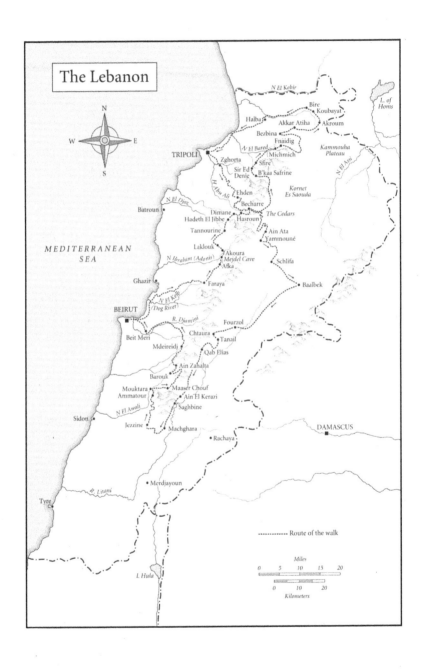

The Lebanon

N El Kebir

L. of Homs

Bire
Koubayat
Halba
Akkar Atiha
Akroum
Bezbina
Fnaidig
Kammouha
Plateau
N' El Bared
Michmich
TRIPOLI
Zghorta
Sfire
Sir Ed
B'kaa Safrine
Denie
H. Abu Ali
Kornet
Es Saouda
Ehden
Becharre
N El Djoz
The Cedars
Batroun
Dimane
Hadeth El Jibbe
Hasroun
Tannourine
Ain Ata
Yammouné
Laklouk
N Ibrahim (Adonis)
Akoura
Mejdel Cave
Schlifa
Afka
MEDITERRANEAN
SEA
Ghazir
Faraya
Baalbek
N' El Kelb
(Dog River)
BEIRUT
R. Djimini
Fourzol
Beit Meri
Chtaura
Mdeireidj
Tanail
Qab Elias
Ain Zahalta
Barouk
Maaser Chouf
Mouktara
Ammatour
Ain El Kerazi
N El Awali
Saghbine
Sidon
DAMASCUS
Jezzine
Machghara
Rachaya
R. Litani
Merdjayoun
Tyre

·········· Route of the walk

Miles
0   5   10   15   20

0   10   20
Kilometers

L. Hula

ONE

We prepare our trip and arrive at Faraya

'FOR GOD'S SAKE don't take a *gendarme* with you. That's asking for trouble. People won't have any confidence in you at all, and you'll find yourself being shot at on principle. Pin your faith on Arab hospitality, drink only spring water and watch out if you meet a man by himself high up in the mountains. He's probably an outlaw, and what he'll want is cigarettes, food and news, and if you give him those you should be all right.'

This was the considered opinion of our quarter in Beirut on the walk we proposed to take with our children through the high mountains of the Lebanon. Our servant Elias Aboujaoude was our channel of information, and we made our decision on the advice he passed on to us.

The walk started as a fancy which grew rapidly into a possibility. We had been living for three years in the Lebanon, and had been very happy there. The news that we were to be recalled to England that autumn had come as a great blow and we determined to use up the three months of leave due to us in enjoying all those things we had liked in the Lebanon to the full. These were the beauty of its landscape, the interest of its history and the friendliness of its inhabitants. Our family consists of four children, and the expense of moving us and keeping us anywhere as a group is one that has to be taken into account. The heat of summer on the coast is considerable and we decided to go up into the mountains. How to live cheaply was the problem. The experience of our excursions and picnics around the country came to our aid. Very frequently, when making for some point of interest, we had had to abandon our car and walk across country to our objective. On these occasions we sometimes hired a donkey from the peasants to carry our youngest child, a sturdy boy whose weight had to be taken into consideration when any long-distance porterage was in prospect.

The possession of donkeys was seen to be the key to the whole idea. Enquiries around the countryside showed us that for a sum of between ten pounds and fifteen pounds sterling we could acquire a young and sound animal, equipped with saddle and harness. The best place to buy donkeys was a district where the farmers depended on them, in default of other means, to carry the produce of the steeply terraced hillsides up and down to the roads. The best way for us to buy donkeys was to get some knowledgeable middleman to do it for us.

As always happens once an idea takes hold, circumstances conspired to help us. A young Lebanese friend, Sami Kerkabi, worked in the Government Tourist Bureau. An enthusiastic speleologist, mountaineer and skier, he had walked over large areas of little-visited country, and understood immediately what we wanted to do. With his help we got maps and roughed out an itinerary, which was to take us northwards up the seaward flank of the Lebanon mountains to the Syrian frontier, over into the Beka'a and back by the lake of Yammoune and the Col des Cedres to our starting point, as yet undecided, in the Metn or Kesrouan districts of the central Lebanon. He also arranged for us to receive an invaluable letter of identification from the Director of Tourism, M Michel Touma.

Discreet enquiries and soundings out by Embassy friends among officials of the Ministry of the Interior and officers of the *gendarmerie* and security services produced very unfavourable reactions. The northern mountain and forest area was unsettled; it would be very inadvisable for foreigners to go beyond the usual summer-resort areas. Certain areas were quite impossible without escort, the inhabitants being notoriously turbulent and hostile to strangers. This reaction was so unpromising that we did not dare pursue it further, lest knowledge of our plans should impel the authorities to obstruct them. Many of our Beirut friends were equally discouraging. 'You must be mad,' they said, 'to go trailing about in the mountains with all those children. Think of the discomfort, the dirt, the impracticability of it all.' Bedouin, bandits and bugs were spoken of in equal terms and unsubstantiated accounts of outrage and extortion were called to mind. But other friends were more resolute, and demonstrated their sympathy by practical assistance. A tent was lent us, and arrangements made for contacting and financing us.

Our servant Elias, in the meantime, had been following the discussions and plans with the keenest interest. Nominally engaged as a cook in our first month in Beirut, he stayed with us our entire time in Lebanon as general factotum, gardener, nursemaid, adviser and friend. The son of a landowning peasant farmer, a Maronite of the Metn district, Elias had a quickness of wit and invention, a good humour and a capacity for complete absorption in the moment which made him an admirable companion. Brave, impetuous, improvident, agile, enquiring, optimistic, he was a friend and favourite of the children from the moment he entered our household. His English was erratic, but in the course of time we evolved a pidgin Anglo-Arabic which we all used with versatility, supplementing our varying command of Arabic and English.

Our life being lived on the open plan, he entered into the problems of the family with zest and sympathy. 'My father used to have lots of donkeys,' he said to us; 'as a younger man he was well known as a pack-driver in the Metn and Kesrouan. I learned how to handle donkeys from him when I was a boy, and as I am a mountain man myself, I'd better come with you to give you a hand.' This decision on Elias' part was of inestimable value to us, and he amply fulfilled his promise as pack-driver. Unconvinced by the reaction to our oblique enquiries about our route, we confided the result to Elias and suggested he seek out in our quarter such people as he could find from the northern mountain area, and bring us what advice he could from them.

This was quickly done. The man who dug our garden, the shoemaker around the corner, the lodgekeeper's uncle, Elias' father, the grocer across the street, the man who sold fruit, were all passionately interested in our project and pleased and excited to give us their help and advice on it. The message Elias brought back was the one at the beginning of the chapter. It confirmed our own feelings and we decided to follow them.

* * *

The period from the inception of the idea to the putting of it into practice was a matter of only a few weeks. Our preparations were scanty and haphazard in the extreme, and we laid in the minimum of stores, being determined from the beginning to live off the country and to adjust ourselves to the conditions in which we found ourselves. The only concession we made to our alien status was a knapsack full of books and an old tea-chest filled with small necessities and luxuries such as a looking-glass, scissors, first-aid kit, cream, talcum powder, soap, toothpaste, lavatory paper, sweets, packs of cards and a set of dice. Our medicines consisted of a bottle of mercurochrome, a packet of elastoplast and tubes of aspirin and entero-vioform, in case of stomach upsets. As it transpired, we could have done without any of them. This treasure-trove was known as Pandora's box, and was regarded with fascinated interest by the children.

We fixed on Tuesday, the 16th of July, as our starting date, and at ten o'clock that morning we were ready to go. Our bedding and gear was stuffed into three duffle-bags, relics of the War. We had two Lilos and a collapsible army cot, three sleeping-bags and a neat tent which packed into a canvas container. The kitchen gear and stores went into two cardboard cartons, and consisted of a few tins of sardines and meat, porridge, rice, sugar, some garlic, a box of salt, a bottle of oil, some plates, cups and glasses, coffee and the necessary apparatus to make it, a primus stove and a primitive charcoal grill made out of tin. Three aluminium pots, a kettle and two water-bottles and a jar made up our total. A length of nylon climbing rope, an old felt mat, two mosquito nets, a child's pillow and two air cushions were added, and we were ready to go. Our clothes were the oldest we had, and the children wore jeans. Apart from a pair of climbing boots, the family footgear consisted of sandshoes, sandals and a pair of walking shoes each for the children and their mother. Everyone had a straw hat, but these proved impractical and were eventually abandoned for *keffiyahs*, the loose Arab headcloth, which is easily the best protection against the fierce rays of the sun.

Elias appeared in a startling new guise which colours all our subsequent recollections of him. During our Beirut life he had something of the dapper, spiv-like air of the city slicker – glossy hair, pointed shoes, an elegant long nail on the little finger of his clean, well-kept hands. Only his wild flashing eye and a certain deftness and agility in all he undertook, combined with his willingness to learn and experiment, distinguished him from the rest of the sleek, white-jacketed, well-trained manservants of the town. But with the prospect of a return to his earlier way of life before him, Elias shed his city-veneer like a suit of clothes, and emerged before us wiry, neat and hardy, clad in cord breeches and tall boots, an old GI windproof jacket on his back and a straw hat set at a rakish angle on his lustrous black locks.

Our family of four children consisted of Miles, aged nine; Anthea, aged eight; Sabrina, aged six; and Sebastian, aged four. All of us, except Anthea, became a year older in the course of the trip, Sebastian becoming five two days after our return to Beirut. The two youngest children had been born in the Levant; the elder two had been born in India and America respectively, but all had spent the greater part of their life in the Eastern Mediterranean area. Prior to living in Lebanon we had spent half of each year in Cyprus and from earliest childhood the children had been accustomed to make themselves understood in Greek, Turkish, Arabic and French, to eat what was offered to them and to take people on trust. We knew them to be our best passports, an immediately comprehensible affirmation of our confidence and trust in the people we were among. 'A house without children is a house without light', says an Arab proverb, and the possession of our children ensured us a warm and sympathetic welcome wherever we went. The question would never arise of our having to protect them; among a people kind and indulgent to children, they, at a pinch, would probably protect us. For the children themselves, the whole project seemed merely an extension of the picnics and excursions to which they were accustomed. Merry, uncomplaining, adaptable, they presented not the slightest problem, and moved from place to place without doubt or hesitation, entering into immediate contact with the people of wherever we found ourselves, and accumulating vast collections of bottle-tops, cartridge-cases, flints, fossils, caterpillars, beetles, small animals, flowers, sardine tins (used as make-believe cars), sticks and clasp-knives, all of which had to be carefully conveyed down to Beirut for safe-keeping. The only link with their past life that Sabrina and Sebastian retained was two teddy-bears, who went to sleep with them each night, and they were always most solicitous for news of Balthazar, our cat, when Elias went down to Beirut.

* * *

We had decided to start on our walk from Faraya, a small winter-sports resort 3,500 feet up in the Kesrouan, less than two hours' drive from Beirut. Nothing in particular impelled us to choose it, except that the valleys leading up to it were devoted to fruit-growing and donkeys were presumably easy to obtain there, and beyond the village there was a fine spring with a very charming coffee-house beside it, which would serve as a base from which to purchase donkeys.

Ten o'clock saw us all piling into one of our neighbourhood taxis, a huge aquamarine-and-white Chrysler, driven by one Henri, an old friend. We sailed up out of the steaming heat and glare of summer-time Beirut with the radio blaring the latest song-hit and Elias and Henri excitedly discussing the best way to set about purchasing donkeys. Soon the pallid coastline fell away beneath us and we were climbing up through the pine-woods, turning our backs to the sparkling blue sea behind us and moving inland to a landscape of great chasm-like valleys, terraced hillsides and bare, tawny vistas of tumbled mountain peaks. The sun beat down remorselessly out of a pale blue sky but, as we got higher, the sharp mountain air was dry and stimulating after the humidity of the coast, and the breeze fanned us coolly as we sped along.

We were now in the hottest and driest season of the year, the season at which the vegetation god Tammuz, the Adonis of the Greeks, in one version of the great regional legend, descended into the underworld and all plant life languished and died in sympathy until the love-goddess Ishtar succeeded in ransoming him, and brought him back in triumph to the living world. His return coincided with the arrival of the first winter rains and the renewal of growth, and is the key to the understanding of the religious beliefs of the ancient Semitic people of this area. To a primitive agricultural and stock-raising people, control and propitiation of the forces of growth and reproduction by means of worship and magic is essential, and the drying-out of the land in the summer heat is an affliction only to be overcome by the hope of the rebirth and renewal of the next season.

As we neared our destination, the donkey quest started in earnest. The taxi would squeal to a stop and Elias and Henri would leap out to tackle some startled peasant, and a variety of dusty-looking animals would be inspected. No one seemed unduly surprised to be asked if they wanted to sell their beast, and everyone entered into the negotiations with the greatest zest. We ourselves kept modestly in the background, and it never crossed the villagers' minds that we were anything other than harmless foreign tourists. After sundry stops and starts of this nature, we eventually reached Faraya, a village straggling along a tree-hung stream, in a green amphitheatre enclosed by high, tawny rock walls. The road continued on upwards for about a mile, to where the Nebaa el Asel – the spring of honey – gushed out of a rocky cleft and ran turbulently down in a series of small falls and cascades to the village below. Just below the source of the stream is a ford, and a track leads off over the brow of the hill. Beside the ford is a built-up terrace, shady with willows and poplars, and here is the coffee shop.

We unloaded the taxi, and ordered food and beer. This soon came in the shape of skewers of hot grilled kebabs folded in flaps of Arab bread, with a bowl of mint-sprinkled tomato salad and dishes of yoghurt and *hommos* – pounded chick-peas mixed with garlic and oil – to support it. Over cups of coffee we discussed our next moves, assisted by the waiter Shafik, a pleasant young man who spoke good English, having worked with the British Army during the War. The patrons of the coffee shop, a fat man playing tric-trac with a priest, another man talking business with the proprietor, were full of advice and encouragement. The upshot was that Elias went off with Henri, who was returning to Beirut, and we moved our gear into two small rooms above the terrace where we proposed to sleep that night.

The fresh, cool air was a delight after the damp, exhausting heat of Beirut, and the coffee shop, with its rows of small tables and chairs, and the water rushing past in artificial runnels channelled through the terrace, was simple and adequate for all our needs. The pollarded willows and tall, leafy poplars sheltered the terrace from the sun, and the quick, brown stream hurrying among the rocks and boulders of its bed added a soothing background of sound to the drowsy heat of the afternoon. As the afternoon wore on, a clattering of hooves and shouted Arabic roused us from our idleness. The children came running to bid us come down to the ford and, following them, we saw a party of wild-looking Bedouin loading glistening goatskins of water on to the backs of their mares. We watched these harsh-faced, angry-looking men with interest as, with their robes girded up around their waists, they strove and sweated to heave the heavy skins on the racy-looking brood mares. A pretty little foal flirted about madly on the outskirts of the group, and the mares, their eyes starting nervously in their small heads, shifted restlessly among the stones of the pool above the ford. At last the skins were filled and loaded, and with a prodigious shouting and trampling the riders swung themselves up on to their beasts, and rode off up the flank of the mountain. The sight of these people stirred and encouraged us, and we were confirmed in our determination to get off as soon as we could.

Late that evening Elias returned, leading a large milk-white donkey. Everyone flocked out to inspect the new purchase, who cost one hundred and sixty lira (approximately eighteen pounds sterling) complete with his gear. His size and colour showed that he was bred in Cyprus, whose donkeys, like its mules, are famous in the Levant for their strength and endurance. Everyone congratulated us on our acquisition, and we were gratified to discover that he came with a certificate in Arabic to the effect that 'this gentleman has paid his taxes'. Elias was very proud of his purchase and swore he was strong enough to carry two hundred kilos, but we decided to wait over another day and buy a second animal.

The night air was cold up in the mountains, and we were all huddled into pullovers and woollen socks. The events of the day had worn us all out, and we went to bed at half-past eight, the children bundling up into two beds, and ourselves lying awake for a while listening to the shrieks and ululations of the radio in the coffee shop and the slap of the wooden counters on the tric-trac board below.

We awoke at dawn after a marvellously refreshing sleep and lay drowsing until seven o'clock. The terrace was still fresh and damp from the night, and the trees glistened in the early sunlight as we ate our breakfast. Elias was off early to the Bedouin encampment hidden in the fold of the hills and returned eventually with a diminutive grey donkey, a shaggy creature like an animated doormat, but with a hopeless, resigned air of patience that won the children's hearts immediately. The two little ones were delighted with him. The big white donkey had a certain wary aggressiveness about him which was rather daunting, but this new acquisition seemed no more alarming than a stuffed toy. 'He very good donkey,' said Elias, defending the undistinguished appearance of his choice, 'he only need little stick.' This caught the children's fancy, and Little Stick became the small donkey's name, and as a natural consequence the white one was known as Big Stick. Little Stick came to us with very makeshift gear, and cost seventy-five lira, about nine pounds sterling. Elias' immediate concern was to find him a decent saddle of sorts, and he took Miles off with him down to the village, to help with the donkeys while he negotiated a purchase.

We, in the meantime, decided to walk over the mountain in the direction of the Jisr el Hadjar, a natural bridge spanning the narrow gorge of the Nahr el Leben – the river of milk – not far below where the river wells up from the base of a cliff. The small pool it forms at its source is of the clearest, coldest water imaginable, green as an emerald, and the solitude and remoteness of its surroundings give a quality of mystery to its silent emergence. The gorge through which it runs is narrow and tumbled with rocks, and the river works its way down through channels and crevices. On either hand the rounded hillside is terraced by man, and it is surprising to look down from the cliffs above and see the cultivation extending in a narrow bridge from one side to the other, while underneath gapes the dark, shadowy cleft of the gorge.

The sun was hot, and the children soon decided to give up, and ran back across the stony hillside to play under the trees of the coffee shop, and paddle in the stream. We walked on slowly up the contours of the mountain flank, until the swell of the land hid the spring from us. All was dried up and desiccated, only thistles and spurge and a handsome blue teazle still survived among the stones and yellowed bents of the hillside. Above towered the shimmering limestone cliffs of the amphitheatre and we seemed to be alone in a world of rock and shale and bare, burnt-out earth. A sudden distant hail caused us to look sharply to our right, and down below on a sunburnt knoll we saw the black tents of a Bedouin encampment. We turned off across the hillside towards them and found there the horsemen of the previous day. Around the encampment grazed the mares and their foals; donkeys, goats and sheep straggled over the hillside and were discernible high up on the rocky walls of the cliffs.

The chief of the encampment was a lean, grizzled old man in a long grey robe, belted around in his middle with a leather belt. He it was who had hailed us with a cry of invitation and he welcomed us with a warm smile and strong handshake. 'Be welcome,' he said, 'sit and join us in our tent.' Half a dozen other men clustered around him in the shadow of the tent – shaggy, villainous-looking creatures in coarse, yellow-dyed robes and rough sheepskin jackets. Their white *keffiyahs* fell over their shoulders and the long, tangled curls of the young men gave a somewhat effeminate appearance to their sunburnt, rosy-cheeked faces. They all shook hands with us in turn, their downy lips parting to reveal flashing white teeth, the eye-teeth gleaming with gold. We sat down beside the open charcoal hearth, with the beaked coffee-pots standing in the coals, cushions and bolsters at our back, and our feet tucked up tidily beneath us. The tent was pitched north to south and a pleasant cool air fanned us lightly as we sat looking out over the tawny hillside. Our hosts were very affable. They were Syrians from Homs, the great horse breeding district of Syria, and were taking their beasts down to Beirut, presumably to sell the colts to the racing stables there. The goats and sheep helped supply them on their slow march southwards, and what remained would be sold off to the butchers at the end of the journey.

We drank hot, bitter coffee spiced with cardamom from little cups produced from a neat travelling case, and then we had glasses of sweet tea. Cigarettes were exchanged, and paper and tobacco were manipulated for us into the required shape. Conversation was a little halting, owing to our uncertain Arabic, but it went on well enough on the question-and-answer level. There were no women; the group was a party travelling down to the coast on business. Two round-faced, rosy-cheeked little hobbledehoys of thirteen were the youngest there, and they hung bright-eyed and alert on the conversation of their elders. The older men were a hard-bitten, jovial crew, but the young men had a dandified, languishing manner which accorded well with their quick, glancing looks and graceful gestures. The rear of the tent was piled with great sacks of stores, and before we left the Sheikh's brother, a corpulent, good-humoured fellow, disappeared behind the screen and reappeared with a tray of yoghurt, fresh bread, *tahina* and a plate of sticky sweetmeats made of ground peanuts, mixed with honey and rose-water. This we were pressed to eat and the assembled company watched us carefully and encouraged us to further effort. The meal finished, we were free to go, having spent about an hour in their company. We again shook hands all round and amid many expressions of friendliness and goodwill, we thanked our hosts for their hospitality and walked off in the direction of the natural bridge.

Having scrambled down through the gorge to the terraced hillside beyond, we came back towards the coffee shop through terraces of beans and tomatoes, whose owners were busy irrigating them from little channels carried off from the tumbling stream. It was hot and empty on the hillside and we startled two small shepherdesses who, in mauve dresses and straw hats, were idling in the shade of a solitary tree while their goats dozed in the shadows about them.

Our business in Faraya was now done and we were ready to start in the morning. Our first objective was Afka, over the wall of mountain beyond the valley, at the source of the Nahr Ibrahim, the river Adonis of antiquity and legend. The rivers of the Lebanon range run roughly east to west and consequently on our northward progress we should be going against the grain of the country, moving from one river valley to the next, but crossing the ribs of the mountain system as near the central spine as we could. In this way we were to find ourselves constantly alternating between the abundant water and fruit cultivation of the river basins and the bare, harsh uplands of the grazing areas.

Our last afternoon in Faraya was enlivened by a violent fusillade from the terrace below which brought us all out of bed, where we had been dozing through the heat. Two sportsmen and two *gendarmes*, after a convivial luncheon assisted by plenty of *arak*, were having a shooting competition, firing at the stones on the opposite bank of the stream. The children were very excited by this and rushed out to collect the shell cases. We ate supper quietly on the shadowy terrace, settled our bill and went to bed early – our gear piled up in a store beside the terrace and our spirits high in anticipation of the morning.

TWO

Faraya to Afka and the source of the Adonis River

WE WERE UP JUST AFTER FOUR O'CLOCK, shivering in our pullovers in the grey pre-dawn light. Everyone was very silent and excited and as Elias loaded the two donkeys with the aid of Shafik the waiter, the children sat huddled on chairs drinking little cups of strong coffee. At last we were ready and with warm handshakes and farewells to Shafik, we crossed the bridge and started up the winding road into the hills. As we rounded the first bend we could look back and see him standing at the end of the terrace watching us and waving vigorously, and we all waved back for as long as we could see him.

Sebastian and Sabrina were travelling slung in sacks on either side of the small donkey, Anthea perched on the top of the white one's load. The sun had not yet struck over the eastern cliff, and we walked on through uplands of ripe corn, with the valley cleaving its way seaward on our left-hand side. After a while our track turned up into a subsidiary valley and led through plum orchards where the fruit was still ripening on the boughs, and past occasional scattered houses. We were all very pleased with ourselves: 'This is the life,' we thought, as we walked easily along the beaten earth track and breathed the sweet, fresh mountain air.

The track deteriorated and began to wind up through a desolate, stony valley. We were leaving the area of cultivation behind and the landscape became increasingly empty and severe. We drank at a spring which welled out among the stones beside our path, now a boulder-strewn gully in a deserted glen, and continued upward until we came out on a small plateau where two glens ran into each other. Here there was a stone hovel with two women scalding milk over a smoky fire. They appeared very poor and ragged in comparison with the peasants inhabiting the orchards around Faraya. In answer to Elias' queries they indicated the left-hand fork – 'Our men always go that way over to Afka' – and gave us some sour milk to drink, which was very refreshing.

The sun was now striking over the tops of the mountains and the day was beginning to warm up. The right-hand fork led desolately up into nothing, but the left-hand one went up in a series of rocky ridges to what appeared to be a pass. It looked a fairly steep pitch, but we could see goat-tracks leading up the rocky shelves and the women were insistent that this was the right route. The small donkey went up confidently, setting his feet down neatly and scrambling from one level to another. We took the children off the donkeys and, taking the little ones on our backs, made a series of sharp, exhausting pushes to the shelter of an overhang of rocks evidently used by shepherds and goats as a refuge from the heat of the sun.

Meanwhile, Elias was having trouble with Big Stick. At the first shelf he jibbed, slipped his load and sat down. Consternation from above, and a volley of oaths from Elias. The load adjusted – and part taken by the two men – another anxious scramble began, while far below the women gaped up, open-mouthed, at the activities of the strangers. It was a hideous ascent, for we were going up the edge of a dried watercourse and at one point had to cross over its tumbled boulders. It was so steep we could only go a few yards at a time, then we would subside, heaving and panting, on to a boulder. Elias whacked and heaved and shouted like ten men, now coaxing, now shoving, now roaring in an access of rage, and gradually we worked up towards a great mass of boulders we could see right above us and which we felt must be the top of the pass. At last, after an hour, we lay exhausted on a patch of green turf just below these rocks, feeling limp after the arduous climb, but smiling and pleased with ourselves for having been undefeated by this first obstacle. Elias produced some sweets from his pocket and we lay there blissfully for a quarter of an hour, recovering, and trying to get our bearings in the tumbled grey mountain mass before us. The children did not seem put out by the turn of events. The elder two had come up very gamely through the rocks and scree, and the two little ones had done part of the scramble on their own, aided by encouraging advice and porterages from their mother.

Standing silently on the rocks above us, we were surprised to discover a black-clad shepherd who had been wonderingly observing us as we lay laughing below him on the springy turf. Coming up to him, we found that the rocks were not the crest as we had thought, but the edge of a broad, undulating, enclosed grazing area. Another shepherd was perched some distance away, upright on a rock, idly fingering his reed flute. All around were goats, black and brown; apart from them the solitude was intense. The shallow cup-like depression lay open and exposed to the pale sky; only the tinkle of the goat-bells and the occasional long hallooing calls of the shepherds broke the silence. They controlled their flocks by pitching stones. An accurately shied stone was sufficient to turn a beast in the direction wanted and to keep the different flocks from trespassing on another's grazing area, whose boundaries were marked by small cairns.

These shepherds would spend all day up on the deserted mountain-tops with just a twist of hard goat cheese and a flap of bread for sustenance until their return at night for the milking. They wore the usual black baggy *shewals* of the Lebanese mountaineers, a trouser made with a tight-fitting leg like a jodhpur, but so full at the top that the seat falls in folds between the legs, making it a garment giving great ease of movement and providing a comfortable pad on which to sit. On their feet were heavy boots and on their heads a twisted black headcloth wrapped round a stiff pointed felt skull-cap. Their jackets were short and braided, and were open over a collarless pleated shirt. This is a costume worn by almost all the mountain people, varied from district to district by different headcloths and ways of tying them. Occasionally their jackets are navy blue, with black braiding, but mostly they seem to prefer black, reserving any colour they wear for their round-necked shirts.

Directed by the shepherds, we set off across the upland. The ground rose gradually and we began to labour as we dragged on over the grassy slopes. At last a cool, fresh breeze blowing into our faces told us the pass was near and with a final effort we thrust ourselves up. A magnificent prospect spread out beneath us. We were standing at last on the crest of the range, about 6,000 feet up; below us the mountain swooped down in wide, yellow shelves, intersected at intervals by bands of precipitous rock to a point where, far, far beneath us, it suddenly broke off into the deep blue and purple valley of the Adonis. It was an astonishing sight, and beyond the wide gash of the valley we could see fold upon fold of mountain stretching away into the distance. We all stood silent and astonished, so many strangers upon our peak in Darien, and for the first time some concept of the scale of the country entered into our minds. Yet the children seemed completely undaunted, and flopped down in the long, dry grass, then gradually started gathering the few campions and scabious still growing among the rocks, drank some water, and wondered about lunch.

It was now mid-morning, and though the sun beat down, the air was fresh and cool and the donkeys, despite their efforts, plucked at thistle heads and browsed among the bents without any sign of distress. We seemed to have crossed the mountain further down than we had intended; looking towards the right we could see where Afka should be, far up at the top of the enormous mile-wide valley in front of us. Down below, almost on the lip of the chasm, we could see tiny rectangular black objects, like so many matchboxes on the vast tablecloth of mountain. These were the tents of a settlement of graziers, and around them we could see little dots which indicated cattle and livestock. They were a long way away, but so steep was the fall of the mountain that they seemed almost at our feet.

We started off slowly, seeking a way down to the tents so far beneath us. As long as we remained near the crest the going was good, but jutting falls of rock compelled us to traverse downwards across a series of narrow, turfy ledges. The further we descended, the more shaly and uncertain became our footing and the fall of the land so acute that from above it looked as if we were on the edge of a precipice. In fact this was not so, but we were not to know it. The small donkey seemed surefooted and at ease on this difficult terrain, and had probably come this way before with his Bedouin owners; he certainly seemed to know the direction in which he wanted to go. The big one was less happy, and much more heavily burdened, and as we straggled down across the mountainside, the inevitable happened. Stuck on a ledge that had petered out, he lunged desperately upwards in an attempt to cut across diagonally to one further up. His load slipped and, losing his balance, he tipped slowly down the shaly slope in a series of somersaults. We were all aghast, and pressed back, shaken, against the sides of the mountain, while bits and pieces of the load came crashing off and Pandora's box sailed off into the blue in a cloud of soap-powder, sweets and lavatory paper.

* * *

Some of the party had been ahead, reconnoitring a narrow track which had appeared on the mountainside leading in the direction we wanted. To their astonished eyes, the donkey's sudden fall had all the horrifying surprise of an avalanche, especially as from below he appeared to be coming down right on top of them. A large rock broke his fall. Jamming up against it, he was caught and held, and everybody converged as best they could on what we confidently expected to be a dead or seriously injured donkey. But no, once his load was cut, he got shakily to his feet and stood gazing around with a surprised air. Well he might, for behind him up the mountainside was a shattered trail of pots, plates, glasses and kitchen gear, and before him a dizzy drop over a slippery rock-fall. Sabrina was the first to recover and climbed nimbly down to retrieve as much of Pandora's box as lay near at hand. In this way we recovered scissors, some medicines and a few sweets but the bulk of our stores had disappeared down the hillside. This was a blow, and we decided to split the party, for, as our water-bottles were smashed or empty, we were anxious to get to water as soon as possible. The children and their mother should go on down by foot to the encampment below to get help and the two men should retrieve what they could and follow on more slowly.

The people in the encampment below had been aware of unexpected movement on the mountain above but it had been too far away for them to see what had happened. They were a family of goat graziers, whose homesteads were down below in the Adonis valley, but who passed the summer months grazing their flocks in the high mountain. The children were received by two charming young girls who hastened to bring them yoghurt and bread, and spread mats for them to rest on beneath a rough goat-hair shelter. The two little ones promptly fell asleep, while a group of young men hurriedly set off carrying ropes and a pot of water.

They met the donkey party slowly coming down the track and bore them back in triumph to the encampment. The family chieftain – a stocky, amiable old man called Abu Bechara – came himself to greet us, flanked by numerous sons and sons-in-law, daughters and dependants. The young men were a rough, merry crew, but strong and rosy-faced and quick to help Elias unload and unpack the baggage. The family were Christians and lived among their flocks and craggy rocks in patriarchal state. Abu Bechara bade us come and drink coffee with him, and so we followed him through the encampment, where a few fowls were pecking in the scrub, to where he had a leafy shelter constructed on the edge of the cliff, a dizzy drop filling up most of the foreground. Here we reclined on sheepskins and bolsters in airy comfort, while his old wife brought coffee and later tea and goats' milk for the children. We were pleased to discover that Abu Bechara knew the father of our Beirut maid Hanne, a patriarch like himself, who lived a little lower down the valley: 'Why don't you take one of my girls when you get back to Beirut? I should be pleased for them to go into a house I know and earn some money,' and he indicated the smiling, sturdy, blonde Aziza and gentle, dark-eyed Latife who had first greeted us.

We stayed conversing with Abu Bechara until the flocks started streaming in at sunset, hundreds of goats converging in thin streams from the high, bare tops of the mountains. The whole of the encampment was filled with the bleating and baaing of these beasts, the shouts and calls of the shepherds and the cries of the women and children herding them into their enclosures. The dust of their passage hung in a golden haze about the camp, caught in the glow of the setting sun. The milch-goats were separated out into stone enclosures, and soon the spurt of milk and the low speech of the milkers were heard all around, while the rest of the flocks were penned on rocky outcrops of the cliff, and shut off there by hedges of thorn quickly pulled across the neck of the corral. It was extraordinary to see the goats silhouetted against the glowing evening sky, settling themselves down on to the ledges and crevices of their prison, while the cliff dropped down on three sides into a frightening abyss. Long after dusk the flocks came streaming in, and the counting, calling, cutting out and milking continued by the light of smoky lanterns, while the shepherds themselves settled ravenously to the food prepared for them around the different hearths.

We had installed ourselves a little above the camp and were preparing for an early night. We had water brought by the girls from a brackish spring at the foot of the escarpment. Further along, they told us, was an excellent spring where they went with the women of the camp each morning to draw water. We laid our sheepskin jackets on the floor of the tent, then put down two blankets and an eiderdown quilt and pillows, and settled the children in a row, covering them with another blanket and a huge handwoven rug from the Himalayas which covered the whole row twice and still had slack to spare. We sponged off the worst grime from faces and hands, took off their outer clothes and left them to sleep in cotton vests and pants. This was our standard practice throughout the trip. Hardly were they in bed than they were asleep, almost before the sky darkened enough to show the myriad stars twinkling above us. We three adults sat smoking over our cups of hot cocoa, talking over the day and listening to the stir of the encampment below, but already feeling a delicious lethargy overcoming us. But hardly had we settled into our sleeping-bags than a bobbing line of lanterns approached us and a deputation of youths came to invite us to watch the *dabke* dancing. Tired as we were, we rolled out of bed and followed them down to the nearest tent, where the nasal drone of the flutes could already be heard and a coming and going of lanterns indicated some sort of activity. The dancers consisted of four or five youths, black-clad, with scarves tied loosely round their heads, and pretty Aziza and Latife and a little boy of twelve or so. Other people were talking and joking around us in the dark, but these were the dancers of this particular group. From the other side of the encampment came the sound of other flutes and voices, and the glow of a bonfire was bright against the night sky.

The line of dancers stamped and swung in the darkness with their arms around each other's shoulders, their leader giving the measure on his reed flute, with a sudden leap aside followed by a sharp stamp. Round and round they shuffled in the darkness, the little boy tagging on doggedly at the end of the row. Occasionally one merry youth would leap out of line and would perform a series of turns and jumps, waving a cloth in his hand, while the rest kept strictly to the two-four beat, forward and back, forward and back, curling like a snail-shell as the musician turned slowly around in time to his music.

Sitting there under the bright stars, on the cold mountainside, we seemed absorbed into a world utterly apart from our normal existence. Round and round shuffled the dancers, dark shapes dimly seen in the smoky light of the lantern, their heads bent, their whole attention concentrated on maintaining the steady one-two-three-stamp of the step, the flute droning its monotonous, hypnotising rhythm. We might have been watching some mysterious, scarce-comprehended rite of cave-dwellers, so serious, so engrossed in their performance were the dancers. Occasionally the music faltered, the dance stopped and the group gathered in earnest consultation. The girls, with eager gestures, then reorganised the line, the flute began again and away they went once more, the shuffle and stamp of their feet keeping time perfectly to the beat of the music.

We watched till we nearly fell asleep as we sat. The girls would have had us join the dance, but Elias refused – to their disappointment. Long after we had left them the dance continued and we went to sleep to the sound of the flute, and watching the line of the dancers passing darkly across the dim light of the lantern.

At dawn the next morning the flocks were already streaming out to the dewy mountainside and the tinkling of their bells and the cries and calls of their departure awoke us to the first rosy light. Milk and yoghurt were again brought us from Abu Bechara, with many pressing requests that we stay with them another day, but, foolishly enough, we felt it unwise to dawdle so early on our trip. Latife and Aziza came to help us pack up and begged us to take a photograph of them before we left. This we were glad to do, for it was impossible to induce Abu Bechara to accept anything for his help and hospitality.

'If I came to your house in Beirut, would you grudge me a cup of coffee? Would you expect me to pay for it? No, of course not. So it is with me here. Anything we can do for you we are happy to do, and shame it would be to think we grudge any traveller our hospitality.'

This answer pleased Elias immensely and was often quoted by him in the course of our travels, never without effect. It touched some deep-seated spring of pride and respect for the traditional way of life – 'Ah, that was a true mountain answer,' people would say with a gratified shake of the head, 'that was a true Lebanese speaking.'

We had with us some red-and-white checked *keffiyahs*, the headcloths of the Jordanian Arab Legion. The two girls had set their hearts on these, so we gave them as a parting present. They decorated the black cords which hold the cloth firmly to the head with bunches of a small, dry yellow flower which they seemed to prize, for they gave us all small bunches to take away with us. Long after we had lost sight of Abu Bechara's mountain we still carried these little bunches with us, and we found on our return to Beirut a few flowers thrust into the pockets of a knapsack.

Our way now led along the lip of the chasm, while below us the floor of the valley gradually rose towards its culmination in the great amphitheatre where the Adonis river springs out of its cave in the rock face. Looking over the precipice, we could see the rocky channel of the river thrusting its way past wooded bluffs and through steeply terraced cultivation, and on the other side of the great valley the bare cliffs and tawny slopes of the Laklouk plateau. The air was fresh and clear and we could see for miles around us as we walked on through swelling alpine pastureland, with the majestic mountains sweeping up on our right hand, and the blue drop of the river valley on our left.

After three hours we started to come down through a cypress-speckled scree. The cliffs of the amphitheatre began to take shape and loom above us, while from every roothold twisted and distorted trees thrust out from the bare surfaces of the rock. The day was hot and the loose stones of the landslide were difficult and tiring to negotiate. After the spaciousness and clarity of the high mountain the huge encircling rocks produced a certain sensation of awe and oppression. We stopped to take our bearings beneath a magnificent spreading walnut tree, one of the two or three survivors of a famous grove of walnuts swept away by the landslide we had so laboriously crossed.

'What news, O handsome boy?' called Elias cheerfully, to a gape-faced youth of fourteen or so, who emerged from among the rocks where he had been dozing away the noontide, while his goats reposed among the cracks and crannies of the cliffs. 'How far to Afka, and by what track – if you have enough wits to tell us that,' he added, *sotto-voce*. The boy appeared amazed at this sudden apparition of strangers among his lonely rocks and scree, but recovered enough to exchange a few phrases with Elias and to open some green walnuts for us with his sharp clasp-knife. After fifteen minutes we pushed on in the direction he indicated, drawing in closer all the time to the wall of the cliffs.

A sudden scramble over some boulders and up a bank, and a great outcry from Sebastian and Sabrina, who tipped backwards over Little Stick's tail, and we emerged hot and panting on to a road. There before us was a great tumble of rock and blocks of stone, surmounted by a spreading fig tree, and, beyond, the road curved round to a little coffee shop. We had reached the source of the Adonis and our day's journey was done.

The coffee shop was a simple affair of a roughly thatched roof of leafy branches covering a mud-floored terrace. There were two or three levels with a black tent on top providing the nucleus of the ensemble. The proprietor was a lean, springy old man with a drooping grey moustache, garrulous and vain, a barn-yard cockerel on his own dung-heap. The family was Metwali. The Metwalis are the Shia Moslems of Lebanon and Syria. Early Islam was split fundamentally on the issue of the succession to the Caliphate. The supporters of Ali, the son-in-law of the Prophet Mohammed, and his descendants by the Prophet's daughter Fatima, are known as Shias. Their rivals, who held by the principle of election to the Caliphate, are the orthodox Sunni Moslems forming the major part of the followers of Mohammed. The Shia Moslems are known for their fanaticism and the Metwalis in Lebanon share this reputation. Until the early years of the nineteenth century they occupied and dominated the Baalbek district and Anti-Lebanon and held much of southern Lebanon, but their power was broken by the notorious Djezzar Pasha (the Slaughterer) of Acre, who persecuted them with his customary cruelty. It was a Metwali chief, however, the Emir Ganjar, who was one of the most active parties in promoting the revolt of the Lebanese mountaineers against the Egyptian occupation of the 1840s. Getting arms from the British ships anchored off Beirut, he joined forces with the Christian Maronites of the Kesrouan and, among other exploits, blockaded the road to Damascus. The unrest and uprising of the independent-minded Lebanon was one of the chief causes of the failure of Egypt to seize and hold Syria.

Sheikh Abu Adil, as the old man was called, extended a warm welcome to us. Our gear was unloaded, the donkeys watered and tethered, the family bed and palliasses were offered us, and his buxom, masterful wife busied herself over her primus stove.

The main terrace extended to the lip of a waterfall and, standing on a rough stone jutting out into the sweep of the current, we scooped up basinfuls of icy-cold water to wash in. The scene was one of great impressiveness. We were surrounded by shaggy, precipitous bluffs, some 600 feet high, forming an enormous amphitheatre. The birthplace of the stream was a large cave, set like an eye-socket in the wall of the cliff. There were several channels flooding out of the main mouth, or by a bramble-hung subsidiary. They came down through a com fusion of great rocks and gullies, full of clear, pebbly pools and sudden miniature cataracts, until they united to sweep under the bridge and fell with a roar some forty feet into the beautiful pool under the coffee shop. This pool lay shimmering in the sunlight beneath us, its enticing depths changing from emerald green to a shifting, shadowy brown, while around its side curtains of wild mint and yellow-flowered St John's Wort hung down among the tangled sprays of blackberry. A little separate valley, small and steep, led up from this pool to the tumbled mass of masonry we had already passed – all that remained of the great temple dedicated to Venus.

Here in ancient times were practised those rites which so offended the civilised susceptibilities of the late Roman Empire and which led to the destruction of the temple in the reign of the Christian Emperor Constantine. The site is immeasurably old, and long before the Graeco-Roman conquests of Phoenicia the inhabitants of the coast used to make their wearisome pilgrimage up the savage glens and frightening immensities of the valley, to intercede with and propitiate the great powers of fertility and regeneration. Here is localised the classical legend of Venus and Adonis, a graceful mask for older, more primitive beliefs and practices. Here, says the legend, lived Adonis, a beautiful youth born of the incestuous love of his father, the king of Cyprus, for his daughter Myrrha. Myrrha was changed into the tree that bears her name, and after ten months the bark split asunder, and the child was born. Grown to maturity, his beauty was such that Venus, the goddess of love herself, fell in love with him, but her lover Mars, jealous, sent a fearsome boar to kill the youth. It was at this pool that the youthful hunter was surprised and killed by the boar, bleeding to death from a deep gash in his groin, and it was down these wild slopes and glens that the goddess rushed – dishevelled and despairing – her limbs scratched and torn by the thorns and briars, her cries resounding from wall to wall of the valley.

In the spring, the melting snows flood the river and send it down in spate to the sea, bearing with it a reddish-brown mud washed by the weather off the steep slopes of the mountain. The clear waters of the river are discoloured and the stain can be seen from the coast, spreading across the sea where the river comes flooding into the bay. This, said the ancient legend, was the blood of Adonis, renewed annually at the time of his death. Across the green levels of the valley, and clustering in the stones and corners of the terraces, the purple anemones, the Hunter's, grow in their thousands each spring, followed in turn by the scarlet ones. These are Adonis' flowers, said the legend, sprung from his blood as he lay dying beneath the trees at Afka, and renewed each year as a sign and remembrance for his mourners.

For mourned he was, century after century, in all the great centres of the love-goddess's cult. The memories of other loves and other mysteries were incorporated in his worship – Tammuz and Ishtar, Baal and Astarte, Isis and Osiris, the Great Mother and Attis, were all aspects of a duality which symbolised the relations between Mother Earth and her fruit. Old, dark, distant, distorted memories of sacrifice and expiation were caught up in the general exaltation which characterised all rituals deriving from the ancient Canaanite practices of the area. Bands of wailing worshippers trailed up on a three-day pilgrimage from Byblos on the coast, resting and sacrificing at the wayside temples whose ruins mark the stages of the route. In the courts and precincts of the temple the prostitutes and catamites were the last evidences of the rites by which early man sought to ensure the fruitfulness of his flocks and fields. The giving by all women of one day a year to Venus' service, the sacrifice of virginities, the self-mutilation, were rituals evolved with only one object in view, namely to maintain and increase the fruitfulness of the earth. With the increasing sophistication of the area, the old primitive beliefs fell into disrepute, the rites degenerated into licentiousness and display, and the worship evoked that feeling of revulsion which culminated in the destruction of the temple.

But though you thrust nature out with a pitchfork, she comes creeping back. So it is with the ancient beliefs of the Adonis valley. The pool and shrine are still haunted by a goddess, the *Sitt el matrah* – the Lady of the place. To the Christians she is *Sitt Mariam* – the Virgin Mary; to the Moslems – *Zahra*. Sheikh Abu Adil assured us she had appeared in a vision to his wife and cured her of a dangerous fever. A pallid youth, a Christian from Jounieh, was stretched out on a palliasse on the terrace. He had been left there by his family in the hope that the beneficial character of the place and the excellent water would speed his recovery from an appendicitis operation. Abu Adil assured us it would, and that he had already much improved in the few days he had been there.

As Sabrina's nose had bled at intervals coming down the mountain, at the old man's insistence she and her sister scrambled across the stream to where one could perceive a small tunnel about a yard wide, in the foundation of the ruins. This has been made into a little shrine and here the children washed their faces in the water which dripped down the fern-covered sides. Above hung the drooping branches of the fig tree, decorated with little rags, votive offerings from the barren women who still hoped to have their wombs opened by the intercession of the Lady of the place.

Abu Adil was a great climber and knew all the tracks and climbing holds of the cliffs. 'Those are my trees,' he said, pointing upwards to some carobs, growing precariously out of the face of the rock. 'I climb up and harvest them every year.' There was certainly no need to worry about anyone stealing the crop, for they were growing on an almost inaccessible ledge, about sixty feet above the ground. We asked him about the castle the Crusaders once had at the head of this valley – 'Castle,' he said, 'castle. Come with me and

I'll show you a castle up there on that slope. Very big, very old, and there are rooms under it which no one has got into – and treasure. I know all the places around here. All my life – and I'm sixty-four now – I've herded and climbed on these cliffs. Over there, for example,' and he pointed backwards towards the eastern cliffs, 'if you go for about two hours, you'll find a king carved on the rocks, high up, in a narrow crevice. No one except us shepherds knows about it, for no one ever goes there.' As he spoke, he was skipping nimbly across the rocky terrain of the slopes above the road, making for a mass of bush-covered rock some way above us. We went up in a series of panting bursts and desperate clutchings at juniper bushes, asphodel roots and even thistles, as we attempted to keep our balance on the sliding hillside. Sheikh Abu Adil enjoyed our exertions to the utmost: 'Keep moving,' he would call; 'here, let me give you a hand,' and we would be hauled up to stand with trembling knees on some insecure tuft of vegetation on a slope so steep it was unpleasant to look down at the road some 200 feet below. At last, after about ten minutes of lung-bursting exertion, we stood before a great fallen mass of boulder half buried in the earth, and covered with scrubby, thorny vegetation. On one side we could discern three little niches, and someone had stuck a votive candle in one. There were other indications of runnels and a basin on the adjacent stones. Where the rock entered the earth was a sort of hollowed entry. 'Here,' said Abu Adil, 'is the entry to the treasure chambers, but no one has ever tried to dig them out.'

Every ancient recognisable human artefact in this area has its attendant rumour of gold and treasure, and we paid little attention to this one. The site was undoubtedly an ancient one, and the niches and runnels bore some resemblance to the other Canaanite sites scattered in the remote places of the Lebanon. 'Here is the king,' said the old man, pointing to a rough, triangular-shaped stone about three feet in height, and heaving it over for us to see. On its rough surface was the dimly discernible indication of a face so crude and so erased that it might well have been only an accidental play of light and shadow on the irregularities of the stone surface.

Stones like these can sometimes be seen in museums; they are among man's earliest representations of God. They are the Semitic *El*, whose name is familiar to us in the Bethel of the Methodist church – *Beit El* being the house of God, and God being housed in the stone. Throughout the pre-Islamic Semitic world certain stones had a ritual significance, and the circumambulation of the Ka'aba stone at Mecca is a rite inherited from the earliest religious practices of the area.

As we looked wonderingly at this rough stone shape, Abu Adil gave it a shove with his foot, and launched it off down the steep slope. Gathering momentum, it went sliding through the shale and scree of the hillside, crashing through the bushes that impeded its progress, with the old man in hot pursuit. His technique of descent was similar to that of the Gurkhas – go as fast as possible and rely on speed and agility to keep upright. We came crashing and sliding down after him, grabbing at whatever we could to steady ourselves, and wondering what would break first when we hit the road, and whether someone would be unlucky enough to be there when the stone came down. A few wild 'Ho-a's' from Abu Adil, and the stone skipped like one of those flat stones children skim over the surface of the sea, and broke in two as it hit the road. Breathless, we arrived a minute later, a miniature avalanche of shale and dust following us. The old man seemed a little disconcerted at the breaking of the stone – he had probably expected to sell it to us – but we propped it up under a small tree at the side of the road and fitted the two halves together, and there it probably stands to this day.

THREE

Afka to Laklouk and across to the Kadisha Valley

THE DAY CLOSED IN EARLY in the shadow of the enormous cliffs, but before we could settle for the night our party was augmented. A Venezuelan of Lebanese descent, visiting his native land, drove up in a large pink Lincoln car, and a jeep brought up a police surgeon, enquiring into a village shooting affray which had ended in the killing of a man. We had quite a sociable evening before we all settled down for the night among the chairs and tables of the terrace. We slept with our heads a few feet away from the rush and roar of the waterfall, the Venezuelan slung in a hammock, the sick boy on his palliasse and the numerous women and children of the household all fitted in somewhere within the shelter of the family tent.

Early the next day we were awoken with cups of strong black coffee and we sleepily roused ourselves in the bright white light of morning. We washed and bathed in the icy stream-water where it ran through the rockfall on its exit from the cave, and Miles found some large fossil clams, which we carried with us in one of the knapsacks. We left at about seven o'clock, parting most cordially from the old Sheikh, who escorted us over the bridge and cheerfully promised to show us the carving of the king next time we came back to the Afka spring.

Our road wound on around the flank of the hill, orchards of apple and plum and pear on either side, and a hedge of blackberries and dog-rose twined with wild clematis separating the terraces from the road. The upper part of the valley was terraced with orchards and rose gradually in tidy steps to a great mass of mountain blocking off the end of it. We had an introduction here to the family of the Sheikh Germanos, a notable and landowner and, as the day was early, and we intended to make only a short stage, we decided to make use of it. We found two of the Germanos sons – handsome, fair young men, who spoke English and French – picnicking in their gaunt, villa-like family house with a peasant to look after them. The rest of the family had baulked at coming up to bury itself here for the summer, but as the apple harvest was due to start any day, some members of the family had to come and supervise it. Dotted around among the orchards were other solid, stone-built villas, the property of cousins and uncles. In each of them all or part of the family was spending its summer and worrying about the crop. The talk was all of apples: the growers were anxious to know whether Egypt would buy, for it is on the Egyptian market that the prosperity of the apple industry depends. A leading member of the Opposition, Hamid Frangié, had just gone to Cairo in the hope of persuading President Nasser to relax the ban on Lebanese apples, and hopes were high that he would succeed. 'The crop is good,' said the young Germanos, 'but if we don't sell, what good is it to us? The home market isn't sufficiently developed to absorb all we grow if Egypt doesn't take the crop, and you can't run everything down to Iraq and Saudi Arabia by truck. The Syrians make all sorts of difficulties and in any case the demand isn't great enough.' The question of trade relations with Egypt and Syria was one which was to crop up regularly throughout our trip. The pro-Western policy of the Lebanese Government was already bringing the country into conflict with the rising tide of Arab nationalism in Egypt and Syria and, to a certain extent, within her own borders. Damascus is the gate through which all Lebanon's exports to Iraq, Jordan and the Gulf must go, unless they are shipped round via the Suez Canal. Until the port of Latakia is fully developed, Syria remains largely dependent on Beirut as a port of entry for goods destined for Damascus, and this mutual dependence accounts in some way for the endemic awkwardness of the Lebanese and Syrian frontier and customs controls. 'The Lebanese are soft,' say the Syrians; 'they are niminy-piminy people who are only interested in making money.' 'The Syrians are mad,' say the Lebanese; 'they can afford to sell themselves to the Russians. They're so poor they can't even finance their wheat harvest without us.' For the time being, both countries have to accommodate each other for their mutual convenience, but little opportunity is neglected by either side to pin-prick and harass the other.

'We will show you something interesting, if you like,' said the brothers, 'we'll show you the Mejdel cave, which is just near here.' So we left Elias and the three younger children, but we took Miles with us to inspect the cave. This was a huge natural grotto opening at the base of a cliff. One got into it from above, sliding down a steep, grassy slope on to a natural bridge spanning a cavity, then traversing beneath it to the cave mouth. Long ago, probably during the Roman period, the cave had been used as a necropolis, and coffin niches were carved in the walls of the entry. Thousands of bats hung palpitating in the fusty recesses of the great vault and an *arak* distillery occupied the open floor of the entry. We picked our way in by torch and candle-light for half an hour or so. We wore pullovers, and slipped and scrambled on the greasy boulders and icy trickles of the streamlet inside. The cave has no end, say the inhabitants, and though some pot-holing enthusiasts from Beirut have penetrated a certain distance, the further recesses have not been explored. It is rumoured to be a haunt and refuge for outlaws, and *afreets* and *djinns* are said to inhabit it, despite the protection extended by St Peter, who has a shrine in it, with the saints' names written on its walls in the old Syriac *strangelo* script.

There are caves and grottoes all over the Lebanon, for the mountains are hollow and the water of the melting snows is stored in them to burst out in the springs and streams of the lower slopes. Sometimes it is a small river that rushes fully formed out of the flank of the mountain, to hurry through ferny, tree-hung glen and boulder-riven gorge to the terraced slopes of a valley; sometimes it is a small, silent pool, green as glass, welling up mysteriously from the base of a cliff, crystal-clear and enticing, and cold as the snow from which it came. The beauty of these mountain valleys has to be seen to be realised – no matter how remote, how stony, how poor the surrounding landscape, where there is water there is life. The carob and plum and Judas tree grow out of rocky crevices, the ilex and terebinth and pine straggle up the shaly sides, and down in the miniature world of the rock-pools and cascades the maidenhair, the silver fern and hart's tongues make a small-scale jungle of their own.

In the hospitable manner of the country, the Germanos brothers insisted we lunch with them, so we shared a large spread of sardines and corned beef which was all their bachelor housekeeping ran to. When we came to load the donkeys we noticed their peasant gazing at us with interested surmise: 'You have a revolver?' asked one of the brothers; 'Our man is longing to look at it. Like everyone around here, he only thinks of firearms.' Alas for their anticipation! The only revolver we could produce was a toy cowboy pistol, a present to Miles from a school friend before we left. Sticking out of a knapsack, it was sufficiently lifelike to give us an added prestige in the eyes of the Germanos retainer, from which Elias had not hesitated to extract the fullest advantage.

With laughter all round, we said goodbye and continued on to our night's destination, Akoura, at the base of the Laklouk plateau. Akoura has had a bad name among travellers for a long time. It is the custom of all the people of this area to travel without supplies; they know they will get hospitality from any house they stop at, on the understanding that the host will receive the same treatment when he has occasion to travel further up or down the mountain. This simple system applies all over the Laklouk area, Elias told us, but the Akoura people, who are Greek Catholics, do not subscribe to it and hence have a reputation for meanness. The Swiss Burckhardt, travelling in 1810, had great difficulty in obtaining anything for himself or his horse in Akoura. Only by representing himself as a Kurd in the service of the Damascus Pasha did he manage to frighten the Sheikh into sending him a few loaves of bread and some cheese.

'Go to the *Mukhtar* (headman),' the Germanos told us. 'They've had a row there. He's a good old fellow and speaks French – served under the French, but got into trouble for killing a sergeant.' What the trouble was we soon discovered as we came into Akoura – a charming whitewashed village straggling down from a backcloth of precipice, with cottages surrounded by fruit trees and wreathed in vines. An air of hesitation and constraint hung over the place, which was hardly surprising as the two rival families of the village were not on speaking terms. We met the *Mukhtar* by one of the village fountains, a small, foxy old man with the long nose and fierce waxed moustachios of the mountain-dwelling Lebanese. He welcomed us courteously enough, and a chance encounter with our Beirut landlord's gardener's uncle's wife's brother helped identify us. The *Mukhtar* led us to his little house – a terraced verandah with a few rooms off it – and a garden of fruit trees all around. Our gear was offloaded on to the verandah and the donkeys led below to the stable under the house, while his elderly wife prepared coffee. We sat in a tiny room almost filled by a plush sofa and a set of plush chairs. On the walls were photographs of the male relatives of the family, all very fierce, including one of the *Mukhtar* himself as a young man, wearing a sword and flourishing a rifle in one hand and a hand-grenade in the other. Seeing the direction of our glances, he sighed and shook his head: 'Those were the days when a man's life was his own,' he said, 'and life was worth living then. We used to raid and feud with the Metwalis over the mountain there' – and he indicated the great mass of mountain rising up behind the cliff face and sealing off the valley – 'and the Government didn't interfere with us all the time, like it does now. Nowadays you can't even have a quarrel with your neighbour without the *gendarmes* coming and settling on you like a lot of blow-flies.' Gradually the story came out. An inter-family quarrel two years ago over a load of firewood had sparked off a feud in the village that had cost fourteen lives and several dozen wounded, and had led to the eventual despatch last year of a force of two hundred *gendarmes* by the Government to restore order to the district. The *gendarmes* had been quartered on

Akoura for six months, living off the inhabitants, and this calamity had damped down the angry emotions of the village, especially as the *gendarmes* had confiscated all the arms they could find. The *Mukhtar* had lost several rifles and six hand-grenades in the process and was obviously chagrined at their loss.

Over an extremely good supper of rice and string beans, eaten on the terrace by the light of a hissing acetylene lamp, while in the shadowy recesses of the house various babies and children prattled and whimpered their way to sleep, our host told us of his problems. 'People here shoot for nothing: they like guns and a dead man doesn't mean much. There are always rows about irrigation water, grazing rights and woodcutting. Somebody is always shooting at someone else, and when things get really bad we just close the shutters, and take care not to get too near the windows. The first sign of bad trouble is usually someone shooting out all the lights and people take pot-shots at each other from their roofs and houses, and sometimes one can't get out for days. Of course, no one attacks the women and small children, but a boy of twelve or thirteen is already some use as a fighting man. The families usually take shelter down in the stables or cellar and the men fight it out from their houses, or from up in the cliffs. It's a sad waste of life, I know, but it's the kind of life we're used to and really' – and here his eyes flashed and his moustaches trembled – 'if a man can't settle his own affairs without outside interference, I don't know what things are coming to.'

'*Mukhtar* good man,' Elias confided to us as we settled our bedding for the night on the terrace; 'this rich village before, but Hashim family make it big trouble, *gendarme* come, now all poor. *Mukhtar*, he very sad.' Very sad indeed for him, we felt, as we struggled into our sleeping-bags on the mud-floored terrace, the night air sharp and cold around us and the snores of the household resounding from every corner. Our terrace dropped on three sides some ten feet on to the orchard below, but we slept comfortably enough beneath the trellises of the vine, the tops of the apricot trees level with our faces, and the brays of the donkeys, the crowing of cocks and the sudden caterwaulings of the village cats forming a scarcely apprehended background to our sleep.

At four o'clock the village stirred into life, and we stirred with it. The *Mukhtar* gave us some apricots from his trees and helped us load Big Stick, who sat down as soon as his load was on. Half a dozen men got him up and pushed and prodded him up the narrow stone steps from the stable entrance to a level space above the house, where he was once more loaded, this time successfully. We were beginning to have a growing conviction that we needed another donkey, for despite Elias' confidence in his strength – 'He like Antar, very strong donkey' – Big Stick seemed to be making heavy weather of the rough mountain work.

We started off soon after five and began a slow, two-hour slog up a bad mountain road to Laklouk. The *Mukhtar* had assured us that it was possible to drive a car to Laklouk, but it was difficult to see how this was done, the road being split and scoured out at several points by spring torrents. The morning sun struck full on to us as we slowly crept up the flank of the bare, weather-eroded mountainside and in a very short time we began to feel hot and fagged. The higher we got, the more coherent became the plan of the valley below us. We amused ourselves tracing our route from our first emergence over the crest of the mountain, and were amazed and impressed to think we had come so far in so short a time. A few flowers still grew in the sides of the road: daisies and dandelions and straggling vetches. Sometimes we would pause in the shade of a scrubby, wind-bent tree or overhanging rock, or wait for each other on the airy promontory of a cliff edge, but mostly we straggled up in a rather languid manner, for we all seemed to be suffering from a reaction to our previous exertions. As we neared the top the short turf and dried yellow grass was full of grasshoppers, quite small ones with wings of every colour. They hopped and chirped all over the road so that it was impossible to avoid treading on them, their wing-cases flashing red and yellow and blue. Miles dawdled a long way behind us, so that we waited and then finally went back to him. With tears in his eyes he upbraided Elias and ourselves for our cruelty in killing the grasshoppers. All the way up he had been attempting to give honourable burial to those he found squashed on the road, but without assistance, he said, it was impossible to send their souls in peace to the grasshoppers' underworld. 'Come, O Friend of all the Grasshoppers,' said Elias at last, when this problem was laid before him, 'you shall walk in front of us all, and in that way the grasshoppers can have warning. If they still hop in our way, then obviously it is God's will that they be killed and we shall have done all we can.' In this way the matter was arranged and we continued more briskly, but Miles' Arabic nickname stuck to him, and to the end of our time in Lebanon Elias would still sometimes laughingly call him The Friend of all the Grasshoppers.

At last we reached the watershed, and the long drag uphill was over. The Laklouk plateau is a curious, isolated upland pasture, some two or three miles in length, surrounded by craggy grey rock summits, except where it dips over into the ramparts above Akoura. Some 6,000 feet high, it is under snow most of the winter, and plans are afoot to turn it into a winter-sports centre. But at present it is little visited. A road runs up to it from the Adonis valley, zigzagging up a rock face, and continues across the plateau to Tannourine, where it stops. The few inhabitants are cattle-grazers who cultivate the fields around their cottages, but depend in the main on their cows and goats for their livelihood. We had been here before, picnicking from Beirut in the spring, for Laklouk has a rare iris growing among its rocks and turfy slopes, the iris *sofariana*, a splendid dark purple flower with magenta sepals, which only grows in a few places in Lebanon. The snow lies in drifts as late as Whitsun, and underneath its melting eaves one can find colchicums and celandines; on the rocks hang cushions of pink and white arabis, and a sort of mauve aubretia, while in the green meadows and streaming hillsides one finds the splendid scarlet tulip with its crossed petal tips, like the tulips on Turkish tiles and Persian miniatures.

Late though spring comes to the heights of the mountains, we were still too late to catch anything of the swift-following summer; only the green of the meadow grass remained, the wind moving in shadows across its surface, and the solitary trees marking the springs shivering their leaves together.

We directed our steps towards the summer house of the Bishop of Jebail, a curious dwelling we had visited on previous occasions. The Bishop is a man of taste and ingenuity, witness his garden in Jebail, where he uses sarcophagi and fragments of carved capitals to decorate his courtyard, and wreathes them in vine and jasmine and casually growing flowers with the happiest effect. Here in Laklouk he has excelled himself, and has contrived the strangest house imaginable close to an abundant spring. A great, ragged, grey outcrop of rocks sticks up on an isolated hillside; at first sight it seems another wind-eroded, jagged mass of stone, such as one often sees in these limestone mountains. But on approaching closer one observes a sort of plan in some of its formation and gradually one realises that a house has been built on to the central core of rock, made of blocks of the same stone. One understands slowly how extremely clever the whole thing is; fantastic, eroded shapes of rock line the approach, like so many grotesque Kinges Bestes, others peer like gargoyles from the edge of the flat roof. Steps are cut in the fissures of the rock to lead to other levels, vaults and hollows are utilised as shady rooms or store-chambers, gaps being blocked in with cut stone and thick, weathered doors and shutters fitted where necessary. Between the two main outcrops of rock extends an open space, a sort of courtyard; here the involutions and hollows of the rock have been used to make a dining-room. Slabs of stone are roughly cemented on to a base as tables, and other stones fitted against the wall to make benches.

While we rested in the shade of the towering rock pinnacles, we were fortunate enough to encounter a young official from Jebail who was picnicking at the house with his French wife and a friend. On our asking if he thought the Bishop would mind us camping on his site for a day, he assured us he had no hesitation in placing it all at our disposal. 'The Bishop is a great friend of mine; he is a most charming and obliging man, and he will be only too happy for you to use this house. He himself has not been well, and is unlikely to come up this summer, so don't have any hesitation in staying here,' and summoning the peasant who had the key, and acted as guardian to the place, told him to be sure to do everything he could to assist us and to make our stay at Laklouk comfortable. This was indeed a stroke of luck and gratified an ambition we had long nourished, to spend some time among the Gothick extravagances of the Bishop's fancy.

We spent a most delicious week in Laklouk, resting, re-packing, getting in stores and buying another donkey for one hundred lira (about twelve pounds). The negotiations for the latter took us half the week, being conducted in an atmosphere of leisurely enjoyment between Elias, ourselves and a handsome young Metwali who rode over from the other side of the plateau with a choice of three donkeys to offer us. These Metwalis spend the winter on the sea coast at Chekka, working in the big cement factory there, but in the summer they revert to their ancestral ways and come to spend the hot weather camping among the grazing herds of the plateau. We had passed by their long, black tents as we came over the watershed from Akoura, and remarked the donkeys and horses grazing on the slopes around them. Now came the opportunity to do a horse deal, to make their happiness complete. Every afternoon Hussein came, accompanied by a brother or two, and once by his father, a ragged old man on a gaunt, breedy Arab mare, who galloped straight up the slope to our tent and stopped dead amid the admiring applause of the onlookers. They would sit gossiping in a desultory way with Elias, drinking coffee and letting their donkeys graze casually in front of us. They would mend harness and saddlery with him and sometimes gallop off with one of the children up behind, to fetch us stores or cigarettes from the little tin shop beside their encampment, a mile or so away across the meadows. Once we went over to have coffee with them in their big black tent, partitioned down the middle with reed screens. Around the sides were cushioned benches on which we reclined and a pile of great black-and-white woven sacks in a corner indicated the family stores of grain and flour. The old Sheikh's wife, a big fine woman with auburn hair hanging in ringlets beside her ruddy, weather-beaten face, hastened with her daughters to her hearth to make us coffee, then, bringing up a curious little wooden stool like a hobby horse, squatted beside us to join in the conversation. 'My mother very good woman,' said Hussein, who spoke a sort of halting English, less versatile than Elias'; 'she give my father seven sons, four daughters.' The family were all around us, the youths and boys clad in American jeans and trilby hats, the girls in bright cotton dresses and cheap white sandals. Hussein himself wore an elegant pair of twill jodhpurs, so well cut that we asked him who his tailor was. Apparently they were made in the *souk* in Tripoli. Only the old people retained their native dress; the old Sheikh in rusty black *shewal* and jacket, his black headcloth fringed low over his shaggy countenance, his wife stately in her long, braided, bright blue gown, with chains and necklaces dangling over her bosom.

The Christian farmers of the plateau distrusted these Metwalis, but shared a cigarette and a gossip with them comfortably enough, if circumstances forced it. The farmers lived in isolated stone cottages, dark and smoky, with a small kitchen garden beside them. Every day, at first light, the flocks of goats would stream up the hillside behind us, to disappear among the cracks and crannies of the rocks. Behind them came the herds of red and black cattle to graze on the lower slopes and idle in the shade of the tall trees beside the springs. Our nearest neighbours were a young brother and sister called Fehme and Fehmia; she was a pretty girl, but a cripple, who limped badly as she busied herself about the yard and living-room of their cottage. They used to bring us fresh milk and yoghurt, and eggs and tomatoes, though these were scanty as they ripen late up in Laklouk. Another neighbour was Boulos, a tall, blue-eyed man who had the key to the house. He used to come by each morning on the way to pasture his cows and later in the morning we would hear him having long hallooing conversations with his brother high up on the crags above. All the dwellers on this upland plateau could converse easily from valley to hill-top and crag to crag. They pitched their voices to a particular note, and claimed they could easily speak with each other at half a mile's distance. Certainly it became a commonplace for us to see a man standing by the spring and engaged in long, bawling conversations with another scarcely discernible on the rocks of the crest, while his goats moved about him like specks on the hillside.

We received many casual visits from people passing up and down the road, such as a party of youths shooting whatever birds they saw with an ancient shotgun which they loaded with shot and powder from a flask, pushing it all down with a ramrod. On another day a posse of *gendarmes* arrived. They were escorting their officer on a tour of inspection and stopped for coffee. Once the Germanos brothers came by on their way to a funeral in Tannourine. Elias took a *service* taxi down to Beirut one morning, taking with him a duffle-bag of things we had discarded and coming back next day with stores and money and newspapers. This was a practice we followed regularly throughout the trip. Whenever we stayed any time at a place and there was a bus or *service* taxi in operation, we sent Elias down for a day or two to see his family, do some washing in our house, get stores, money and the mail. We never carried any great quantity of money with us, perhaps ten or twelve pounds at the most. As this became depleted, we had to try to get into position for Elias to make a trip down; we ran it very fine sometimes, once indeed we were reduced, in his absence, to a tin of sardines between the six of us, but these were only temporary embarrassments and on the whole we managed to keep a small reserve of food and money in hand.

The days sped by in the utmost content. A little bucktoothed, dotty boy called Moussa, who herded bullocks on the far side of the road, showed us a swimming-pool the Bishop had constructed among the rocks beside the road. It was a rough stone tank lined with cement, with water piped in from a nearby spring. It was used as a reservoir for irrigating the fields, the water being drained off every four days and led away in stone irrigation channels. Here we all bathed every day, for the tank was long enough for the children to swim in and deep enough for a dive. The climate was just right, for though the sun shone effortlessly all day, the air was always fresh and dry, full of little breezes, while the nights were colder than any we had as yet experienced. In the evenings we would stroll across the meadows towards the spring, while the children urged the donkeys into a gallop and periodically fell off with wild shouts and laughter. The courtyard of the house was full of flints; it must have been a caveman's factory, the ground was so full of broken and discarded knives and scrapers. Miles would spend hours pacing slowly around this site and another across the road, picking up flints, and the big fossil clams we also found here. The others would ramble to chase butterflies and catch grasshoppers, or pick the few flowers still found on the spiny hillside, or help Elias in the kitchen. Boulos had opened up the house for us and we used the refectory, a big, roughly vaulted room with barred and shuttered windows high up in the wall, as kitchen and dining-room. There was another room next to it, most of whose walls and ceiling were natural rock, dynamited out to the requisite shape. Here the children slept, on the huge iron frame of a rusty bed we found there. Light only entered these rooms through their low doors and they remained cool and shady all through the day. At night as we sat at the rickety table eating by the light of candles and a lantern, the shadows loomed up enormous on the vaulted ceilings; Elias, with his head wrapped in his *kefiyah* against the cold, looked like a bandit. Outside the night was cold and silent, and sometimes we would sit for a little while huddling over a fire of twigs and dried asphodels, for wood was scarce on the plateau, and listen to the donkeys stirring among the stones. The solitude and silence were intense, yet the whole atmosphere was peaceful and friendly, and lying in bed reading by torchlight, one was only conscious of the night wind sighing outside the tent walls and the pleasure and contentment one felt at the prospect of yet another day.

* * *

The time came at last for us to go. We were all rested and refreshed, our stores and baggage in order, the donkeys in better shape than when we arrived. Our new donkey was a pretty, soft-eyed, long-eared black creature with a mealy coloured nose; he came to us with the

name Bedu, but because he was midway between Little Stick and Big
Stick in size, he was known to us as Middle Stick. Part of the reason
for our extended stay at Laklouk was the condition of the donkeys.
Middle Stick was badly galled when we bought him, and he had a
great open sore all over the root of his tail. His legs were sound, but
it seemed he must have been foundered at some time, for there were
the scabs of a burn on his belly. When an animal is down, as a last
resort, the Arabs will sear his belly with a hot stone to get him up. If
this treatment does not get him to his feet, nothing will. We felt sorry
for Middle Stick and bought him partly out of pity and partly for his
pretty looks. He was an amiable donkey, gentle and untroublesome,
unlike Big Stick, who was a most turbulent animal. A week's rest
and good feeding brought Big Stick into excellent condition, and his
constant hee-hawing and braying and aggressive attacks on the other
donkeys earned him the admiration of all our visitors. Hardly a night
passed in which he did not break away from his tether, or rouse us
all up with an outburst of wheezy honking and hideous brays, but
despite these annoyances Elias cherished him dearly. Apparently the
amount of noise a donkey stallion makes is regarded as an indication
of virility. We had no cause to complain of Big Stick on that score, for
apart from the noise he made, he periodically broke his head-rope
and careered off in pursuit of any she-ass which happened to be in
the vicinity, followed by a rout of children, Elias and any onlookers
who were about. Little Stick remained dopey and undistinguished to
the end. His air of thoughtful melancholy never varied, even when
he was detected wandering into the kitchen and eating a dishcloth or
food left out on the table. He and Middle Stick became firm friends
and would graze peaceably together, or stand drooping in the shade
leaning their heads on each other's shoulders, but Big Stick disliked
Middle Stick and would kick or savage him whenever he got a chance
so we always had to tether them well apart. As can be imagined, these
donkeys were a source of unending delight to the children. They
treated them rather like toy tricycles, to be used and abandoned at
will, so that we would see a small figure manoeuvring a donkey up
against a rock in order to scramble on to it, and a little later the animal

would be casually abandoned on the hillside while the child busied itself with other pursuits. Little Stick was an ideal animal for such treatment; mild and indifferent, he allowed himself to be pushed and pummelled and dragged even by Sebastian. He would stand patiently while the two little ones wove daisy chains for his neck, or scrambled on his back, or slid down his tail; to the end he remained their favourite donkey and we felt most grief at parting from him. Middle Stick had a similar temperament, but being taller was more difficult for them to manage. He was the laziest of the donkeys and was the most awkward to get going at the pace one wanted. Elias' favourite – Big Stick – was undoubtedly our best animal; he was strong and fast, always eager to lead and very game and willing. Being tall, he was almost like a mule to ride and would whirl off gaily with Elias or Anthea on his back, cantering over the green turf with a rocking-horse motion. Elias lavished much attention on him. He was always fed first and had the most beads and ornaments around his neck, where they showed up splendidly against his milk-white skin. We preserved his complexion by washing him down with detergent, then we would anxiously walk him up and down until he dried, to prevent him rolling himself dirty again. Although he was a good donkey to us, his personality was not one to inspire affection. He lacked the wistful hopelessness of the other two. There was something self-sufficient and disagreeable about Big Stick, and when he was awkward, he was very awkward indeed. On these occasions Elias would shout and roar like a man possessed: 'Father of devils,' he would cry, booting Big Stick vigorously as the animal cunningly shifted weight just as the load was being balanced, 'try that again and you know what I'll do.' The children copied his tone and phrases exactly and would whack and pull the donkeys into line, shrieking and abusing them in shrill Arabic, or urging and encouraging them as they picked their way down steep and difficult places.

Each donkey came to us with its saddle and gear. The saddles were coarse black woven rectangles, padded underneath with wool and hay; the edges were embroidered with coloured wool and the cruppers were also ornamented. Their bridles were leather headstalls ornamented with cowrie-shells and tufts of coloured wool, pink and yellow and orange; their girths were strips of brightly woven webbing. Around their cruppers were more tufts, so the whole effect was very bright and colourful. In addition they wore necklaces of blue glass beads to ward off the evil eye. These were interspersed with more tufts of wool, and had little bells hung on them so that we jingled pleasantly as we went along. The bridles had no bits, but a steel chain acted as a curb. This was attached to the lead-rope which, in turn, was hooked up on to a ring on the saddle so that, when travelling, the donkey's head was kept up as if by a bearing rein. When we stopped, a hook at the side of the headstall undid to let the animal graze or drink; as soon as we were in motion Elias hooked it up again. The animal would not walk out well, he said, if its head was allowed to droop.

We fed the donkeys twice a day on barley and chopped straw, mixed up in a nosebag. This was supplemented by any grazing they could obtain from the thorny hillsides, and chopped melon-peel, fruit and vegetables as they occurred. Middle Stick's appearance gradually improved under our care and his worst galls were cured by the application of coffee-grounds. These dried in a hard crust over the raw surface and a new skin formed in a day or two. The open sore on his tail took longer to heal and had a tendency to break open during any hard exertion, but eventually we got it closed up and a few hairs began to grow over it again. Big Stick and Middle Stick were both shod, and periodically their feet needed attention; they both had new shoes in the course of the journey. Little Stick was unshod, and was the most sure-footed animal of the lot. None of them was ever lame and none except Little Stick ever gave us cause for concern, and that was only a temporary alarm.

Our baggage was now much more compact. Our clothes were reduced to a minimum – what we wore and one change; pullovers for everyone, headcloths, spare sandals made up the rest. We decided we must carry more water and fewer books, and thus got rid of a knapsack. We never replaced Pandora's box and found we could do very well without it. The kitchen gear and stores were fitted into two large cardboard cartons and wedged into the sack sling in which Sebastian and Sabrina had started the trip. This was easy to sling over a donkey's back and did not require the careful adjustment which Big Stick's burden needed. With three donkeys, each of the younger children had an animal of its own to ride. Big Stick carried the tent and baggage, Middle Stick the kitchen gear, and Little Stick the donkey feed and the day's provisions, the drinking bottles and usually Sebastian. Sabrina, being the lightest, was perched up on Big Stick, in a hollow between the diamond-hitched duffle-bags, and Anthea rode Middle Stick. Occasionally they would swop mounts and Sabrina would have Little Stick, who was her favourite animal. Miles walked the entire distance.

* * *

Our last night at Laklouk was enlivened in a manner we had not anticipated. After supper Elias and Miles set off on Big Stick to buy cigarettes. Hardly had they disappeared into the darkness than the whole district seemed to rock with a series of dynamite and hand-grenade explosions, while from all around came the cracking of rifle and pistol shots. Going quickly to the door and peering out, we were astonished to see that every cottage had its bonfire burning brightly, and across the valley we could hear the voices of the inhabitants calling happily to each other. Much mystified, we waited anxiously for Big Stick's return. It would be unfortunate, we felt, if another feud had broken out in the district and Miles and Elias were to ride into the line of fire. But the bonfires and fusillades continued and the joyous voices, which hardly seemed the atmosphere of doom and disaster. After a while we heard the donkey returning, with Elias as mystified as any of us. He and Miles had nearly fallen off at the first explosions, so startled had they been. We stayed up some time watching the bonfires blazing from all corners of the plateau, while the shots echoed in the bright, starry sky, and finally went to sleep with the noise of the explosions still ringing in our ears.

Next day we were up early, ready to pack and go. From the cowherd Boulos we learned the reason for last night's excitement. The news had just reached the district that Hamid Frangié, the Opposition nominee for the next Presidential elections, had obtained from President Nasser the release from prison of one Sheikh Georges Beg Yussef, a landowner of the district. Georges Beg Yussef had been sentenced in Cairo to life imprisonment for hashish-smuggling; he had been arrested while boarding an aircraft in Cairo. Marked banknotes planted by agents of the Narcotics Bureau served to convict him. Fourteen months of his sentence had been served when Hamid Frangié's intercession obtained him his release. The whole district was in a ferment of excitement and all along our route that day we heard people talking happily of the news. The popularity of this release seemed to augur a strong vote for Frangié among the Christian farmers of this district.

We left Laklouk with the feeling that, had we lingered any longer, we should never have stirred ourselves away from it. We parted from Boulos and Fehme and Fehmia, and dotty little Moussa, with regret tempered by the anticipation of new scenes and new people. Our way led gently downhill along the tarmac road to Tannourine, with a new prospect of jagged mountain gorge and shaggy mountainside opening before us. We met our young friends the bird-shooters on our way, and they begged us to stop at their home, a cottage set in orchards above a glinting stream, but we were determined to get on to Tannourine.

At last the tarmac ended and a white stone road replaced it. We were now winding down the steep sides of a gorge and below us we could see the roofs of a village half hidden in fruit trees and piles of chaff beside the circular threshing-floor. A stream fell in a cascade down the face of a cliff and ran down the narrow valley under a stone bridge, shaded by huge walnut trees. The descent of the gorge had been hot and tiring and we were grateful for the shade which enveloped us as soon as we entered Tannourine. The village straggled down the side of the stream, shut in on three sides by tall cliffs, but open seaward for a dazzling glimpse down the valley of a wide sky and distant fall of cloud-wreathed escarpment. We were greeted by several women and taken to a house for coffee and repose, while Elias sought about for a suitable camp site. At last one was found for us, a charming situation beneath two large walnut trees, comparatively secluded. The stream ran gently beside us, like a Scottish burn, falling over rocks and forming little pools. A fresh spring bubbled up by the roots of one of the trees, supplying us with drinking water. Even in the heat of the day the place was fresh and cool, for the stream was edged with planes and poplars and ran through quiet groves of apricot and olive trees. The villagers were very friendly and showered us with gifts – a basket of apricots, bunches of fresh chick-peas which are eaten raw, a basin full of mulberries. 'Me big friend this fruit,' exclaimed Elias joyfully, as a withered old man poured them out before us and watched with a smile while we scooped them into our mouths. Another old man was threshing corn on the other side of the stream; we could see his brown ox patiently circling the yellow threshing-floor, while his driver dozed on the chair fixed to the flint-studded sledge which is used to separate the grain from the ear. There was an old stone mill a little downstream from us, the water led in by a rough stone channel, and falling out in a thin stream. Here the pools were deep enough for the children to swim in, and they spent the afternoon scrambling over the rocks and sending leaf boats down on long, adventurous journeys to the distant sea.

We were surprised to notice a large hashish plant growing in a patch of potatoes and from casual conversation with the villagers learned that they were all admirers of the hashish smuggler, Georges Beg Yussef. In fact, they were hoping and expecting him to pay a triumphal visit to their village so that they could offer their congratulations to him. This probably explained the *gendarmerie* jeep which we noticed patrolling at intervals along the road, full of heavily armed *gendarmes*. 'That's nothing,' said our hosts; 'we had a celebration last night when we heard the news and let off some rifle-shots, but they don't know whose rifles they were, and they can't do anything about it.' Relations between the village and the *gendarmerie* appeared to be warily cordial, neither side wishing to provoke the other. It was a fruit-growing village, sending down late apricots to the coastal markets, but it supplemented its income by the cultivation of hashish. Prices, however, were bad this year, and a cause for concern. A plant was worth only three lira now, showing a fifty per cent drop on last year's prices. Like the apple growers of Lebanon, the hashish growers are also feeling the economic squeeze applied by Egypt, but, unlike the apple growers, they are not entirely dependent on one crop.

Hashish is mostly grown as a very profitable sideline, a cash crop that brings a quick return for very little outlay. Egypt is the principal customer, as hashish is a drug used to counteract the impotence caused by bilharzia, said to afflict eighty per cent of the Nile-valley population in some degree or other. The Egyptian buyers this year had cut the price drastically and the peasants were faced with a considerable drop in profits, but as the hashish traffic is largely illegal in Lebanon, it was not a matter they could very well raise through their parliamentary deputies. As far as we could understand from our hosts, the growing of hashish is not actually illegal, though we had heard of cases of crops being destroyed on the ground. Presumably in such out-of-the-way districts it is difficult to enforce any regulations which may exist, so what cannot be stopped is tolerated. The toleration extends to the harvesting and threshing of the crop, which is done in a windowless, air-tight room draped in sheets, in the grower's house. The plants are cut at the end of summer, when the green leaves are beginning to turn yellow. They are laid in rows on the floor of the dark room to complete the drying process, then they are gently beaten. The light dust resulting from this threshing clings to the sheets and is scraped off. The first threshing represents prime-quality hashish, for which the highest price is paid; subsequent threshing produces a coarser powder, for which there is a corresponding lowering of price. As long as the hashish remains in the grower's house, he is relatively immune from police action; it is only when the sealed-up packets of the drug, usually the size of a cigarette tin, are moved down to the coast that the police net comes into action. Stoppings and searchings on the main roads, running gunfights, secret motor-boat runs are all commonplace incidents in the smuggler-versus-excise-men intrigue which occupies a large part of the attentions of the Lebanese coastal patrols. There are check points along all the coast roads and it is nothing to see a whole busload of people being turned out on the roadside, while the excise men and *gendarmerie* search the vehicle.

The buying is done by agents who come up early in the season to estimate the crop and fix the price. When the hashish is ready for collection, a runner starts off on the dangerous job of getting it down to the collection centre. This is when the authorities try to intercept the traffic, and it is their wits against those of the smuggler and his agents. The big smugglers never leave town, and are men with considerable commercial interests; the carriers are armed and often shoot it out rather than surrender to a police-trap. Graft and corruption both play their part in this variation of the classic cops-and-robbers theme and famous smugglers have a sort of Robin Hood glamour in the remote mountain areas.

The peasants and mountaineers who grow the crop can see no reason why they should discontinue this profitable source of income. They never use it themselves, and wrap their faces carefully in their headcloths when they are threshing the dried plants, to avoid intoxication. Possibly an old man smokes it occasionally in his hubble-bubble pipe, we were told, if he is very old and ill, but that is unusual. Certainly we never saw any being used and were never offered any, though it is easy enough to obtain hashish-filled cigarettes in any bar or coffee shop in the seedier quarters of Beirut.

Our map indicated a route up a fork of the lower valley, which would bring us to Tannourine Tahta, lower down the mountain, but all the villagers assured us this route was impossible with the donkeys. A man on foot could do it, they said, but the track was too steep and too narrow for animals. 'You must go that way,' they said, 'that's the way to the Cedars,' and they pointed to the top of the steep cliff overlooking the village. A man named Nahlé, who had been gossiping with Elias most of the afternoon, offered to guide us as far as Hadeth el Jibbe, a small town on the edge of the Kadisha gorge. His fee was to be five lira, about ten shillings – the price of a day's labour. We were glad to accept this offer and whenever we could we used a local man to guide us over country where our map was faulty and unreliable.

Nahlé was a sturdy, well-set-up man with light tawny eyes. He had a slight cast in one which gave him a curious, enigmatic glance and this, with his ruddy sunburnt face and white teeth, made him look rather like a large, sinister Cheshire cat. But he was a guileless, garrulous soul, a great chatterbox and scrounger of cigarettes. He arrived at our camp at a quarter past three next morning and aroused Elias. 'In the name of God,' we heard Elias sleepily protest, 'what are you doing here in the middle of night?' Nahlé settled down imperturbably to pump the primus and make coffee, and gradually we dragged ourselves awake and lay listening to the birds in the soft, drowsy grey light. The children still slept huddled in their nest of blankets under the tree and we hesitated to awake them. 'Come on, come on,' we heard Nahlé urging Elias, so we rose and breakfasted, washed and packed, and then clattered up in the bright morning light to Nahlé's house, where he collected a bony young mule about two years old. With his well-cut breeches and tall black boots and a light-coloured headcloth twisted dashingly around his head, Nahlé looked infinitely superior to the rest of us, and he glanced complacently about him as we passed up the road through the village square, where the butcher was jointing a sheep he had just killed and the few small shops of the place were busy with customers. Before we left the square we passed by a small stone chapel, obviously older than the church on the other side of the square. Nahlé hopped off here and beckoned us to follow. Inside was a large oil painting of St George killing the dragon, the saint wearing a fierce black moustache with curled-up ends similar to a mountaineer's. The altar was decorated with silver and gold paper in a Byzantine pattern and around one of the columns supporting the arched roof were tied wreaths of flowers mixed with human hair. When we had admired all this we asked why the hair was there. Apparently it is cut from the head of any woman who dies in the village, but Nahlé's explanation was rather confused and perhaps we misunderstood him. He, having muttered a prayer, was now ready for departure, and it was about half-past six as we started to climb up through the village.

At first the track was moderately steep, but as we got higher it became increasingly difficult. It was a rough, rocky path leading up between the stone walls of the houses, with here and there a flight of steps to be negotiated. Then it became just a track, zigzagging steeply up a boulder-strewn slope. We started to labour early on, while the donkeys heaved and scrambled and the children hung on precariously. Ahead of us we could see Nahlé riding up with cheerful indifference, while we toiled on behind him, urging the donkeys and calming the children, who began to find the effort rather more alarming than they had anticipated. Below us we could see the flat roofs of the village, almost between our feet, it seemed, and the rim of the cliff opposite gradually came level with our eyes, so that we could see over it to the humped grey plateau of Laklouk. The sun was now striking clearly over the mountains and we could understand why Nahlé had been so anxious to get us off to an earlier start, for the heat of its rays could already be felt. At last we staggered up, puffed and panting after our twenty minutes' climb, to find him rolling a cigarette beside a big grey rock and pointing over to the west, where far away beyond the fleecy-white curl of cloud we could see the pale, shimmering line which indicated the sea.

We were now in a secluded fold of the hills and on looking about we saw we were passing by terrace after terrace of hashish. Sometimes it grew mixed in with other crops – potatoes and beans and other vegetables – but the farther we got away from the village, the more undisguised it was. Here and there tall sunflowers grew along its edge and the pink spires of mallow mixed with its pretty green leaves and cornflowers and other simple flowers of the English countryside. The plant itself is graceful and grows to two or three feet in height. It is only the female plant which produces the drug, from tufts of brownish-green flowers rather like overgrown mignonette which decorate the ends of its feathery spires. The male plants are much taller and can grow higher than a man. We had a splendid one growing beside our front door in Beirut, which reached ten feet high. It was a chance seed from a packet of bird food and was carefully tended by Elias in the hope of getting a good price for it, until its sex was established. One male plant can fertilise a considerable area of female plants, and here and there in the level terraces we could see one plant taller than the others – presumably male.

We were cutting over a bare upland which separates the valley of the Nahr el Djoz – river of walnuts – from the gorge of the Kadisha – valley of saints. Now that we had made nearly all the height that we needed, we were spared further scrambles, but instead had long hours of steady up and down slog. The sun beat down very fiercely and Nahlé took off his coat and tied it over his head as added precaution. The landscape was incredibly bleak and forlorn, for we had left the hashish terraces behind and now appeared to be straying through a desolate, stony waste, like some land afflicted by a biblical curse. We were high enough to look over vast tracts of country, the whole barren sweep of brown and thorny upland, with the purple line of the mountain hanging over the Adonis gorge far away on the horizon. Very occasionally we would see a poor, stony cabin beside a bare, ploughed field; once we came to a stretch of sparse chick-peas which Nahlé told us were his. Getting off his mule he stumped down in his heavy boots to pick us some bunches, for they are sharp and refreshing to chew. His mule promptly lay down and rolled, then galloped madly around the field until caught.

After some hours we began to ask Nahlé when we would reach Hadeth. 'Oh, in half an hour,' he would say airily, borrowing another cigarette; 'it's just over there,' and we would groan pathetically to each other, for we were beginning to know that half an hour in Nahlé's language was a mere figure of speech. On we toiled, drooping in the heat of the sun, gazing longingly at the implacable distances of the plateau in the hope of seeing our destination. Once we came over a shoulder of mountain to see below us a huddle of two or three stone hovels and a small church, white and dusty in the glare. A few fowls were picking about the doorsteps. The inhabitants sheltering in the shadowy recesses of their houses, and gazing out lethargically through the clouds of flies, saw too late that an event was passing through their village. We pushed on doggedly up the further slope, feeling that El Arissa was unlikely to provide anything to make delay worth while, and in the course of time came to a wide cup of terraced cultivation, green with young maize. The pale, stony ground gave way to a richer dark earth, and streamlets glinted along the irrigation trenches of the crop. The few houses we saw were coarse rectangles of stone piled together and ringed with thorn fences – primitive smoky troglodyte dwellings, though the people who crept out of them to see us were civil enough, ragged and backward as they might be. A spring trickling into a stone pond provided us with much-needed water and a plot of lettuces growing beside it with deliciously fresh, cool cos lettuce leaves which Nahlé commandeered from a youth and which we crunched gratefully as we went along. They tasted infinitely better than the most carefully dressed salad we might have eaten at home.

At last we topped a rise to see before us a landmark we had been expecting to see for the last two hours – the Cedars of Tannourine. Speckling the side of a grassy-green hollow, and clustering in a thick clump at its lip, they lay bathed in sunshine across the shallow declivity in front of us, and reassured us that we were not wandering in thrall to some demon king across his deserted kingdom. It was now about noon and we seemed to have been travelling since early daylight. Our feet were bruised and sore from the rough stones of our path and our ears dulled by Nahlé's constant stream of conversation. 'Like phonograph,' groaned Elias, 'gur-gur, cigarette, cigarette, that man he make me crazy.' As we breasted the rise at the level of the Cedars we at last saw Hadeth el Jibbe, pale and heat-washed across a desiccated landscape, with the sun flashing blindingly on the cars parked among the villas. Nahlé would have left us here, for he planned to sleep at an uncle's place down among the Cedars, but we persuaded him to come on with us to eat some food at a coffee shop. 'That Kadisha valley is a terrible place,' he muttered; 'even a drink of water costs you something. Think of that,' he repeated unbelievingly, 'a drink of water costing money. You don't want to stay in the town; get out as soon as you can and go on up the road to Dimane, where you'll find a spring.'

An hour elapsed before we finally trudged into the town, hot, tired and dusty. The first coffee shop we saw received our custom, and amid the wondering glances of the middle-class townsfolk who make up the summer clientele of the resort we tied up the donkeys and called for food and drink. An immense ilex tree shaded the terrace where we sat and a group of sportsmen at the next table were taking pot-shots with an air rifle, and amid great jubilation finally brought down a linnet. Nahlé looked incredibly out of place among the holiday-makers, with his big cat's face and strong, sinewy body; we also found the blare of taxi horns and scream of tyres disconcerting after the rustic quiet of our recent days. After eating, we prepared to be on our way. Nahlé led us with his pin-toed horseman's walk to a small store, where we bought a new bridle for Little Stick, some stores and some beads and ornaments for the other donkeys; then we shook hands all round and parted. With a last warning against the rapacity of the shopkeepers, he swung himself on to his beast and rode away into the hot afternoon.

FOUR

Up the Kadisha Valley to the Cedars, and across the High Lebanon

OUR ROAD WAS NOW LEADING through the very heart of the Maronite Christian Mountain. Owing to the isolation and intractability of its inhabitants, the mountainous area of Lebanon has always enjoyed a considerable degree of independence. Its essential apartness from the rest of the area was gradually recognised by the Ottoman Turks after their defeat of the Arab Mamluk caliphs in 1520 and the enormous expansion of their empire which then took place. By the next century the growing spirit of Lebanese independence was already becoming troublesome, and it became customary to refer to the area, its people and its problems simply as 'the Mountain'. This recognition of the peculiar status of the people inhabiting the Mountain was not tied to the supremacy of any particular religion. Christians, Moslems, Druzes, lived side by side in varying degrees of amity and alliance, linked together by a common determination to remain free of outside interference. By the mid-nineteenth century the autonomy of the Lebanon had been recognised by the European Powers, and it continued as an autonomous principality under a Governor until the outbreak of the Great War of 1914. The term 'the Mountain' has always had a certain political significance, and it is in that sense that we use it here.

We were edging up the lip of the great gorge which splits the mountainside beneath the most famous group of cedars in Lebanon. In a land riven on its seaward side with a succession of gorges, which cut down sharply through the soft limestone rock, the Kadisha valley is still considered remarkable for its depth and inaccessibility and the grandeur of its rocky scenery. It was here in the seventh century of our era that certain Christians of Syria, in religious conflict with the Byzantine Empire, retired under the leadership of Johannes Maroun, who bore the same name as the patron saint of their church, a fifth-century ascetic named Maroun. Under the leadership of Johannes Maroun the community developed into an autonomous nation, and safe in its gorges and wild mountain ranges maintained a precarious independence from Moslem caliph and Byzantine emperor alike. With the coming of the Crusaders, the Maronites entered into those friendly relations with the West, particularly with France, which they have maintained ever since. They provided guides and archers for the First Crusade and, with the establishment of the Latin Kingdom, found themselves accorded first place after the Latins, priority over other Christian denominations and the same rights as the Latin *bourgeoisie*. King Louis IX of France is regarded by tradition as their first and greatest friend, who wrote in 1250 that he considered the Maronites as part of the French nation. The protection and *amitié traditionnelle* which France extended to the Maronites continued through her intervention in the Druze and Maronite conflict in 1860, until her assumption of the Mandate at the end of the Great War in 1918.

The Latinisation of the Maronite rite commenced in the thirteenth century, but complete union with Rome was only effected in 1736. Traces of its Eastern origin remain in its use of a Syriac liturgy and in the acceptance of non-celibate clergy; but from the early days of the Latin intervention its relationship with the Roman Church was so good that the Maronites are described as 'roses among thorns' by one of the popes. This cordial relationship between the two Churches allowed the Roman Church to maintain missionaries in Lebanon almost without interruption throughout the whole period of the Arab and Turkish conquests, and from the seventeenth century onwards the presence of Capuchins and Jesuits contributed enormously to the intellectual awakening of Lebanon and through it to the rest of the Arab world.

The Maronite state was a theocracy, and the Patriarch its chief figure. To this day he has great prestige, and is an important figure in the Lebanese Republic. The President of the Republic has to be a Maronite. The Prime Minister is a Sunni Moslem; the President of the Chamber of Deputies a Shia Moslem, and the Cabinet portfolios have to be distributed in an established convention to members of the other religious denominations which make up the population of Lebanon. The Minister of War is a Druze, and other communities supply nominees for the rest.

The valley of the Kadisha retains its Syriac name, which means 'holy' or 'saintly', and it acquired this designation in medieval times, when Maronite hermits and monks took refuge in its caves. The gorge starts at the base of the amphitheatre in which the Cedars stand, and splits into a frightening chasm, sometimes 1,700 feet deep, which carves its way in a series of bends to the foothills above Tripoli. The stream which rushes out of the grotto at the head of the valley and falls in a long, thin waterfall on to the rocks below is joined farther down the gorge by another falling from the rocks below Mar Sarkis, and these are the two main sources of the river which eventually runs through Tripoli under the name of the Abu Ali. The summits of the cliffs are decorated with villages and small towns, whose church bells ring out sweetly on the mountain air. Down below in the gorge are the monasteries and hermitages which gave the valley its name, and in the walls and crevices of the cliffs are the caves and retreats of the anchorites. This withdrawal from the world was from early on a feature of primitive Christianity, and the first Maronites probably brought the concept with them from their original home in the Amanus mountains on the Turkish frontier. Some of these cells are almost inaccessible, more like eagles' nests than human habitations. The most important of the monasteries, Kannoubin, is itself carved in part out of the solid rock of the cliff, and hangs two-thirds of the way down the cliff, reached in half an hour's walk from the floor of the valley. Said to have been founded in the fourth century by the Byzantine Emperor Theodosius, the monastery became the seat of the Maronite Patriarch in the fifteenth century. Before that time he had tended to move from village to village, depending on the state of the country. The tombs of the Patriarchs are here, the coffins propped up vertically against the wall, and their glass covers allowing the relatively efficient conservation of the corpses by the dry air to be seen. Other monasteries and chapels are to be found along the entire length of the valley, the most notorious perhaps being that of Mar Antoun Beddawi (St Anthony of Padua), where as late as the last century lunatics were brought to be chained to the rocks in a dark cave, and fed on bread and water until the madness left them.

The sun was sinking towards the west as we finally dragged ourselves out of Hadeth in obedience to Nahlé's instructions. The great chasm was veiled in bluish obscurity, but the sun's rays, striking obliquely, lit up the sloping flanks of the mountain in a soft gold light. Far away up the valley we could see the dark smudge of the Cedars, like a tuft of pubic hair on the great sprawled mass of the mountain; along the cliff edges the pine trees and bell towers stood out in silhouette against the impending sunset. This was a scene frequently described by nineteenth-century travellers doing a tour of Syria and the Holy Land; 'sublime', 'grandiose', 'awful', are the words they employ, and indeed the whole has all those ingredients of large-scale scenery and romantic interest so dear to the travelling Victorian. We found it very hot, and the road very long. It ambled on through the tidy fruit orchards and past knolls of pine trees; on the other side of the valley we could see the same pattern repeated. We were all tired and dusty and dirty, but so trim and cultivated was the roadside area, we could see nowhere to camp. At last, rounding a bend, we saw ahead of us the Maronite Patriarch's modern summer residence at Dimane, a vast, sprawling stone building surrounded by pines growing right to the edge of the precipice. Here there was a spring, running out of a stone terrace beneath a straggle of acacia trees, and, bending down, we all drank gratefully and filled up our water-bottles. On a bluff overhanging the road was a pleasant, whitewashed, verandah'd house in a grove of pine trees, with a rough track slanting up the hillside towards it. We determined to camp somewhere up there in the woods, for they looked moderately secluded from the busy summer traffic of the road. Our approach seemed to alarm the household, for a woman came out to look at us, then retreated to reappear later with a pleasant-faced young matron and two little boys in cowboy jeans. On asking her if there was a spring in the vicinity, to our surprise we discovered she spoke fluent English; not only that, she invited us to camp beside her house, and to use its washing and cooking facilities as much as we wanted. With the easy hospitality of the East, beds and sofas were found for the children, and we settled ourselves in for the night on the wide verandahs. Mme Nassim, our hostess, was the wife of a Lebanese merchant trading in Nigeria, one of the many prosperous traders who left their native villages at an early age to make their fortunes in a foreign land. Their children now having reached the age of ten or thereabouts, their mother had brought them back to Lebanon to be educated at the French schools in Tripoli. The father returned every eighteen months to see his family, which in the meantime was wrapped close in the cocoon of family relationships and interests, and was secure from the pressure of loneliness and disorientation common to divided families.

'We're from Zghorta,' explained Mme Nassim, 'and normally our family always goes to Ehden for the summer. We've always had the same house, and it's much nearer and convenient for us, but after all that trouble with the Frangiehs and Douahis I simply couldn't risk it this year. Last year was bad enough – people were shooting backwards and forwards across the square, and in the end we had to give up our house and go down to Zghorta again. I was determined not to risk that happening again, so we took this house, which belongs to the Patriarch, and although it's rather far away from everything, at least we're not likely to be caught up in a shooting affray.'

Mme Nassim was referring to an incident in the clan warfare which still breaks out at intervals in these areas. Ehden, on the other side of the chasm, is notorious for the toughness and intractability of its inhabitants, and the blood feud is an accepted local custom. It was from Ehden that Yusuf Karam, a nationalist hero patterned after the European Risorgimento model, struggled to obtain the Governorship of the Lebanon from the Turks after the Druze–Maronite war and the European intervention of 1860. The son of the Maronite Sheikh of Ehden, handsome, lively, educated by the Jesuits, he struggled to obtain the supremacy of the Maronite cause, was deported by the Turks, returned, was captured, and ended his life in exile, following in the footsteps of those others who had attempted to slip Lebanon out of the grip of the Ottoman Empire.

The fierceness of the people of Ehden was one of Elias' favourite subjects of conversation. 'Women very strong at Ehden,' he would say, 'take it gun like man and Bang, Bang! they kill it other family, other man. In Ehden when they kill sheep or cow, all small boys he come stick it knife, make it blood, he no worry, he laugh, make him strong man.' We used to translate to him as well as we could the reports of the most horrible crimes we could find in our English newspapers. His eyes gleaming, he would respond with famous accounts of revenge and disaster. In this way we covered many a weary mile, the accounts of murder and chicanery being occasionally varied by descriptions of terrible road accidents, whole busloads and bridal parties destroyed, no difficult thing in a country where everyone drives as recklessly as in a Hollywood car chase.

Mme Nassim was kindness itself, and did all she could for us. Her maid, a strong, sullen, red-haired woman from Ehden, recovered enough to heat up a big kettle of water for us to wash in, and to exchange rather wary conversation with Elias. 'We couldn't think what you were at first,' said our hostess; 'my maid came in and said we should lock the house up, as some suspicious-looking people were coming up to it. We thought you must be gypsies, but when we saw the children we realised you couldn't be.' The children meantime were running gaily over the hillside with the Nassim boys, trying to get some chickens and guinea-fowl into their pen for the night, and came with reluctance to be scrubbed and put to bed, while the two little Nassim boys larked about in their bedroom, and the radio played, and the dark came welling up from the quiet floor of the valley.

We sat talking with Mme Nassim for a while, who was glad enough of company. It was interesting to think that M Nassim, like many thousands of present-day Lebanese, was following in the footsteps of his Phoenician ancestors, and seeking his fortune in a foreign land. From 3000BC onwards, the inhabitants of the coastal plain had turned their eyes westward to the sea, and struck out boldly for unknown shores. The towns that are now in many cases sleepy, sandy, forgotten fishing ports were then thriving city-states, jealous and independent of their neighbours, only coalescing into short-lived federations when danger or invasion threatened. From these early Canaanite settlements evolved the Phoenicians of history, receiving their name from the Greeks (*phoinix*: purple) with whom they traded, who identified them with the great purple dyeing industry of Tyre and Sidon. This industry, whose mounds of discarded murex shells are still piled up outside the walls of the shabby modern towns, was one of the chief factors in promoting the wealth and growth of the Phoenician city-states. Their situation and the enterprising nature of their inhabitants did the rest, for the caravans from faraway Mesopotamia and Arabia brought in goods from the borders of the known world, and the merchant adventurers of the coast traded them as far beyond the confines of the Mediterranean Sea as they could go. They were the great middlemen of the ancient world. They were not inventors, except possibly in the sphere of navigation. Rather they were utilisers and transmitters of other people's findings, among other things giving to the Greeks the prototype of the alphabet from which our modern writing is derived.

With the Graeco-Roman conquests not only the trade-goods and skills, but also the religious concepts of the area spread to the West. Long before the Christians set up their Church in Rome, the Phoenician merchant communities had brought their concept of death and redemption, personified in the Adonis legend, and the intense, emotional worship of the Great Mother, to all the maritime cities of the Occident. They set up colonies and communities in Europe from Hungary as far west as Spain, trading silk and linen, spices, glassware, ironwork, slaves, timber, dried fruit. Enthusiastic Christians from the fourth century of our era onwards, these merchant communities provided two popes during the early centuries of the Roman Church. It is to these popes that the Roman Catholic Church owes practically all the feasts in its calendar in honour of the Virgin Mary.

Our night was a disappointment to us. Ideal though the setting was, the dark pines clustering around us, the great valley in front, the last streaks of light lingering in the west, we did not sleep well. Hardly had we slid into the first layer of sleep than the mosquitoes attacked us and, worse than the mosquitoes, the sandflies – pigmy insects who by their size deny one the pleasure of slapping them dead. Through the succeeding hours of the night we tossed and turned, now falling into sleep, now roused to a restless irritation. At last, creeping in the night to our duffle-bags, we found a mosquito net and, dropping it over as many of us as it could reach, passed at last into peaceful slumber. We awoke next morning in the cool, piny mountain air, with the trees around murmurous with birds, and the new day bathing the huge prospect before us in the clear white light of morning. The sound of the bells up and down the valley rose clearly in the fresh dewy morning, mingled with the voices of people passing on the road below.

The Kadisha valley was in all its aspects something of an anti-climax for us. The days were blazingly hot, the nights tormented with sandflies and mosquitoes. On leaving Mme Nassim's house next day we had barely twelve miles to cover to the Cedars, but it was to take us another day before we reached them. The road climbed slowly but perceptibly as we approached the head of the chasm, and though the air was crisp and dry, the sun beat down fiercely and unrelentingly. At Hasroun, a small stone-built town, the houses built over vaulted stables and warehouses, we stopped to buy stores and new shoes for all the children, who by now were almost barefooted. The little town had a gentle, summery atmosphere, with people sitting about at open windows or on shaded terraces, roses and dahlias and fuchsias climbing and sprawling over the balconies and stairs and different levels of the houses, while every open space was green with fruit trees. The strong, solidly cut stone houses grew right to the very edge of the cliff, and fruit trees were cultivated at what seemed from afar almost unreachable terraces on the cliff face itself. The townspeople were friendly and courteous, and the shopkeepers in their cool, shady, vaulted stores, the fruit and vegetables spilling out of their containers all around them, did not laugh too much at the sight of our string of donkeys, and weighed and measured and took their money in a leisurely, good-humoured manner. The main street was a winding, narrow affair, and crowded with people, either summer visitors idling from store to store, or peasants from the surrounding country busy about their own business.

Once clear of Hasroun we made a better pace, but by the time we had come level with Becharré, on the other side of the gorge, and were beginning to descend slightly as we approached the bridge spanning the Kadisha River at the head of the chasm, it was obvious we would not reach the Cedars that day. We decided to camp and make an early start next day, so sought around for a suitable place. A chance encounter in a charming coffee-house at the side of the road solved our problems for us. A neat, wiry, sunburnt man was sitting under the shady vine trellis of the coffee shop, where a spring gushing from the mountainside behind was channelled through the terrace to fall with a refreshing sound into the stream bed beside the road. Clean and inviting with its white paint and bright advertisements and signs, the place was further enhanced by enormous clumps of dahlias and cannas, whose bright flowers formed a small hedge around the terrace, so one sat surrounded by flowers in a rush of sound. Our new acquaintance proved to be Nabil Geagea, one of Lebanon's ski-champions and an instructor at the Cedars ski-resort in winter. He owned some terraces of land not far from the coffee shop, near a stream, and professed himself only too happy to be of use to us and to lead us up to the Cedars. With his help we hoisted our gear up on to a very narrow cultivated terrace just above a pool, and by making a detour got the donkeys up on to the levels above us. It was rather like living in an apartment house but without the lift, and although the drop down into the pool or on to the stony stream was hedged off by trees and bushes growing to the lip of the terrace, it was essentially a place in which to avoid sleepwalking. We took the precaution this evening of hanging up our mosquito nets from various trees, and consequently slept better, but the croaking of the frogs below, the buzzing of the baffled insects and the snores of Elias all combined to disturb our night again.

Next morning Nabil was with us bright and early, and we got off to a good start. We crossed over the head of the gorge and started up towards the Cedars, skirting past Becharré. Nabil took Miles off with him on a mountaineer's short cut, all skip and hop and short, sharp rushes along goat tracks. We sedately decided to follow the road, which had begun to climb the mountainside above Becharré. Would that we had stuck to it, for Elias took the advice of a peasant boy we met, who pointed out to us what he considered the best way for a donkey to go up to the Cedars road. A few minutes later we found ourselves toiling up what appeared to be a staircase cut in the white limestone rock of a cliff. The donkeys had to turn and change direction every few yards, as the track went up in ever-narrowing angles. It was fascinating to watch how neatly they placed their feet, their wiry legs and small, strong hooves much more like a deer's or goat's than a horse's, their scrawny quarters coming right down on their hocks as they thrust and scrambled their way up the narrow track. The children hung on for a while, but finally preferred to walk, while Elias pounded and heaved and shouted, and we all panted and pushed, and finally got to the top. We met another family there, whose donkeys, laden with brushwood, were picking their way down as best they could, and whose bulging loads threatened to cause a traffic jam. Their children, little tiny things of barely walking age, were being brought down by a harassed-looking father, half leading, half carrying two toddlers, while three or four others were already bearing their share of the family burdens. Luckily we were just emerging on to easier going as we impinged on each other, and each party managed to get clear with its donkeys and children intact. We were completely exhausted by the time we scrambled back on to the main road, and had to flop down on the tarmac while we eased our trembling limbs.

The road now went up the mountainside in a series of zigzags, while the valley fell into perspective beneath us. We were dragging up to the rim of the amphitheatre, and seemed to hang like flies on the side of a bowl. Occasionally we would pause for a few minutes, to smoke a cigarette or rest our legs; then it was pleasant to sit on the roadside, on the angle of a turn, and catch the cool mountain wind on our faces, while below us the sunbaked valley dropped down into the hazy blue immensity of the chasm.

At last we came up to Miles and Nabil, nonchalantly sipping *gazoozas* at a wayside stall: they had arrived half an hour before, having followed the river bed and then sprinted straight up the mountainside. Where they were waiting was the entrance to the Kadisha grotto, from which the stream rushes out of the mountain, to fall in a long plume of spray to the valley below. A ceaseless noise of *service* taxis and buses testified to the popularity of the grotto as a tourist attraction. Family parties of plump, perspiring matrons and anxious fathers, their sallow offspring clutched to them, teetered in groups along the narrow path which leads along the flank of the mountain to the grotto. So dizzy is the drop that many prefer to avert their eyes, until safe in the galleries cut out of the side of the mountain. The grotto itself is not so impressive as the Jeita caves from which the Dog River, nearer Beirut, emerges out of the mountain. Those are indeed the 'caverns measureless to man', and the river rushing turbulently over cataract and waterfall in the dark, unmeasured recesses of the caves widens at the last into a silent, limpid, icy-green lake beneath a vast, cathedral-like vault, then sluices through a narrow cave mouth into the sunny sylvan luxuriance of its valley. The Kadisha is a smaller affair, and its stalactites and stalagmites and grotesque rock formations are lit up and displayed by the electricity which generates it and which supplies the town of Tripoli with light.

The commercial aspects of tourism are in considerable evidence all around the Cedars: soft-drink sellers, ice-cream men, touts, souvenir-sellers. The souvenirs are all objects made out of cedarwood and highly varnished. We pleased Elias by buying him a cigarette box with the national emblem of Lebanon – a cedar – carved on it, but even that cost us approximately the price of a day's food. The children were all agog to spend money, but we hurriedly removed them, and amid the sardonic comments of the taxi-drivers – monopolists these, who viewed our donkey transport with disfavour, as smacking of dangerous independence on the part of visitors – crawled on upwards towards the top. Nabil now varied the tedium of the ascent by lightly springing up a goat track from time to time, thus cutting off an angle, while we heaved ourselves up after him, clutching at clumps of sage and cistus and arriving on the level above with our breath coming in painful heaves. At last the road made the necessary height, and ran quietly along the edge of the amphitheatre. The remains of a military camp, whose huts had been turned into winter-sports chalets with names like 'Bambi', 'the Sherpas', 'Kozy Knouk', indicated that we had reached our destination. The road rambled up past a hotel and a few stores, turned a corner, and there we were. Several shopkeepers immediately darted out of their shops with demands for custom – postcards, soft-drinks, souvenirs, etc. – and another contingent broke into a brisk argument as to who was to extract an entrance fee to the Cedar grove from us.

The Cedars themselves grow in a hollow, surrounded by a stone wall, to whose construction Queen Victoria contributed. One descends a stair to reach the enclosure. The trees belong to the Maronite Church, whose Patriarch once a year holds an open-air service at an altar in the middle of the grove, attended by thousands of people from all over the Lebanon. This ceremony occurs at the Feast of the Transfiguration, in the early part of August, and the celebration is not entirely religious in character. From earliest daybreak bus and carloads of people drive up to the Cedars, laden with picnics and children and babies and musical instruments, and camp out all day, and even sometimes the night, in and around the trees. Among the local inhabitants the trees have a certain quasi-mystical reputation: they are known as the Cedars of God, or the holy trees. The movement of their boughs is said to indicate the coming of snow, and various legends still surround them. They are said to be endowed with perpetual life, and great care is taken to preserve them from injury, though probably the banishing of the goatherds and the presence of a forester do more to ensure their continued existence than anything else.

Elias and our friend Nabil between them routed the horde of importunate shopkeepers and we all descended into the grove. It is very fine. The trees themselves, about four hundred in number, grow on and about a few stony knolls, and the enclosing wall has a circumference of something over half a mile. A dozen of the trees are very old – perhaps over a thousand years – and the biggest is about seventy-five feet high and measures thirty-six feet around its trunk. The age of the others is variously estimated as ranging from two hundred to eight hundred years, and apart from these there are several very young seedlings and saplings, the reward of the prohibition of goat grazing. We had been prepared to find the Cedars something of an anticlimax, but the trees themselves were not. Perhaps it was the contrast of the shady cool beneath their boughs with the glaring heat of the sun outside, perhaps the tranquillity and calm of the deserted grove after the stress and strain of the negotiations preceding our entry. We chose a secluded spot on a grassy knoll and prepared to unload our gear. Now we found the explanation of the vague, soothing hum which had followed our wanderings among the majestic trees. It was the noise of innumerable bluebottles and blowflies living off the debris left behind by picnickers. Examining the long grass, we found sardine tins and bully-beef cans by the hundreds, old bottles, cartons and containers of every description, rotting fruit, human faeces – every manifestation, in fact, of man's ability to turn a noble site into a rubbish dump. With every step the insects rose murmurously in the still, cedar-scented air, then settled into contented clusters on whatever was engaging their attention. Even Elias wrinkled his nose in disgust, and in unanimous agreement we turned towards the remotest end of the enclosure. We decided to leave the children and gear in the cool and quiet of the grove while we looked for a camp site outside. This was easier said than done, and after having rejected two suggestions – one in a half-finished house used as a lavatory by the neighbourhood, and the other in a field already occupied by a hundred very active beehives – we threw ourselves on the mercy of the Hotel des Cèdres. This was a large, rambling building with two fine cedars on its terrace, and no clients. A site was found for us in an orchard of young walnut trees, near the hotel's water-tank, with splendid views of the mountains around us, and a faraway glimpse of the sea.

The Cedars has some reputation as a summer resort, but we could see very little evidence of much activity in this respect. We stayed five days in our site behind the hotel, and were the only people to use the place. The other hotel, at the entry to the village, seemed equally deserted. Occasionally a car would bring up a party of tourists, or a bus unload a school excursion, or similar group, but there was no resort life of any kind. The quiet and seclusion were not unpleasant, only the sun beat down fiercely on our site all day, and we were forced to take refuge in the shadowy recesses of the hotel. No doubt in winter it is a jolly place, with winter-sports enthusiasts clumping about, but in summer it has a rather meaningless atmosphere – its rooms too big, its ceilings too high, its corridors too long. We, however, had nothing to complain of. A lavatory and bathroom were placed at our disposal, and hot water in cans produced from the kitchen by a succession of wild-looking serving youths. Elias went down to Beirut for two days and came back furious at having had to pay twice as much as usual for his seat on a *service* taxi. The service up to the Cedars being a monopoly, the drivers charged what they liked, and such is the reputation of the inhabitants of the Ehden and Becharré, nobody dares challenge them. The taxi-drivers of the Lebanon are a very tough and very important part of the community. Apart from the village buses, which in remote parts make perhaps one trip up and down a day, almost all the country traffic is in the hands of *service* taxis. Wherever the roads go, the taxis go, and sometimes farther. Cram-jammed into their seats, the passengers ride five or six at a time, each paying a standard fee calculated unerringly on the price of petrol per gallon. Sometimes the driver owns his car, sometimes he rents it, sometimes he is employed by a taxi company. In the towns the taxis are the newest American Fords, Hudsons, Chevrolets, brightly coloured and with enormous fins. The farther up into the mountains one gets, the more battered and disreputable the cars become, but they all have one characteristic in common. Their drivers are skilled, tough and fast, and the competition among them is extremely fierce. With them, it is possible to move from one end of the country to the other, and over into Syria, very cheaply and very fast. Without them, the whole country bogs down into immobility. There is no railway system worth speaking of, except for the transport of goods, up and down the coast, and laboriously racked up over the mountains between Damascus and Beirut by a small-gauge line.

* * *

Our camp lay alongside the spiny hillside where wandering families of shepherds grazed their flocks. We used to hear them tootling on their flutes as they led their animals among the rocks and pastures of the mountain flank, or came themselves to fetch water from the spring. They used to bring us cans of foaming fresh milk, and cheese curds, and sometimes trade a few eggs for a handful of tea or soap-powder. Their women were ruddy, sunburnt creatures, their brown hair bleached tawny by the sun, their limbs gaunt and wiry from the rough open-air life they lived, and they usually had a child or two to carry or load on their little asses, already heavily laden with cans of water slip-slopping against their sides.

From these people we enquired the best way down the mountain flank to Mar Sarkis and the forest of Ehden, from where we intended to make our way around the mountain to Sir ed Dénié, at the head of the next valley. We wished to avoid using the tarmac road again, and hoped that by following the goatherds' tracks we would be able to travel more quietly and easily. An alternative route was to cross the mountain here, over the pass up which the ski-lift ran, and then bear away leftwards to the source of the River el Bared, and drop down on to Sir ed Dénié. This we decided against, as the huge bulk of the mountain looming above us whenever we raised our eyes seemed too formidable a project for our ramshackle organisation and load of small children. But as events turned out, we were forced to take it.

In the meantime, it was decided to reconnoitre the route along the mountainside, prior to departure next day. The two men and Miles rode off at dawn on the donkeys. Following a faint track in the thistly foothills, they at last reached the base of the mountain proper and then turned west. A ride of nearly two hours through the expanse of barren hillside, with here and there a terrace of hashish making a wedge of green against the tawny slopes with their tangles of grey rock and awkward sprawls of dried-up watercourses, brought the party in sight of Ehden, lying ominously quiet below them. A wild, ragged shepherd running three hundred yards through the scrub to cadge a cigarette gave them their first indication of trouble down in the valley below, but his story was confused and his dialect difficult for Elias to follow. Having beaten off a pack of dogs which flew at Little Stick and Miles, they started back along the same route, passing by the tents of the shepherds on a craggy promontory overlooking Becharré. Near here they encountered a party of prosperous-looking citizens from a village near Ehden, who had prudently taken to the hills at the news that fighting had broken out in Ehden between the Frangieh and Douahi families. Elias and Miles drank in the news with the greatest interest. A minor clash one day had developed into a major battle yesterday, lasting from six a.m. to six p.m. The quarrel seemed to have been over irrigation water – a fruitful source of discontent in an area where every terrace depends for its survival in the dry summer months on a careful system of irrigation. An officer of the *gendarmerie* had been shot dead while examining a disputed claim, whereupon the major in charge of the *gendarmerie* withdrew his forces and called on the army for aid. 'If you want to see men being shot down like birds out of the sky, go to Ehden,' said the village worthies, all agog with the disaster. 'Would you believe it? They're even knocking the houses down with their cannons.' The army had apparently moved into Ehden overnight, bringing tanks and mortars with them. One house had been destroyed by mortar fire, which had impressed everyone immensely, and the troops were mortaring the surrounding woods and hillsides where the warring families had taken refuge.

This news put our projected route out of the question. The army was in control of the area, the road was cut, and the whole mountainside would be full of people taking their traditional refuge out of the immediate reach of the forces of law and order. This Frangieh and Douahi feud was one of long standing. Both families are notables of the Maronite community, and both claim descent from Crusader families who with the end of the Latin Kingdom sought refuge in the mountains rather than follow the Lusignans to Cyprus. Already in spring the ill-feeling between the two families, and the Frangiehs' allies, the Awads, had burst into open violence at Miziara where during Mass one Sunday morning, and in the presence of three bishops, members of the warring families shot it out inside the small stone church, killing seventeen people and wounding twenty more. This shocking outburst had been in part occasioned by the electioneering tactics of a priest belonging to one of the families concerned, and with the election of the new Parliament it had been hoped that the trouble would end. But now it was obvious to everyone that the area would be unsettled for a long time, and that the army would probably be quartered on Ehden to damp down trouble, rather as it had been in Akoura some years previously.

Back at the Cedars, we decided to cross the mountain at the ski-lift, and make our way around Kornet es Saouda, the highest mountain in the Lebanon range, over 10,000 feet high, and so on westward to Sir. In order to put ourselves in a better position for an early start we decided to camp the next night at the foot of the ski-lift, where there was a coffee shop, and send the donkeys up the pass unladen, very early the next morning, while we followed up with the children and luggage on the ropeway.

Not far from our camp, and just opposite to the entrance to the Cedars, was a small coffee shop, conveniently sited under the shade of an enormous old cedar tree. Here we formed the habit of taking our main meal of the day, while Elias was in Beirut. It was pleasant to idle away a hot noontide under the shade of a coloured umbrella, with bees and insects humming drowsily in the banks of golden rod which formed a sort of hedge around the terrace, and watching the occasional tourists in their bright clothes being mulcted by the inhabitants. Sometimes a party of wild, gipsy-like drovers or horse-dealers would come past on their way down to Becharré and the coast, for a rough stone road runs past the Cedars and continues up the mountain in closely angled zigzags to the Col des Cèdres, then down into the Beka'a valley the other side. It is a military road, built by the French, and only practicable in summer, when the snow is gone. Being rough and unsurfaced, it is little used except by herders and the occasional lorry freighting goods by the shortest route, instead of making the long descent to the coast and then up the main road from Beirut to Damascus by the Dahr el Baida pass into the Beka'a.

The owners of the coffee shop were a pair of tall, thin, lantern-jawed young men, grim and reserved in their manner, rarely smiling or speaking unnecessarily. Helping them was their mother, a scrawny old woman in rusty black, two grey pigtails sticking out peasant-fashion from under her black headcloth. It was with great surprise that we realised one day that she was addressing us in perfect English, although pronounced with a strong American accent. It appeared she was the child of Lebanese immigrants, born and grown up in Chicago, and although the family had long since returned and settled into its original environment, she had never forgotten her second language. They were a curious family, more like rather morose hillbillies than the usual open-faced mountaineers. They held aloof from the other inhabitants of the settlement, and concentrated entirely on running their business, which they did very efficiently. During the course of our stay there they became less forbidding towards us, and their mother was always most helpful about stores, and shopping, and lending a primus when ours broke. Elias came up from Becharré one day with shining eyes: 'Very strong family this, six, seven brothers, three sisters – one brother he shoot it sister, one year jail, mother she no say nothing.' Apparently a report having been brought to one of the brothers that his sister, a girl of about twenty, had been seen flirting with a *gendarme* – they were sitting at neighbouring tables in a cafe in Becharré – he seized his gun, ran straight to the cafe, shot his sister dead. The *gendarme*, warned in time by a friend, made his escape. The brother, arrested, claimed he was defending his family's honour, and was given a year's imprisonment. He is now free. Cases similar to this occur frequently not only in the distant mountain areas, but also in the towns and villages of the coast. Brothers are particularly zealous in defending their family's name, and woe to the sister or mother who is indiscreet or unchaste, and the man who is rash enough to tamper with another man's family. This fierce and primitive concept of honour ensures a very high standard of behaviour among the poorer Lebanese, and among the Christians divorce is very uncommon. Marriages are arranged by the families, perhaps with the aid of the priest or a professional matchmaker. The dowry and the girl's future inheritance are questions of the greatest importance. The whole family enters into the affair, and although it is now becoming rarer for a girl to be married off willy-nilly to a man of her parents' choice, considerable pressure is brought to bear on her by all her relatives to fall in with the family's wishes.

Our last day at the Cedars was a Sunday, very hot and stifling, with coachloads of tourists arriving from early morning and flocking into the cedar grove. Next week the Patriarch was due to celebrate the yearly Mass at the altar in the grove, and we began to have some idea of what it would be like. The tourists were mostly people from the towns out for the day, clad in brightly coloured cottons and jeans, the youths bearing guitars, accordions, drums and other musical instruments, the girls frequently wearing toreador pants or American style play-clothes. Every group had its elderly female relatives with it, for the Levant seems to have more old women per family than seems possible, and scores of little children and babes in arms added to the confusion. The soft-drink and ice-cream sellers did a roaring trade, and so did the postcard and camera-film men. The sacred grove resounded to the thump and twang of popular song-hits and the delighted squeals of sportive youth, while the pop-pop of airguns indicated that the small birds of the vicinity were being pursued by shooting enthusiasts. It was a noisy, animated scene, in contrast to the somnolent calm of the previous days, but we were glad to think we were leaving it behind.

As soon as the sun began its decline, and a light cooling breeze rose up, we struck camp and loaded. A great agitation arose among the children as to the carriage of their caterpillars – splendid fat green things with tufted bodies diamonded with pink and light blue warts, which lived in the walnut trees of our camp. They were the larvae of the Great Peacock Moth, and were the object of much jealous attention on the part of the children. We finally persuaded Elias to surrender two porridge tins, whose lids we pierced and which we filled with walnut leaves, and in these containers we carried with us a few favoured specimens. Anthea was particularly assiduous in collecting caterpillars and beetles, and enjoyed coming up to press a squashed and furious-looking spider into one's hand. It was always unnerving to see a child coming towards us with an oddly distorted face, until we realised that it was a grasshopper or praying mantis clinging to a nose or eyebrow which was responsible for the changed appearance. They used to put their trophies into the tent, and would sprawl happily playing cards or quarrelling over dominoes, while insects of various kinds crawled and flopped and hopped about them.

We parted amicably from the Armenian hotel manager and the Keyrouz family at the coffee shop. They commended us to their elder brother Selim, who kept the coffee shop at the foot of the ski-lift, where we proposed to spend the night. The ski-lift is a mile or so above the Cedars, where the tarmac road ends and is succeeded by the stone road. It is nearly a mile and a half in length, and takes one to a pass overlooking the whole sweep of the Kadisha valley.

Selim Keyrouz welcomed us warmly at his little establishment, and offered to go up himself with Elias and the donkeys next morning, or to send his son Dib. He was a much gentler, simpler person than either of his younger brothers down below, tall, thin, with large dark blue eyes like theirs, grizzled hair, and the loose black trousers and handwoven shirt of the mountaineers. He had a little daughter of whom he was very fond and a pet quail in a cage. His coffee shop was small, but conveniently situated for the tourist traffic at the ski-lift, which remains in use summer and winter. We settled down comfortably enough for the night on the floor of the coffee shop, with the baggage piled in readiness for the hoist up next morning. Little Stick caused a momentary alarm by wandering off towards a shepherd's encampment behind a flock of sheep. Having been bred as a shepherd's donkey, he seemed to suffer a compulsion to follow sheep whenever he saw them, but the boy Dib retrieved him, and we tethered him firmly for the night. Early the next morning Elias and Selim set off riding the unladen donkeys; we could watch them creeping like tiny specks up the steep face of the pass. It took them an hour and a quarter to reach the top, riding for all except five minutes of the time. We in the meantime waited until the ski-lift began operations at nine thirty a.m., then sent the luggage and ourselves up on it. The children were very excited to see the duffle-bags and gear being slung on to the chairs by the attendants and moving inexorably away up the mountainside. They were even more excited when their own turn came. Miles and Anthea travelled by themselves, and we took the small ones on our knees. It takes about a quarter of an hour to reach the top, and the lift travels quite high above the ground, spiny and sharp with rocks. Looking back, one saw the valley dropping away below one with a sickening fall. On the landing platform one had to look sharp to jump clear of the chair before it swung round on its downward journey, but with the help of the engineers we all got off safely, to find Elias and Selim waiting for us. Loading the donkeys, we straggled off up a stony gully in a muddle of goats, tourists and children, come like ourselves from the valley below. A few minutes' walk brought us to the very head of the pass, the tourists waved us goodbye, and the whole vast, blue-shadowed horseshoe of the Kadisha valley, with its curving enclosure of mountain, its sweeping fall and sharp-shadowed gorge, disappeared from our sight. Before us stretched an essentially Central Asian landscape – a shallow stony valley patched with snow leading away into the distance between bare brown peaks, and a brilliant blue sky over all. Coming towards us was a nomad family on the move to the valley below, where they hoped to obtain work during the threshing season. They passed us silently and aloofly, with their brightly caparisoned camels padding softly across the rough ground, their fierce, shaggy dogs snarling suspiciously, their women and small children riding or walking among the little asses, the babies carried on their mothers' backs and small, sun-bleached children of three or four stepping out manfully in the file. There was a disciplined purposefulness about their long, striding march and silent, self-contained demeanour that put our untidy organisation to shame. Strung out against the pale brown hillside they looked bright and barbaric and remote from any contact with our own day.

Aided by Selim, we pitched the tent in a hollow below the skyline, near a patch of snow. Noon was approaching, and rather than risk a late start and the possibility of not getting through the high mountain plateau that day, we decided, perhaps unwisely, to rest now and start the next day at the crack of dawn. Shortage of water was our great worry, for there are no springs in the central plateau, and travellers rely on melting snow-water for their needs. According to Selim, Sir was about six hours' march away, provided we did not lose our way, but experience had already taught us the unreliability of local estimates in relation to our own performance. Consequently we decided to risk the water, and make sure of getting off to a good start the next day. The donkeys did not greatly care for snow, which they refused to touch, even when it was melted down for them into water. We made snow tea, which was drinkable, but not very appetising. Around the rocks at the head of the pass grew a pretty mauve vetch of some sort, some eighteen inches high, with a rich green leaf, but apart from this there was very little vegetation of any sort. The donkeys grazed away industriously at whatever there was, and the children played in the snow, and we checked over our baggage for the morning. As soon as the sun dipped behind the mountain, the cold rushed at us. We huddled into all our pullovers, made supper and prepared for an early night. It was bitterly cold, and even our down sleeping-bags were hardly adequate protection. The moon and stars shone down brightly, while a bitter wind whistled over the crest of the pass, and crept into our bedding. We were up at the first grey light of dawn, and on our way very quickly. The donkeys had not drunk properly now for thirty-two hours, except the little snow water we had eventually induced them to take, but they were well fed and rested, as were the children. 'Go straight down the valley,' Selim had told us on parting the day before, 'and take the third valley on your left, before Kornet es Saouda. You can't miss it if you count carefully, and that will bring you eventually to a place we call Samarra. You've got to go westward all the time, once you're clear of Kornet es Saouda, but don't worry, there are shepherds in all these mountains; you'll find them near the snow patches, and they will put you on the right track.' We set off down the wide, barren valley, following the track of the nomad family we had seen yesterday. On either side stretched the naked, tawny mountainside, swelling so that our view was confined to the prospect before and behind us. Occasionally a big patch of dingy snow lay glistening in the early sunlight, and the dew still pearled the small plants sparsely covering the bare brown earth. It was not unpleasant striding down this steppe-like waste, with only the empty hills around us, and the track sloping gently downwards into the pale, stony distance. By and by we saw a larger mass humping itself up among the rocks and boulders on our left. This was Kornet es Saouda, the highest mountain of the range, and our landmark for the first leg of the march. Here we turned left into a stony, boulder-strewn valley, and continued onward into a complex of dried-up watercourses and thorny open spaces. On either hand the barren, rocky mountainside lay tumbled about us, with great screes of fallen rock and curious circular hollows, of considerable extent, filled with a loose debris of rocks and boulders. Presumably it is through these funnels that the snow drains down into the underground hollows of the mountain range, whose reservoirs keep the springs of the mountain flanks flowing throughout the dry season. Once we were challenged by a fierce shepherd's dog, which sprang snarling at us from behind some rocks; his owner, equally shaggy and fierce-looking, indicated we should follow the track we were on, but his dialect was almost unintelligible to Elias. The track eventually brought us out on to a wide, open grazing area, with valleys running into it from every angle. We could see the marks of campfires and the tracks of camels, so presumably the nomads had camped here on their way to the pass. The place was littered with curious stones and sharp slivers of rock, and as we crossed it the children amused themselves by picking up rough and ready axeheads. We were far from sure of our direction by now, but continuing along the track we came over a small rise to find ourselves looking down on to a grassy green hollow in which were some tents.

Our appearance on the skyline brought a small crowd of women and children out of the tents, and we were greeted with friendly curiosity as we came down into the hollow. Here the turf was green and smooth, and we were glad to slacken the curb-reins and let the donkeys graze. The sun was hot, and the shade of the tents looked inviting. Our hosts were a family of poor graziers and cheesemakers who spent the summer season with their flocks, carrying their cheeses down once a week to market in Sir. With many hospitable words and gestures we were led by the hand to the largest of the tents, where the housewife was busy heating a great shallow iron dish of goats' milk over a smoky wood fire and, with the aid of her daughters and other womenfolk, preparing the cheese for market. Most of the men were out on the mountainside with the flocks, but the headman of the family, a tall, striking giant of a man, partially paralysed down one side by what appeared to have been a stroke, was in the camp. They were a very friendly, hospitable family, shaggy and unkempt though they might seem. The long, black tent was scrupulously tidy, the quilts and bedding stacked up neatly, pillows and bolsters ranged comfortably around the sides, so as to give support to the back. With cheerful insistence, they brought us plates of delicious cool fresh yoghurt, wonderfully refreshing and stimulating, and flaps of thin mountain bread. Their sustenance seemed to consist mainly of goats' milk, for except for the flour and sugar and oil they had brought up with them when they moved up for the summer, they had only a few chickens to supplement their diet. Presumably on their weekly trips down to the market the women might bring back tomatoes and cucumbers from their gardens down below.

'Stay with us for the day,' they said; 'some of us women are going down to Sir with the cheese this afternoon or tomorrow. Wait till then and we will show you the way down – it's only two or three hours away.' We were tempted, but there was no water near the site, even though the headman led Elias off to a small seepage half a mile away. It was so slow and dried out as to be useless for us and, being anxious for the donkeys, we decided to press on alone. We had some sweets with us, which we distributed among the children of the encampment, to the great delight of the headman's little curly-haired son Yusuf. While everyone was still speculating as to who and what we might be, Yusuf had told his mother that the strangers in big boots might very well be bringing sweets for him, and, behold, his belief was justified.

Having spent nearly three hours with these friendly people, we set off once more, guided by a young girl who led us back to the grazing plain, and into a desiccated valley leading off it. Here she left us, after having explained carefully to Elias the landmarks we were to follow. The valley led down steeply beneath a soil-eroded hillside, speckled with the dry grey stumps of a ruined cedar and cypress forest. At one time the whole of this western slope of the mountain must have been thickly forested, but steady cutting had cleared off huge tracts of it. Our way continued downwards till the valley ran into another, more chasm-like, with steep, precipitous walls hung with stunted trees and shrubs. The track was rough and uneven, and not always easy to follow. We were obviously coming down from the high central massif into the head of a valley system, for the farther down we came, the thicker and more established was the growth. The exhausted forest gave way to a curiously malformed one, the trees having been systematically deprived of their main trunk, and a subsidiary growth having been allowed to take its place. The trees were all consequently lop-sided, the secondary development being all on the left-hand side. Presumably, when this was sufficiently matured it in turn would be lopped, and a third limb encouraged to grow in its place.

The sides of the valley grew rougher and wilder, as the track twisted down ever more steeply. Elias and the two larger donkeys, with Anthea and Sabrina riding them, drew farther away from us. Little Stick, with Sebastian up, made increasingly heavy weather of the descent, and in the hot afternoon he began to lag badly. We took part of his load ourselves, in an attempt to hasten his pace, and to no avail. We continued on through the solitude, and the valley began to show unmistakable signs of human occupation. Once we came to a woodcutter's cabin, a small, smoky, stone house in a small stone enclosure. Sitting silently outside the locked door were three small children, hardly more than babies; beside them was a bucket and tin mug, unfortunately empty. The children gazed at us speechlessly with enormous eyes, too startled by our strange appearance to cry out. Their parents were apparently cutting and carrying wood far up the mountainside. At last a narrow terrace of cultivation appeared below us – yellow corn ripe for plucking. We scrambled down laboriously with renewed energy, and had our reward in a pannikin of cool, fresh water begged from a young woman in a cottage among the corn. She was a pleasant-faced young matron, wearing the frilled trousers and cretonne petticoats of the Moslem peasants. 'There is a spring over there,' she said, pointing up towards a shaggy, wooded bluff overhanging the valley, but seeing our hot and travel-worn appearance, she hastened to bring us a full pannikin from her day's store. We shared this among the four of us gratefully, so delicious did it taste, it being the first fresh spring water we had drunk since we left the Cedars forty-eight hours before. Rather to her surprise, we gave Little Stick what remained in the bottom of the pannikin, which he sucked up in two or three draughts. The knowledge that we had passed over the worst, and were down within reach of water again, cheered us up, and we set off in pursuit of Elias. He, meantime, was far ahead, and we caught up with him waiting for us an hour later.

The narrow valley now curved around and opened into a cultivated plateau, which stretched broad and smiling in front of us as we emerged out of the rocky defile. All around we could see trees and fields and people busy about the harvesting of their grain, and dotted among the trees we could see flat-roofed houses and farms. After the sun-scorched solitude of the high mountain tableland, this Breughel-like scene of peasant activity and summer fruitfulness was entrancing to observe. 'Let's stay here,' we said, 'and go on down to Sir tomorrow.' 'There are no springs here,' we were told by the first farmer we encountered; 'such water as we have is rainwater stored in tanks – here, have some,' and he handed us a kettle full of warm, rather tasteless water. 'There are springs there,' and he pointed up the shaggy flank of the bluff enclosing the plateau, 'and there's a splendid spring straight ahead, only an hour's walk, the Cold Spring (Nebaa es Bared) which has all the water in the world, and which supplies Sir Dénié.'

This dashed our expectations, and we decided to go on, for Elias was always very firm and insistent on using nothing but spring water. The golden glow of afternoon was flooding the whole plateau as we stepped out along the winding path. People took little notice of us, being busy with their crop. Occasionally we would meet a pair of sleek oxen on their way to a threshing-floor, or a woodcutter riding up on his tall, gaunt mule. The mules were enormous brown brutes, sixteen hands high, with great round hoofs and big flat knees. They were very splendidly caparisoned with carefully worked crimson meshes over their quarters, hung with blue and scarlet wool bobbles. They clinked and jingled with beads and bells as they drew near, and their riders, rough, wild men with fierce moustachios and thick, black, fringed wool turbans worn at swashbuckling angles over one eyebrow, clattered past us with the barest of greetings. We had not seen people like these before, and realised we had moved into country entirely new to us.

An hour elapsed, and we were still threading our way through fields and orchards. Our spirits again began to flag, especially as we found that the path was starting to climb once more. As the day drew in, and the soft afternoon light began to dull, we noticed men and women were streaming in from the fields and converging on the path we had been following. We could hear the calls and shouts from group to group and the tinkling of goat-bells and donkey-bells as they slowly drew away from their fields. Some of the donkeys had great sheaves of grain tied to them, others bore sturdy black-clad peasants and little brown, shaven-headed boys. 'Where are you going to?' asked a jolly young man on a tall chestnut mare, seeing us resting disconsolately under some fruit trees. 'We're trying to reach the Cold Spring, in order to camp for the night,' we replied; 'everyone tells us it's just ahead, but we never reach it.' 'It's up there,' said the young man, pointing to the right of the track, 'under that clump of big trees which you can see right on the skyline. But by the time you've got up there, you could be down in B'kaa Safrine, the village to which all this land belongs, if you follow this path.'

Fleecy white clouds had been gathering in the sky for some time, and even as we spoke the faraway clump of trees was obscured in a drifting cloud of mist. We decided to stick to the track and follow the rest of the people down into the village. The climb up to the pass was steep, and Elias again soon left us behind. On reaching the top, to our surprise we looked down into a sea of mist. The path twisted around a rock and disappeared down into the cloud. This was an unexpected development, and we stood hesitant in the eery stillness. By and by we heard below us the distant noises of human habitation; somewhere under our feet, it seemed, was a village, and even a road, for we heard once the ghostly hoot of a car horn. The track down was extremely steep and narrow, turning constantly on itself, so that it was like going down a very awkward stair. The mist closing in around us enabled us to see only what was immediately in front: we had no idea of what sort of a drop was below us. Sebastian now decided that walking was safer than riding, and leading the tired Little Stick by his head-rope, set off resolutely down into the cloudy unknown, accompanied by his mother. It was an interminable descent, made doubly tiring by the sharp drop of the rough steps and the extreme narrowness of the angles, so that Little Stick had sometimes to be manoeuvred around with the utmost care. Halfway down a tremendous clattering, muffled by the mist, warned that something was coming up, and shrinking back against the rocks Sebastian saw a huge mule brought to a sliding, stone-rattling halt beside him, while the wild, bandit-like rider glared down at him. The child, with commendable assurance, in view of the circumstances, stared boldly back and, after a pause, the man's face split in a flashing white smile, and he leant down and handed our small son two sweets, then with a clatter of hoofs swept on upwards into the mist.

An hour later we at last reached level ground, and the mist began to clear, although the cliff above us remained wreathed in cloud. We found the rest of the party beside a beautiful clear spring which ran out beside a pear orchard. And here at last the donkeys could drink their fill, while a pretty curly-haired boy of twelve or so brought us a pitcher of fresh water from his cottage, a few paces away. We were now in B'kaa Safrine, a predominately Moslem village at the head of the valley of the River Bared (the Gold River), which eventually flows into the sea between Tripoli and the Syrian frontier. Evening was closing in fast, and in the mournful half-light we hastened to set up the tent in the first open space we found, a sort of green on the outskirts of the village. We were all very tired, it being eleven hours since we set out from the head of the ski-lift pass, and our longest and hardest day's march so far. The worry about water, and the inadequacy of our water-bottles, had been constantly at the back of our minds, but the children had borne up very well, and had endured the heat, the long hours on donkey-back and the restricted drinking supplies with patience and considerable fortitude.

FIVE

Sir ed Dénié and north towards Kammouha

THE MIST CURLED AROUND US as we lay sleeping on the open green, and the cloud brought with it a penetrating damp cold, sufficient to disturb but not to interrupt our heavy, exhausted sleep. Next morning we roused ourselves with an effort in the dim grey early-morning light, but we were anxious to be clear of our rather public camping place before we attracted too much attention. B'kaa Safrine is a Moslem village, and as we came into the main street we were courteously greeted by various bearded old men, dignified and sedate in their long gowns. Some were well-to-do merchants from Tripoli, summering up here among their orchards and comfortable villas, others were prosperous inhabitants of the community. The village straggled down the hill, losing itself gradually among the fruit trees, and as the sun rose and the misty indetermination of our surroundings sharpened into the shining brightness of morning, we began to make out where we were. Looking back above us we could see the jagged white face of the cliff we had come down yesterday evening, sharp and defined now, with its bosky fringe of shrub and tree on top, and the thin line of track slanting diagonally across its face. Even as we looked, we could see tiny men and women toiling up it to their fields above, and disappearing from our view as they neared the top. The cliff face formed a rampart stretching as far as we could see, as if a jutting shelf of the mountain had been broken off like a sliver of mushroom, and nibbled here and there by giant teeth. The great, barren, tawny central massif across which we had

100

come yesterday was hidden from view, and the horizon commenced
with the wall of cliff and the trees fringing its rim. Before us the fruit
terraces descended in orderly rows wherever we looked. Where the
fall of the land hid the detail of the intricately patterned landscape,
a wider view took the eye in a dazzling sweep of pale foothills and
paler coastal strip, to the curve of the bay with the cloudy cobalt
blue of the sea merging into the blue of the sky beyond. The town
of Sir was an hour's walk from the outskirts of the village, and as
we started to clear the last habitations we were aware of stones and
pebbles falling about us. We looked back to see some hobbledehoy
boys shouting abuse and pitching stones from a safe distance up
the road. 'A nice welcome you keep here in Safrine for strangers,'
remarked Elias, to a man mending a ditch beside the road. 'What
do you mean? Ah, I see,' and seizing his stick, the man hastened
purposefully up the road. As we rounded the next bend, we could
hear from above the sounds of argument and abuse and the angry
admonishments of our protector, and laughed among ourselves at
the probable fate of the boys when the matter was reported to their
fathers, for Moslem fathers are stern.

The farther we went on, the more overcome were we by the
extraordinary richness of the mountainside we were descending. It
was the height of the fruit season, and every tree was laden with its
crop, and the crates of fruit were piled outside every garden waiting
for the lorry to come and pick them up. Peaches and plums and
greengages, pears, apples, melons – there seemed no end to the
profusion – and even the tall poplars clustering around the springs
and rivulets that gushed so eagerly from the hillside were wreathed
in vines, that hung dangling their tendrils in the breeze. Not only
did the fruit and water abound, but flowers grew with unimaginable
vigour in and around the courtyards of the farms – great dahlias
glowing red and purple among the leaves, and sweet-scented old-
fashioned roses, their crumpled pink faces nodding down at us
from among the blackberries and honeysuckle of the hedges. After
the scorching heat of the Kadisha valley and the solitude of the High
Lebanon, this land flowed with milk and honey, and the smiling

fruit-growers busy in their gardens, who called cheerful greetings to us and sent their little children running down the road to press peaches and apples into our hands, seemed like the happy denizens of a new Eden.

A little above Sir we passed a well-built new structure of stone, a long modern building rather like a school; it was on a terrace with a splendid view over Sir to the distant sea. The town itself occupies a rock promontory jutting out above the two rocky gorges which enclose it; the valley narrows just below, at the confluence of the two streams, which force their way through the barrier of rock to expand further down into the characteristic cultivated valley of the foothills, before winding in pebbly, oleander-tufted shoals across the plain of Akkar to the sea. Sir is the centre of the Dénié region, and its position tucked beneath the shelter of the mountains of Akkar and the Kornet es Saouda massif makes it the richest fruit-producing district of the north. A million boxes of apples alone are produced per season. The town itself is small, but has an hotel, an agreeable climate and two charming coffee shops beside a rushing mill-stream at the entrance to the town. Here, under the shade of an enormous oriental plane tree, we lunched off freshly grilled kebabs and plates of sharp, refreshing tomato-and-cucumber salad, while the crystal-clear stream sluiced past our feet to fall in a spume of spray over a little weir. Splendid peaches as big as grapefruit were brought to us, their crimson-and-purple skins smooth and unbruised, their flesh dissolving fragrantly in our mouths.

Various suggestions were made as to suitable camping sites for us – above the mill-stream, on a terrace beneath the sombre ilexes sheltering the old cemetery, in the school-house. The best came from the young, bespectacled, campus-style college boy, from Cairo University, doing a summer job as assistant manager of the Sir Palace Hotel. 'Go back up the hill for a mile until you come to the Social Centre, and ask the director to let you camp there. They've got space, and tell the director I sent you – he's a friend of mine.'

We toiled up the hill once more to find our destination was the modern-looking building we had noticed in the morning. In response to our enquiry a handsome, thick-set young man of about twenty-eight came to the front entrance; he spoke little French or English, but Elias acted as interpreter for us all. He seemed astonished at our appearance, but acceded to our request with shy good grace, and placed the terrace around us at our disposal. The Centre, he explained, was not really complete. He regretted that no water was laid on, but anything that he or his caretaker – a bright, friendly, grey-eyed peasant – could do, he would be very pleased to do. It was very quiet up here, the Centre closed at two p.m. each day and did not open on Fridays, but the farmers and peasants around were very friendly, decent folk, and everyone would be happy to have us there.

The problem of the camping site being solved, we next attacked that of getting ourselves clean. We were dusty, sweaty and unshaven, and the children's sandshoes were once more splitting open and in need of replacement. Having got the tent up, we left Elias to recite our saga to a small crowd of interested onlookers. We descended by a short cut through the orchards to the town, and returned to the hotel for the bath our young friend had promised us in the morning. The hotel is a big, tall, yellow building built in 1934, standing in a charming garden at the very edge of the promontory, with streamlets gushing down the hillside below its walls, and being drawn away to irrigate the orchards below. Its owner traded for many years in South Africa, and now in middle age has retired to being a prosperous citizen of his native town. He has a passion for dahlias. His whole garden was planted with them, of every variety. They blazed in every colour, scarlet, purple orange, yellow, white, big shaggy flop-headed ones and neat little pom-poms. They grew in orderly files inside the iron railings of the entrance, poking their big yellow-centred faces through the bars, they filled up every patch of ground except for the terrace around the water-tank, and even there they crowded in so close to the awning that one sat with a wall of dahlias at one's back. During our stay in Sir we spent many pleasant interludes sitting beside this water tank, which was circular, some ten feet in diameter, and lined with blue tiles. In the centre was a small pressure point, from which the icy-cold spring water bubbled in to fill the tank, and to set the watermelons cooling in it swirling gently around in the limpid water. The striped awning filtered the sun's rays, and we would sit there drinking fresh cool beer, while the young Arab Sheikh from the Gulf in his spotless white robes played tric-trac with the Cairo student, and a handsome Greek priest, bearded like a Rasputin, sat smoking a hubble-bubble, his stove-pipe hat on the chair beside him, and his long, wavy hair caught up in a bun at the back of his head.

The proprietor's love of flowers was not confined to the thousand or so dahlias he had in his garden. He also grew begonias and carnations, and sweet-scented double jasmines and plump fuchsias. These filled the big pots lining the terrace and, interspersed with ferns, formed splendid formal arrangements decorating the scrubbed white marble spaces of his hotel. We would encounter him, a small, sleek, stocky man, sitting beady-eyed in his over-stuffed office with a large portrait of Nasser staring down from the wall, or pausing enigmatically beside a basin crammed with whole armloads of creamy roses. He rarely spoke, but tolerated our untidy incursions into the ordered calm of his establishment, so cool, so shadowy, so remote, a relict of an older, more sedate age, flavoured with unpretentious prosperity.

Our baths cost us ten shillings a time, and entailed setting the hotel's whole water-heating system in motion. We had two during the five days we spent in Sir, and on each occasion the bath waste must have looked like the Nile in flood, so brown and discoloured did the water become. We used to scrub and wash the children in pairs in the enormous old-fashioned tiled bathroom, and emerge hours later shining and resplendent in clean clothes, our discarded garments in a bundle ready to sling on to Little Stick's back. Little Stick was now rather well, and firmly established in the children's affections. It was a rude surprise to them to hear the shopkeepers and corn-chandlers joking and teasing about his undistinguished appearance, and they defended him vociferously in shrill, indignant Arabic. The local inhabitants favoured sturdy black donkeys and enormous mules like the ones we had met coming down to B'kaa Safrine. These mules and their wild, uncouth drivers frequently clattered down the road past our camp, great baulks of timber slung each side of the beasts, and in the afternoons they would come rattling and hallooing up on their return journey, their bells and harness jingling as their owners hastened their pace in the afternoon hush. Half the town seemed to be making packing-cases for the other half to use, and every day the fruit lorry used to grind up and down the mountain road, picking up and putting down crates for the farmers busy with their families in their orchards.

Everyone was engaged in picking fruit, even small children of seven or eight years old. From earliest daylight, people were out in their terraces, and hour by hour the pile of crates grew beside the road. Wherever we went, presents of fruit were showered on us. The widow from whose spring we drew water pressed enormous apples on us each time we washed our teeth, her children would shyly unload an apron full of pears and plums beside our stove each evening when they brought us over a pail of fresh milk from their cow. The jolly farmer whose land surrounded the Centre delighted to load us with gifts and favours – 'It's yours, it's yours,' he would say, his shaggy face splitting into a delighted laugh, when we tried to stem the flood of his generosity. His plump, comely wife took our washing, and brought us eggs, and would only take soap-powder or tea in exchange, until on leaving we managed to press two liras (five shillings) into her hand on the understanding she buy a toy for her little daughter with it.

The Social Centre remained oddly apart from the busy rural prosperity around it. Punctually each morning the director and his two young woman assistants would arrive; one, a pretty dark-eyed young woman, came up each day from Tripoli by *service* taxi. We were invited to visit the Centre, and to have its work explained to us. The only one of its kind in Lebanon, it had been financed by the Egyptian-dominated Arab League in conjunction with the Lebanese Government, and had been built less than a year. Funds seemed to have run out, and we heard it rumoured in the town below that the Lebanese Government was chary about advancing more. The director and his assistants had all been trained in Egypt, he having had a year's training in welfare work, and the two girls six months each at the Social Teachers' Training College in Cairo. They were all ardent Arab Nationalists, and Nasser's picture was prominently displayed in the Centre, as it was throughout the town. The actual aims of the Centre seemed a little vague. They took in small boys, and girls up to the age of twenty, and claimed to have a potential two thousand members to draw on. The building was solidly constructed, and ambitiously planned; there was a volleyball court, a recreation hall with a small stage at one end, a dispensary, various classrooms and a kitchen. There was, however, no electricity or water laid on, the telephone in the director's office was unconnected, the library had no books, the dispensary did not function, and the place was empty except for a pair of boys playing tric-trac in the hall and a handful of high-school girls giggling around the paper cut-out of a dress. 'This is a cat,' said a scrawled sentence on a blackboard, followed by 'This is a fat.' The director was engaged in a conference with a group of earnest young men of about his own age when we arrived, which had all the appearance of a political meeting, but the young women invited us to take coffee with them. This we did amid a giggling bevy of schoolgirls and their rather tongue-tied mothers. Conversation did not flow. 'How do you see us Arabs?' we were asked. 'Not as savages, I hope.' We hastened to assure them of our repudiation of this view, and another long pause ensued. The young female assistants were charming girls, enthusiastic and high-minded. It was impossible not to feel sympathy for them, naive and undiscriminating though their devotion to their cause might seem to be. They were very typical of the educated Moslem girls of good family, all over the Arab world, whose social conscience and fiery political convictions have led them to identify themselves with the cause of Arab Nationalism. To modern young Arabs Nationalism is equated with progress; and the emancipation of women, higher education, hygiene, social services and greater opportunities for development are all part of the ideal socialist state towards which the educated youth of the Arab world are convinced they are progressing.

After five days in Sir we were ready to continue our journey. We were clean, rested, well-stocked with stores. Elias had been down to Beirut, and had been brought up by friends in a car loaded with newspapers, books and food for us. He also brought a very welcome supply of money, as we had run out during his absence, and had been reduced to our last cigarette. Little Stick had a new saddle, Middle Stick had a new bridle, and the children had new shoes. We had a splendid new water-bottle, cork-covered, and holding two gallons, to supplement our tins, and had lightened our load considerably by sending down to Beirut various stones, fossils – including scores of small, fossilised, acorn-like spheres, which littered our camp site – insects and a charming small tortoise, whom we still have, which Anthea picked up one afternoon on the hillside. Sir Dénié, as he is called, is even now only a finger in length, and has a glossy black and yellow shell. He has made the transition very well, and goes to school with his owner. The small fossils, we found later, were sea-urchins and at one time were much prized by East Indians as charms, and were the object of a small export trade at the turn of the century.

Our plan was to go inland along the flank of the mountain to the high grazing area of Kammouha, a plateau lying enclosed on the forested slopes of the mountain above Akkar. The Lebanon range, now nearing its northern termination, swings slightly eastward as the coastal strip widens into the broad plain of Akkar, a grain-growing area watered by several rivers. The Syrian frontier runs right around this northern tip, where a depression between it and the Nosairi mountains of the Syrian coastal strip forms the famous Homs gap which is the natural route from the coast to the fertile grainland of the northern Syrian plain. To get to the plateau we had to cross over the shoulder of mountain separating the Bared River on which Sir stood, from the valley of the River Abu Moussa, whose headwaters emerged on the mountain flank below Kammouha.

Our maps were those made by the French during their Mandate and, although revised in 1942, were not completely accurate when relating to areas off the beaten track. The secondary roads of northern Lebanon run just so far up the narrow gorges of the rivers, and then stop; the central mountain area is consequently comparatively isolated from the main current of Lebanese development, and large areas of mountain and forest land are virtually beyond the reach of the central administration. These areas are inhabited by semi-nomadic Moslem and Christian tribes who move up and down the mountain with the seasons, spilling down into Syria and the Beka'a around Hermel in the winter, moving up again with their flocks as soon as the snow is gone. Several tribes compete and combine for the control of the grazing – the Dandache and Jaafar being the most powerful. Fierce, turbulent, lawless, they are left undisturbed by the Government, which rarely intervenes unless tribal disorder threatens to spill over into the settled areas.

Sir was our entry into the predominantly Moslem north, and a sharper political feeling was noticeable immediately. People were at first suspicious of us and our manifest foreignness. 'Are they not Jews?' they would ask Elias anxiously. 'Everyone knows that Jews are different from Arabs. Are you really sure they are what they say they are?' There was always someone at the back of the crowds that gathered around us to suggest that we were spies, and that we would poison the water of the springs if people weren't careful, but at the first personal contact these doubts and suspicions would be resolved, and shamefaced smiles and offers of assistance would replace the earlier reserve. Our English nationality meant little to them; among the more educated it was automatically associated with acts unfriendly to the cause of Arab Nationalism, for this was little over six months after the Suez Canal incident and the bombardment of Port Said. But once a personal contact had been established all these considerations assumed a secondary importance, and we on our part looked for no trouble, and found none. Elias, with his quick wit and ready tongue, had a good-humoured tolerance of the foibles of these remote mountain peoples. His Maronite Christian background and name were of no assistance to him here, and very early on he started slipping in and out of his secondary personality, that of Abu Talal, a sheep-dealer, a relic of his youthful days as a drover on the mountains of the Kesrouan.

The possession of our three donkeys also never failed to amuse and impress our audience. At first it was always assumed that Elias was their owner, and that they were on hire to us. As soon as this misconception was rectified our stock rose. The financial advantage of owning rather than hiring was obvious to everyone, for the day's wage of a man and his donkey is in the region of one pound, depending slightly on the locality and the work. That we should have shown such acumen was a point in our favour. Obviously we were not the usual kind of foreigners, of whose gullibility and shocking disregard of values everyone had heard tell. The uncomplicated assurance of the children, with their quick command of Arabic and obvious familiarity with the habits of the country, was another point in our favour, and the extreme simplicity of our way of life – for we lived very much country-style – was comprehensible and reassuring. Only Ralph's habit of silence was a puzzle to them. 'What is the matter with him?' people would ask Elias. 'Does he never talk?' And they would shake their heads in commiseration at such a fantastic renunciation of the joys of social intercourse. Elias would tap his head sagely. 'Too much in there is the trouble,' he would explain. 'He is thinking all the time about things and so has little time left over for talk.' 'By God,' our interrogators would wonder, 'to think that he thinks like that all the time. What a misery for him, what a burden to bear,' and they would gaze in sympathetic concern at him, as he sat immobile and abstracted by the fire, occasionally stirring to receive or offer a cigarette.

Talks during our various halts and encounters followed a fairly similar pattern – greetings and polite exchanges, then a gradual unfolding of our past and an indication of our immediate future objective – never more, as this only served to confuse. Our Moslem interlocutors lacked the volatile friendliness and unashamed curiosity of the Christians, but there was a natural dignity about them, and a calm acceptance of our status as strangers which was undemanding and reposeful.

From Sir the first stage of our journey was clear. A road led up to Sfiré, allegedly two hours' walk away, but there it stopped, and from there on we would have to make our way across country as best we could. We packed up and left the Social Centre after a cordial farewell to the director, who had come early to see us off, and were on our way by six-thirty. As we started down the road, the friendly farmer and his wife leant over their hedge and filled our hands with wonderful ripe peaches, more almost than we could carry, and as a final gift picked the sweet-smelling pink roses from the hedge, so we went away with our hats and hands full of fruit and flowers. Looking back, one recalls with a pang the spontaneity of the gift and its acceptance, and the ease and well-being of that golden morning seem to contain all that was happiest and best of our life in the Lebanon.

We passed through Sir all astir with the business of the day, mules, donkeys and black-clad peasants thronging in the street, and the noise of the carpenters' hammers resounding from every narrow alleyway. Our road dipped down through green, shady orchards, winding in serpentine curves to the bottom of the Kattin valley, the tributary of the Bared which joins it at the narrow bottleneck below Sir. All was cool and fresh and green, the hedges sparkling with dew, and the flank of the mountain we were descending protected us from the sun's rays. There was water everywhere, gushing in torrents from the brambly recesses of the hedges, and spreading into miniature rivers and lakes beside the roadside. The familiar crates of fruit were piling up along the roadside, and the ruddy faces of the peasants peered down at us from the trees they were busy stripping. The descent was long, but at last the ground levelled, and we crossed over a rushing stream by a concrete bridge, with a Moslem tomb embowered in oleanders beside it. Now began a long steady pull upwards, and as we rose from the valley bed the hot sun began to strike full on to us. Our earlier spring and enthusiasm evaporated, the children clambered back on to the donkeys, and we began to wind slowly up the steep flank of the mountain. A heavy, sinister drumming began somewhere up the mountain in front of us, and a confused sound of shouting and wailing drifted down to us where we stood hesitant in the shade of a huge mulberry tree, whose fruit stained our lips and hands as we ate it. The steady throbbing continued uninterruptedly, quickening occasionally to a wild, barbaric frenzy, then regaining its sinister, sullen note. 'Someone dead,' we remarked to each other, but the deserted road, the hot sunlight and the dark shady groves of ilexes that seemed to mark the successive stages of the climb all conspired to produce a sensation of oppression and unfamiliarity. It was not difficult to imagine ourselves as victims of a malevolent trap, with unfriendly natives summoning their allies by drumbeat to the kill. We knew well enough that the drumming portended a Moslem funeral, but it was with a certain relief that we saw a procession of scarlet-and-white banners emerging from a cabin far up the hillside, heard the last frenzied throbbing of the drums and the wild skirling of the mourners, and knew the ceremony of mourning was over, and that the corpse was being taken out for burial.

It was very hot as we toiled up through the pear and peach orchards to Sfiré, a hamlet straggling along a bold spur of mountain. We could look over Sir on its headland to the great ring of mountains dominating that sunny bowl of sheltered fruitfulness. From below, this was hidden by the rocky clamp of the converging hillsides, with Sir like a wedge between. Another enormous dark grove of ilexes occupied the extreme edge of this spur, and scattered in among the trees were the whitewashed tombs of the dead, one newer than the rest indicating the morning's addition. This was the road-head, and piles of empty crates were being unloaded from a lorry and snatched up by waiting boys. All over the flank of the mountain were ant-like files of laden donkeys being driven into the collection centre by youths and men, the crates slung in careful balance across the animals' backs, then heaved by their owners on to the lorry tailboard, while the donkeys waited in patient dejection for the return and repetition of the manoeuvre. So busy was everyone about their business that the addition of our three donkeys to the scene hardly attracted any attention.

A young man who had joined us on the last part of the walk up now led us to the general store, for we were all parched and thirsty and glad of a rest before the next steep pitch up to the Roman temple at Nabi Nasr, our destination for the day. The store was crowded with strong, fresh-faced peasants in their rusty black clothes, their shirts and headcloths stained with sweat. To our surprise a beady-eyed old man with a bristly white beard, whose headcloth and cummerbund and baggy trousers made him look like a tribesman from the North West Frontier, addressed us in twanging Yankee accents. 'You folks American? I'm from New York, from New York City, oh yes, sir!' His fellow villagers listened in amused interest to this exchange, and appeared gratified by our astonishment. 'You want to go to Fnaidig by this road – you can't do that, sir, not with donkeys. There ain't no road, and the country's too rough for you to get across. You'd best go on up to the Bared spring, that's real nice, then get on down back to Sir, and go down to the coast, if you want to get up to Fnaidig.' This was disheartening, but experience had already taught us that if we took all the advice offered us we might as well have stayed at home. So we temporised and said we would camp up at the temple today, and decide what to do next day. We bought some bread and eggs from the storekeeper, and were bidden a cordial farewell all round.

The track was up the ridge of the spur, an evil, slippery shelf of rock, scored by minor torrents. Above us we could see the temple, a plain rectangular stone shape on a rocky ledge jutting out from the crest of the mountain behind, and dominating the pass into the valley system beyond. The people of Nabi Nasr, two or three mud cottages scattered beside a clump of evergreen oaks, had a bad reputation with the townspeople of Sir, and even with the villagers of Sfiré, but we were beyond caring and flopped down in the shade of the oaks in grateful relief exhausted by the scramble up. We were just over the crest of the pass, and from where we lay we could see the temple on its shelf above, its entrance steps encumbered with fallen stones, and its three doorways meaningless in the roofless facade. We were now over 3,500 feet high, and on the threshold of a wild, tumbled landscape which sprawled out in front of us for as far as we could see. When we had recovered ourselves a little, we set to work to unload our gear and prepare some food, watched by a few men squatting in the shade of a stone dyke. A threshing floor occupied the level stretch of ground beside the tall oaks, and a little boy was urging a scrawny chestnut mare around in circles, while he balanced on the flint-studded sledge she was pulling. It was a stony landscape, tufted with bushes and carob trees, whose umbrageous spread was further enhanced by swags of vines trailing in neglected exuberance, and sometimes looping from tree to tree like the creepers of a tropical jungle. The earth was a reddish brown, liberally sown with sharp grey stones, so that one needed stout shoes to protect one's feet, and scored with dried-out torrents wherever the rocky outcrop terminated in the head of a small glen. When later in the afternoon we climbed up to the temple and from its well-laid stone platform looked out, back and front, over the whole enormous range of landscape, the country we proposed entering fell into the context of its surroundings. From the temple we had a bird's-eye view of where we had come from, and where we wanted to go. Behind us and below was the lop-sided bowl of cultivation out of which we had climbed, funnelling to its lip at Sir, while around it we could clearly see the massive shapes of the High Lebanon lying with folded paws like beasts of prey. A great shaggy shoulder of this mountain mass ran down to the pass where we were, projecting into a craggy, tree-grown peak above the temple. It continued northeastwards in a long, forested rampart which we could see in the distance merging with the indistinct dark-blue knot of another spur of the chain. We were standing, as it were, on the crest of a watershed, and before us the mountainside fell steeply into what must be the valley of the Abu Moussa, hidden as yet by the bulging hillside. Our destination lay at the far end of this valley.

The temple itself is of little architectural interest, being devoid of all ornamentation. Its four walls, however, are still intact, and a concealed stairway within the wall of the facade allows one to climb up on to its top. The stone is well-cut, and a Greek inscription, which none of us could read, is incorporated in the right-hand wall. There seems to have been some other edifice alongside it, but all this is tumbled down in ruin, and blocks the flight of steps leading to the main building. From its situation, it would appear that the temple was built on the site of an ancient Canaanite High Place, a frequent practice of the Romans, whose tendency was to adopt and modify the religious concepts of their conquered territories, and by a gradual process to obliterate characteristic features of native life in favour of an overall standardisation. It was under the Romans that much of the language and custom of Phoenicia, which had survived contact with Egyptians, Assyrians, Babylonians, Persians, and the increasing Hellenisation of the area after Alexander's triumph against the Persians at Issus, finally became extinct, and the independent city-states of Phoenicia were merged into a province of the Roman Empire. The Roman settlement and the Roman peace led to a notable increase in population, and gradually the tide of settled agriculture crept further up towards the then still heavily forested upper slopes of the Lebanon range. But the Mountain did not emerge as a political unit until the seventh century, when the early Christian sectarians, taking refuge there, coalesced into the Maronite community, a process repeated four hundred years later in the southern region of the Mountain, when dissident Moslem units evolved into the Druze nation, and the two communities succeeded in maintaining the precarious independence of the Mountain from the flood of succeeding conquests which washed around its feet.

Among the men who had watched us unload our gear was one Achmet Mohammed Harmouche of Sfiré, a handsome, wiry man of thirty or so, who owned an orchard on the western slope of the watershed, where a spring trickled slowly out of a recess under the shelf on which the temple stood. While we were talking casually among ourselves of our plans for the next day, we were surprised to hear a voice in good English joining in the conversation. This was Achmet. 'I will show you the way to Fnaidig, if you like,' he said quietly. 'I know the way, and I can get you all there.' We were delighted to receive such an offer, for his quiet, steady manner and frank, dignified gaze inspired immediate confidence. 'I learnt English from the English officers during the War, when I worked as a mess-boy in a camp near Tripoli,' he explained. 'Now I'm back here in my village, and as my fruit is not ready for picking, I've got nothing to do, so I might as well spend my time helping you.' An animated discussion now broke out among all the men present as to the best route to follow. We, working from our maps, suggested the high level route along the lip of the valley, at forest level, rounding the basin at its source. 'No,' we were told, 'that is impossible. There is no water, and there is no track. You must go down the Wadi Gehannum [the Valley of Hell], cross the river, and get up the other side to the motor-road, which will take you into Fnaidig.' This was news to us, for our maps did not show any road on the other side of the valley, but we were content to abide by Achmet's decision.

We passed a reposeful, relaxed afternoon at Nabi Nasr, undisturbed in any way by the inhabitants, who seemed to accept our presence with tolerant indifference and a certain unobtrusive kindness. People came and squatted down beneath the trees, and drank tea and smoked cigarettes with us, and brought us offerings of fruit, and chatted quietly with Elias. The women were baking *tannoura* bread, made of cornflour pasted to the sides of a hot mud oven, and we had some of this, hot and fresh. The children, having exhausted the possibilities of the temple and its interior staircase, wandered over to a deserted cottage on the hillside beyond. From here one had another sweeping view of the wild, shaggy country we were to traverse tomorrow. The cottage had long been abandoned, and its timber-baulked mud roof was falling in, but it was charmingly situated on its grassy terrace, with the irrigation stream running in a well-made stone trough behind. Walnut and carob trees almost shielded it from view and an enormous vine, looping from tree to tree, made a wonderful leafy swing.

As the sun started sinking towards the sea, the goats came streaming down from the rocky, scrub-covered peak above the temple, and converged in a piebald flood on the irrigation stream and its little stone bridge. With their elegant mincing steps and neat clicking hoofs they raised a sparkling golden dust about them as they drank, then to the flutes and shouts of their herdsmen, moved off towards the village in a malodorous confusion of sound. The small boy ceased goading his old mare around the threshing-floor, and ran off cheerfully to his mother, who had come to call him; the birds came in to roost in the trees above us, and the bats to skim low in the soft grey evening light. Soon we were courteously bidden goodnight, and left to prepare our beds on the open ground, while Elias curled himself up among his cookpots and kitchen stores, and the donkeys stamped and jingled among the stones. The full moon rose up in the cloudless sky, and sauntered languidly above us, sending down a clear cold light that made fantastic shadows on the undulating ground. An enormous silence descended on everything around us, and lying there in the bright silvery moonlight we saw the stars brilliant above us, and Orion wheeling splendidly through the dark night sky.

Before the sun was up the boy was back at his threshing, the cocks crew, the birds flew and the new day began with us gulping sweet, soggy porridge and mugs of *café au lait*. Achmet arrived very punctually wearing a wool cap, sandshoes, *shewals* and shirt, and carrying a large black umbrella. We made a good start and were soon working our way through an intricate network of narrow paths, fenced on either side by the stone dykes containing the terraces with which every cultivatable strip of hillside was scored. Sometimes the track was used as a channel for irrigation water, and then we would splash through the gushing stream, or clamber up on to the enclosing walls, and make our way as best we could among the brambles and thorns which grew in their crevices. In this way we went some miles, slanting slowly downwards across the flank of the hill. After a while Achmet pointed out a shaggy, tree-crowned hillock with a village on it, towards which we were descending. 'The Australians were there during the War; they used to signal with mirrors to Nabi Nasr, where they had another camp.' That probably explained the bullet-scars we had noticed on the stones of the temple. After about two hours our path became much steeper and more difficult, as we edged down towards the river cutting its way through the enclosing rocks. The baggage got caught and torn on projecting stones and thorny bushes, and the donkeys had to balance delicately as they painstakingly manoeuvred their way across the dried-out watercourses which intersected our path. Elias and Achmet sweated and strove mightily during this difficult descent, for the donkeys required constant attention, their loads jamming frequently in the narrow confines of the track, especially when it degenerated into a sort of goat tunnel between high, thorny hedges of scrub and secondary growth. The land was all cultivated painstakingly by hand, and occasionally we would encounter a peasant busy pulling his corn or controlling with a long hoe the irrigation of his crops. Such villages as we passed were nothing more than poor, straggling mud hamlets, fenced with brushwood and cactus; a stand of tall ilexes marking the village cemetery, remote and poverty-stricken on the harsh mountainside. The fruit cultivation of the Sfiré area gave place to Indian corn, the rich green sheen of whose level terraces became more marked as we descended the valley, but the track remained rough and almost impassable. At one place we went down a stream bed, the cascades providing the steps, the water above the donkeys' knees. At another Middle Stick's hind hoof caught in a narrow rock cleft. We despaired of ever freeing him, but with a stupendous heave Elias got it free, and after a few halting paces the animal regained his stride. The children hung on as best they could during this frequently alarming descent, comforted and encouraged in a mixture of Arabic and English, and occasionally slung by hand over some difficult traverse, while the donkeys were coaxed gingerly into a better position.

Having started out at six-thirty, by ten o'clock we were beginning to feel in need of a rest, and it was with relief that we saw in front of us a huge shady grove of ilex trees, towards which we were evidently steering our way. Another half hour, and we stepped into its sombre recesses, the height and obscurity of the trees enhanced by the vines that climbed over their topmost branches. A group of men were seated in quiet conversation under the trees, among the stones of a cemetery, big shaggy fellows with beards and black headcloths wound negligently around their sharp peaked felt hats. They regarded us unstirringly until Achmet and Elias greeted them, explaining our business. Then the headman, a tall, blue-eyed, auburn-haired man in a butcher-blue shirt, shook hands with us all and motioned us to rest in the quiet and coolness of the trees. 'Is it possible to obtain any bread in your village?' we asked. 'For we left too early this morning to get any from Sfiré.' 'Rest a little first,' was the reply, 'and we will see what can be done,' and so leaning on the saddles and gear tumbled on the ground about us – for the donkeys needed a rest as well as us – we exchanged cigarettes and gossip and leisurely information about ourselves. After an hour a smiling old woman, the headman's oldest wife, appeared among us with a large, plaited straw tray of food. There was a pile of delicious freshly baked maize bread, sliced tomatoes, fried eggs, French beans in gravy and, best of all, enormous bunches of newly picked black grapes, the first we had had that season. We were rather overwhelmed by this unexpected gift, but to our protestations and thanks Ali Mahmoud Haimo, the headman, only replied, 'Eat, eat, and do not thank us, but thank God who orders us to be charitable to all wayfarers,' while everyone sitting around him nodded their heads in pious agreement. So, watched by a semi-circle of rough, shaggy figures, many with their guns beside them, we all settled quietly around the tray and in very little time made short work of it. The bread was delicious, still warm from the oven, and the platters of food arranged on the straw charming to look at in their artless profusion. The old woman sat beside us, tucking her bright-flowered petticoat over her frilly pantaloons, and delightedly urged us to further efforts, scooping up extra titbits in a flap of bread for the children, happy when we praised the excellence and generosity of the gift. Three little shaven-headed boys sitting on a tombstone beside us intoned verses from the Koran, for the grove was the village schoolhouse, and the men of the village saw to it that their sons received whatever teaching they could give them. After the meal Elias hastened to make coffee, which with cigarettes was the only repayment we could make for the hospitality we had received, and then, rested, refreshed and impressed by our treatment, we rose to prepare for departure. The donkeys loaded, we began our farewells – a lengthy business this, entailing shaking the hand of every man present, the children following our example with respectful care. The whole party escorted us to the edge of the grove, augmented by a score or so of small children, who clustered merrily among the tombstones and watched us with lively, bright eyes. Here there were less protracted farewells and, with a final word of thanks and gratitude, we stepped out into the blazing sunshine, watched from above by the villagers, until we passed out of their sight.

We were now nearly at the bottom of the valley, and a short descent brought us to a bluff overlooking a ford where the river, emerging from a miniature canyon, widened into a delicious emerald-green pool before resuming its turbulent descent. The line of the ford was easily discernible, and encouraged by the sight of the river we sought about for a means of descent to the pebbly white strand below. The children scrambled quickly down, leaving the donkeys to come down more prudently by a narrow track, and promptly took off their clothes for a swim. Achmet and Elias meanwhile got the animals on to the other side, the water slopping over the tops of Elias' boots, while the children and their father joined a group of naked little brown boys swimming in the stream. It was a wonderful bathing-place, the deep green pool stretching as far as the gorge out of which the stream rushed swirling over the rocks, while carob trees clung to the sides, and pink oleander bushes formed clumps along the banks. Three girls had been bathing and washing their clothes further upstream, and retreated into the shelter of the oleanders, their bright, floral-patterned petticoats and pantaloons hung out to dry on the bushes. Cattle browsed along the bank of the ford, and the goats had tucked themselves up into the shady crevices of the gorge, while their attendants drowsed in the shadow of the trees, or tootled reflectively on their pipes.

If the descent to the river had been hard, the ascent was worse. Above us we had glimpsed the new road shimmering far ahead in the hot sunshine. Now we toiled up what seemed an endless succession of steep lateral gullies, hung with brambles and blocked at every turn by thickets. The pitch was so steep that we could only make a few yards at a time, and the laden donkeys had to be pushed and heaved at the worst places. We all streamed with sweat, and the benefits of the swim were soon lost, as we forced ourselves upwards to the crest of a spur. At last, after an hour's exhausting struggle, we emerged on to more level ground, and flung ourselves gratefully down to drink from a cool spring, welling up into a clear pool at the base of a limestone rock face. Getting clear at last of the thickets and scrub of the lower valley, we were now faced with a long, tiring trudge across bare, brown, stony fields to another tree-grown spur, above which was the road. Our party was soon well strung out, for on top of our other exertions this uphill drag in the heat was very punishing. A cheerful man jingling past us with three donkeys encouraged us merrily in our toil, and a sweating companion astride a skeletal mare carrying two leather sacks of yoghurt took Miles up behind him, and carried him up to the road. With aching limbs and sore feet, our clothes sticking to our bodies, we made the final push up to the road, counting the paces as we made them in the effort to keep going. We were so done in when we reached the top that it was hard to walk the few extra paces to a grass-roofed hut selling fruit and *gazoozas* in the shade of a big carob tree. Here we squatted for ten minutes or so, in a small group of black-clad peasants waiting with their bundles and baskets for the village bus to come up from the coast. We were all pleased and relieved to have reached our objective, and congratulated Achmet on having got us here. From where we sat we could look across the valley to the huge shoulder we had traversed, and we could just identify the temple like a child's brick sitting on the skyline.

It was now four o'clock, and time to part company with Achmet, who would get a lift down to the coast from here, sleeping a night with relations in Tripoli before getting another taxi up to Sir next day. We were very sorry to say goodbye to him, for he was a nice man, energetic, competent, calm and good-humoured, with the natural good manners of the Lebanese mountaineer. We paid him fifteen shillings for his labour and travel, which seemed to please him very much, then started slowly up the road, while he stood waving until we passed out of sight. His ambition was to emigrate to America with his wife and three children, for he had brothers there already, but so far his application for a visa had not been granted.

The road led up in the warm westering sun through broad terraces of stubble and dark green rows of melon cultivation. After the narrowness and constriction of the valley, it was pleasant to walk through an open landscape again, and to see the mountain system stretching away in folds and convolutions as far as we could see. But the exertions of the day were telling on us all, and we were anxious to find ourselves a suitable camping spot, and even the gentle gradient and smooth surface of the road were no inducement to continue. At last, rounding a bend, we saw before us a spreading dark forest of evergreen oaks on a spur overlooking the valley. In its lap, where the road ran through, it enfolded a wide, open space dotted with huge mounds of chaff, where men and women were at work winnowing the grain. This was the village of Hrar, where there was a small police post, manned by mounted *gendarmes.*

There was a check point at the police post and, as we paused here, the *gendarmes,* seeing we were strangers, asked us our destination. 'Kammouha? That's a wild sort of place to want to go to, and its several hours' march away from here. Sleep tonight in our post, if you like, and go on tomorrow.' We accepted this invitation gratefully, and dumped our gear down on to the verandah surrounding the post, while an orderly led our donkeys to the stable inside the post. The two *gendarmes* were Christian, and were glad enough to find someone with whom to talk. 'There's not much to amuse oneself with here,' they said, 'the people are poor and brutish, and the higher up you go the worse it becomes. You want to take care at Kammouha, the people are savages, but there's another police post up there, and the sergeant's a good man.' Just as we were settling ourselves for the evening, a jeep drew up and another pair of *gendarmes* came in. One appeared to be an officer, for we could hear him rattling off abuse and reprimands at our luckless acquaintances. Then came the question we were waiting for, the enquiry as to who and what we were. Elias bore the brunt of this inquisition, for we merely produced our identity papers and letter of recommendation from the Director of Tourism, and relapsed into total incomprehension of anything said to us. Elias was subjected to a searching crossfire of questions, delivered in a very bullying, ill-tempered manner, to which he, wise in his time, replied in quiet, reasonable, confident tones. A satisfactory cross-reference was at last struck, in the shape of an uncle of his, a famous sergeant of police who had been dismissed the service after a shooting affray in which six men were killed. Elias' police uncle was of the greatest assistance; he always cropped up whenever we came in contact with the *gendarmerie*, and never failed to bring us into favourable relations with the service. On this occasion the charm again worked. The tone changed, the atmosphere cleared, and we were bidden a curt but cordial goodnight, and left to our repose. Everyone heaved a sigh of relief when the jeep roared off, including the *gendarmes*, who soon recovered their equanimity and settled down with Elias to gossip around the lamplit table.

The night was warm, and we were bitten by mosquitoes, while inside the post people came and went in the small hours of the morning. We were rather jaded when we arose next day, though the children were ready enough to roll and rollick in the big heaps of straw, as they had done as soon as we arrived last night. As we prepared to go, the peasants were already hard at work, the women and girls in their bright clothes helping the men clad in sober black. '*Fellagh*' was Elias' sole scornful comment, uttered with all the free-born peasant proprietor's pitying contempt for the tenant of an absentee landlord. The whole village belonged to a wealthy landowner resident in Tripoli, who farmed his land on the *metayage* system, he owning the land and providing the seed, the tenants providing the labour and receiving a percentage of the crop.

We were now very near the head of the valley, and the road wound in broad curves through an open, stubbly landscape, dotted with groves of trees. We gradually mounted higher until, crossing a *col*, we came into a more constricted landscape given over to the familiar cultivation of fruit. We were stiff and tired and little inclined to any great exertion, and paused frequently. Outside Michmich, while we rested beside the road, our daughters each lost a milk-tooth, a great event which had been anticipated for days. This little diversion encouraged us all, and we trudged on again through the straggling village. An excited voice calling to us made us look round, to see a plump, well-dressed man in jodhpurs and a spotless white *keffiyah* signalling vigorously to us. 'Come and drink some coffee with us,' he called and, nothing loath, we turned into the yard of his house. It was a half-built modern villa on the hillside overlooking steeply terraced orchards and dominated by a bleak ridge of mountain. The house was our host's, but rented to an unsuccessful election candidate, whose wife, it transpired, was the daughter of the hotel proprietor of Sir. She was a plump, fair young woman who spoke good English. Her husband, a peevish-looking man in a dressing-gown, was recovering from an attack of Asiatic flu, and sat huddled under a shawl most of the time. Our hostess pressed tea and milk for the children on us, and biscuits and buns, while the terrace on which we were sitting gradually filled up with village notables come to quiz the strangers. In the end there were twenty-two people sitting in polite curiosity on the straight-backed chairs, all of whom were served by our hostess with coffee. The family was passionately opposed to the Ghamoun Government, and ardently pro-Egyptian in feeling. The talk turning on the children and their places of birth, the ex-candidate opened his arms wide and called in Arabic to Sabrina (for he refused to speak English or French, though it was obvious he could speak both): 'Come to me, my little Egyptian, come, my best and most precious one.' The children quickly caught on, as did our audience, and the joke was exploited to the full. 'Come,' to Sebastian, 'come, my Cypriot, my little Makarios; you too are a friend of us Arabs,' but Anthea, laughing merrily amid the applauding crowd, was repulsed as an American. 'No, no, go back to Eisenhower; we don't need you here.'

'And me?' queried Miles. 'I was born in India.' 'Then you'll do,' was
the reply. 'Nehru is all right, but your sister – come, Sabrina, come
my eyes, my darling – is the best of the bunch of you.' Despite our
political differences, we passed a cheerful hour, for although our
nation was unpopular, individuals were still liked and accepted. A
fellow national, one Peter Wilkinson, a student of Arabic, had passed
this way some two years ago, on a walking tour, and spent three
days with the candidate's family. He was remembered approvingly
by many of the people present. We received many warnings about
the intractability of the people of the Kammouha plateau, but our
host agreed it was worth visiting. 'It's like Switzerland,' he said, 'but
you'll see how poor the people are and how little this Government
has done for them.' When we came to leave, most of our fellow
guests escorted us to the end of the village, and the children were
kissed and embraced and laden with biscuits as they were lifted up
on to the donkeys.

At last we reached Fnaidig, and the road-head. It was a poor,
straggling, fly-blown settlement, almost mediaeval in its squalor.
The road degenerated into a boulder-studded mud wallow, with
smoke-blackened stone houses squatting haphazardly in the dust
and debris of the settlement. A few people huddling apathetically
under the ilex trees of a cemetery appeared to be suffering from
some malady – Asiatic flu, we were told – while below them watermelons and vegetables spread for sale in the roadway indicated
that some sort of market was in progress. 'You see what a wretched
poor place it is,' said a young man who had walked up with us from
Michmich. 'What's grown isn't worth selling, even if there was any
way of transporting it down to the coast. We haven't any facilities
for moving our produce, there are no schools, doctors, hospitals
or anything, and everyone is poor and ignorant and without
hope.' Certainly on looking around us our hearts sank. Here was
an ingrown misery and squalor and neglect not seen elsewhere in
the Lebanon, except in the extreme south. The people were dirty
and careworn, their eyes bleared with smoke from the gloomy
interiors of their low houses. One had to stoop to enter the village

store, blackened beams supporting a mud roof, and a few tins of sardines, cigarettes, and corned beef supplying the greater portion of the stock. Elias wrinkled his nose in disgust and pity: 'Faugh, fancy having to live here all one's life.' We were glad to get clear of the village and strike out along a straight stony track towards the fir-covered escarpment we could see rising in front of us.

A burly young man in an old pair of corduroy jodhpurs attached himself to us on the outskirts of the village and, learning that we were bound for Kammouha, offered to guide us there. He proved a mixed blessing, being garrulous, hungry and extremely dirty.

SIX

The Kammouha plateau and the forests of Akkar and Akroum

A T LAST WE FELT we were getting into entirely new country. As we entered the forest, the track started rising steeply, zigzagging upwards through pine and spruce trees. Halfway up, our guide led us into a rocky gully, where a stream rushed out of the recesses of a narrow cave, twice as high as a man. This was the spring of Adam and Eve, we were told, and we drank and washed contentedly in its icy water. We picnicked near by under a huge spruce tree, sharing what we had with our new friend, who proved to have a voracious appetite for food and cigarettes. He was more or less an outlaw, he told us, and, though only seventeen years of age, had already served three years in jail, while his elder brother was a wanted man and lived as best he could among the lawless families of the forested mountain above us. He was a boastful, big-mouthed youth, immensely strong, but anxious to please, as if he sensed in us a useful meal-ticket for the future. After eating, we continued our weary way upwards through the forest. The road was steep, and the sun beat down fiercely through the trees. Sebastian began to doze on his donkey and, before we saw what had happened, our guide had seized the child and was carrying him pickaback up the road. This raised immediate doubts in the mind of the child's mother, who hastened forward to take the burden herself, but the damage was done. Contact with our friend's filthy shirtback produced, within a few days, an irritation on Sebastian's chest, which proved to be scabies. It spread in some measure to the other children, but only slightly, and we were able to treat and cure the children at a very early stage.

The reward for our labours came at last as we topped a rise and looked down on to a long, level, semi-circular saucer of smooth green turf, good enough for a cricket-field. It was completely enclosed by a low line of hills covered with spruce fir, juniper, cedar and pine. The plain was more than a mile in length, and about half as broad, and wherever we looked we could see sheep and goats, cattle and some horses, grazing peacefully in the bright sunshine. We were so astonished at this unexpected sight that we stood some minutes on the lip of the saucer, taking it all in, while our guide grinned with proprietary pride. At last we stepped out on to the plain and started towards the blockhouse which we were told was to be found at the far end. As we approached the centre, the black-clad shepherds were matching their rams against each other, a favourite sport we discovered later. The rams – heavy, square brutes with curling horns – were taken out from the flocks and, sighting each other, would run together as hard as they could, their skulls meeting with a sound like a mallet knocking on wood. Several huge dogs rushed fiercely at us, but were called off by their masters, who eyed us curiously, and who greeted our guide with jocular familiarity. We had several such encounters, sealed with formal handshakes and offers of cigarettes, before we reached the blockhouse, a small square Beau Geste sort of fort beside a spring, which commanded the whole central grazing area. We were received here in very friendly fashion by the *gendarmes* in charge of the post, a sergeant who had served in the French Army, Abu Selim, and two troopers, to whom we had brought a note from the *gendarmes* of Hrar. They begged us, however, to camp near their post – 'It's not safe otherwise, we're right on the edge of the Jaafar country, and these people are all absolute savages' – so we pitched our tent on the greensward beside the shallow stream which seeped out of the basin of the spring.

We spent seven full days on the plateau, leaving on the eighth. It was a marvellous place, wild and unspoilt, and the people, in their rough way, were not unfriendly. We suffered a certain amount of pilfering from the small boys who grazed their cattle near the stream, but we recovered, by negotiation, a torch and water-bottle which were the most valuable things taken. We were also constantly asked for aspirins and mercurochrome by the people of the tented encampments scattered in the recesses of the grazing area, and any empty tins we had were immediately snatched up to be used as drinking-cups and food containers. The porridge tins with their lids were especially popular. Elias was away for three days, returning on the afternoon of the fourth, it having taken him most of one day to get from Fnaidig down to Beirut, and during his absence we moved our camp into the shelter of the trees on the slope overlooking the fort. This was a wonderful site, under some spruce trees, all that a forest camp should be.

The donkeys and the children enjoyed themselves immensely, the former being able to roam and graze at will, their fancy being tickled by the presence of various seductive little she-asses, who inspired even Little Stick to amorous activity. The children built forts and encampments in the trees and rocky ledges of the hillside, where they staged elaborate games of warfare, or played cards with the two little cowherds, Dib and Yassin, who were our most constant visitors. Dib was a handsome, wiry little boy of ten or so, a round embroidered cap perched on the side of his auburn head, his quick bright eye like a fox's taking in everything we did. His friend Yassin was a swarthy, wistful boy with a shock of basin-cut black hair, clad in a large khaki GI's service jacket which reached to his knees, wilder and more uncivilised than Dib, who had considerable aplomb and was master of every situation. The pair of them would undertake commissions for us in faraway Fnaidig, bringing up potatoes and melons to supplement our stores, and engage in long, complicated barterings and exchanges with the children of walnuts and knives and useful sticks, and other things of interest to them.

The *gendarmes* used to ride out on patrol in rotation, and reliefs came up to them from their headquarters at Beino, in the settled area below the plateau. The fort was only manned for the grazing season, from May to September. Once the weather broke, the herdsmen retreated with their flocks down to the lower levels, and the plateau was abandoned. It seemed as if the plateau was in reality a lake-floor which was still water-covered at certain seasons, as it was scattered with small pieces of driftwood, which the children used to gather every evening for our campfire. The police sergeant pointed out to us a place, dried out now, near our camp, which in winter became a quagmire, and where a man, woman and boy had been engulfed two years ago. The fort was the farthest outpost of government authority in the area, for the forested mountain land immediately eastward was all in the possession of the Jaafar family. 'You notice that we have no window frames or shutters on our fort,' remarked Abu Selim one day. 'Those damned Jaafars came and swiped the lot last winter, and used them for the houses they're building with bricks supplied them by the Government contractor in Hermel. As if you're going to civilise the Jaafars with presents of bricks and things like that! They just take what you give, and if they want more they come and grab it. That chieftain of theirs is the biggest robber of the lot, and absolutely unprincipled.' The Jaafars certainly had a name to conjure with in that area, and we never heard anything good said of them. The police were horrified when they heard we proposed crossing through their country to Hermel, on the other side of the mountain at the top of the Beka'a. 'You can't possibly do that, you'll be assaulted, pillaged, anything can happen. Those people are like beasts, and with or without arms you're absolutely at their mercy. We never go into their country, and as long as they don't cause trouble here, and interfere with the grazing, we let them alone. Last time there was trouble was four years ago, and that cost sixteen dead. They held that ridge there and shot it out with machine-guns and the latest rifles – of which they muster about a thousand – and in the end the army came up and restored the demarcation line.'

This information caused us to think rather carefully of our next move, for this confirmed what our friend Sami Kerkabi in Beirut had told us. Crossing the Jaafar country on foot two years ago he had been held up, stripped of all his gear and had been lucky to walk into Hermel in the clothes he stood up in. Our doubts were further reinforced a few days later by the arrival of two forestry officials on an inspection tour. They too advised us seriously against the risk.

The plateau is Government property, and attempts are being made to conserve the forests. Cutting in the immediate vicinity of the grazing area is forbidden, and we witnessed the arrest one morning of a man who had the temerity to drive a laden mule under the noses of the *gendarmes*. Despite his protests the load was confiscated, and locked up in the fort. Sharing the life of the *gendarmes* was a big, ruddy man dressed in white, criss-crossed with ammunition and revolver belts, the *natur* or warden, whose flowing *keffiyah* used to be a fine sight as he wheeled and galloped his bay horse across the green turf, practising those sudden halts and charges which are the pride of Arab horsemanship. Sometimes in the afternoon he would be joined by a granite-faced man on a grey mare, and they and the *gendarmes* would race madly across the plateau. Once we saw a superb feat of horsemanship. Having lapped the arena, the bay and the grey came in to a fighting finish at the entrance to the fort. A sharp turn to the right, and the grey slipped on a flat table-top of rock, started coming down sideways, was lifted up, recovered, slipped again, was lifted again and finished game but beaten, all in a matter of two seconds, his rider impassive in the saddle, his long grey moustachios and black *keffiyah* flowing in the breeze.

The days passed quickly in such surroundings. We occupied our time with the domestic chores of the camp, washing our clothes and ourselves in the springs which bubbled out among the rocks of the hillside. We had books and letters to read, and clothes to mend, and kit to repair. Early in the morning the flocks would stream up into the forest, the shepherds pacing slowly in front, their heads bent as they blew into their flutes. Sometimes they would call and encourage their rams by name, holding a handful of salt beside them, so that the animals would nuzzle and lick their fingers as they went along. The morning air was melodious with the tinkling of the sheepbells and the calling and fluting of the youths leading out the flocks. Punctually after noon, they would re-emerge, appearing from every quarter of the surrounding hillside, and converging slowly on the centre of the plain. Seen from afar, the small, black-clad figures of the shepherds in their short jackets and full-bottomed jodhpurs, their fringed headcloths drooping negligently over one shoulder, seemed rather like figures from some Dutch *genre* painting. We used to watch this performance every afternoon, from our vantage point on the hillside, but could never establish the rules which governed it. There was something of the slow stateliness of a *pavane* in the orderly advancing of the flocks, the crossing and recrossing of the files, the calling-out and counting which seemed to be the main business of the occasion. It was rather like an elaborate Trooping of the Colour, though, instead of guardsmen, the participants were sheep. An hour or two was given over to this exercise, then the ram-fighting would begin, and wrestling contests between the shepherds, and a wild, hockey-like game they played with their staves. The cattle and mules and asses which also grazed around the springs frolicked and chased among themselves, and the armed horsemen racing and wheeling full-tilt across the green turf in the warm glow of the afternoon sun were like figures from some old drawing of life under the Ottomans a hundred years ago.

We used to stroll and explore the subsidiary glens and extensions of the plateau in the late afternoon, when the flocks and people had mostly drawn off towards their encampments and the evening milking. One, to the east of the fort, had at its head the trace of a rough road which traversed the steep slope in a series of bends and disappeared on into a wilderness of forest and rock. Strolling there one evening, we encountered a diminutive woman riding on a diminutive ass. She could hardly have been more than five feet high, and she had a comely, sunburnt, high-cheek-boned face. We noticed at once that her clothes were different to those of the women of the Kammouha encampments, her trousers, instead of being jodhpurs with a frill at the hem of the leg, being full-bottomed and loose, as one imagines Turkish trousers, and cherry pink in colour. She wore a long dark robe over her pink shirt, hitched up to allow her to ride, and on her head was a black turban of wool, wrapped so that it seemed wide and flat in relation to her face, and from beneath it her hair dangled in snaky curls over her ears. She was a very gay, good-natured little woman, who told us she had been down to sell some cheese in Fnaidig. We walked on with her for some distance, she chatting merrily all the while, and left her at the top of the *col*, where the track went off through the forest to Beit Jaafar, her destination.

Sometimes we walked in a westerly direction, and this brought us out to the edge of the plateau overlooking the coastal plain, where an old military road zigzagged precariously down the escarpment to the settled areas below. There had been an army camp on the plateau during the War, and indeed the hillsides such as where we had our tent had obviously been levelled for camp sites before. The camp appeared to have been a British one, for we were told once or twice of the Inglezi playing football, and shown where they had a hutted camp. Men like Dib's father recalled with a certain regret the days of full employment and ready cash. The camp seemed to have been established for the purpose of taking wood, but we never obtained a clear story, and at one time the plateau seemed to have been used as an aerodrome.

From the head of the military road, one had a magnificent view, westward to the sea-coast, and north-eastward to the long, shaggy barrier of forested mountain which was the ultimate outcrop of the Lebanon mountains. Where the range dropped abruptly to the plain was Syria, and that would be the termination of this leg of our journey. After long reflection and discussion with Elias, we had decided against trying to get across to Hermel from Kammouha, partly because of the unwholesome reputation of the Jaafars and their neighbours, partly because of our very real fear of running out of water. Our long day across the Kornet es Saouda massif, and our traverse from Sfiré to the Abu Moussa River, had shown us clearly the importance of having knowledge of the local springs. Our maps were very vague for the whole of the area before us, and we had no confidence in the reality of the springs marked on them, certainly not now, in the height of summer, when only the permanent springs were flowing. We had also broken our new large water-bottle, and were once more reduced to two hip flasks and a porous jar. The foresters on their visit had given us a whole new itinerary, which would take us to the tip of the forest range, at Akroum: 'We'll give you a note to Sayyid Ali Adhra; he's a hospitable chap, and he'll tell you if it's possible to get across to the Beka'a. Get him to take you to the Wadi Saba when you're there, it's worth a visit, there's a big carving on one of the rock faces of the *wadi*, and his people know the way down to it.'

Walking in the cool of the evening was very pleasant, with the children skirmishing across the turf on the donkeys, and the forest stretching silent and deserted around us. Kammouha has an incredibly remote and isolated atmosphere, probably due to the sensation of being enclosed by the rim of forest, and it is a feeling that colours all our recollections of the place. As soon as the sun had gone, the night would start to hang in the sky, at first imperceptibly, then, as we turned our steps towards the camp, slowly dulling to the soft grey of the brief twilight. We used to sit around our campfire eating our supper, for the nights were cold, and we were glad of the warmth. Behind us the donkeys would jingle and stir as they champed in their feedbags, and the flames would light up our faces as we sat on the stones and rocks we used for seats. Sometimes the *gendarmes* would come and join us for tea or coffee, and would sit huddled in their *abbas* or big camel-hair cloaks around the blaze, smoking cigarettes and telling us stories of fights and feuds and disorders they had encountered in their service, and about the Jaafars, and occasionally, more simply, of their families and children. At about seven each evening, we would hear our milk for the morning being brought over to us by two shepherd youths who lived in an encampment some way across the plateau. From far away we would hear their voices raised occasionally in shouts and long hallooing calls, to frighten away the evil spirits, while their lantern glimmered erratically in the dark. Arrived, they would squat silently around the fire watching the flames and smoking a cigarette, and then one, Ahmed, would sing wild, plaintive Arab love songs in his harsh cracked boy's voice. Sometimes he would sing two or three – all songs of love and sadness and desperate tragedy – 'The girl with the tooth of gold' and 'When she walks, it is like a field of corn' and 'When I was in prison, you said you would come to me' – tricked out with many mournful cadences and wandering grace-notes. We would sit there listening, even Elias barely comprehending the rough dialect and broken phrases, the children drowsy on our knees in the hot firelight, but all touched and moved by the naive pathos and heartrending simplicity of these songs.

Then abruptly they would rise and bid us goodnight, and we would see their light disappearing into the darkness, while we ourselves tucked up the children in their tent and lay down in the silent night under the stars. Sometimes the quiet was broken by shots and shouts from the encampments, and the frenzied baying of the dogs, so presumably some jackal or wolf had got in among the flocks. Very early each day, before the night was gone and the moon still swam in sickly pallor in the sky, the woodcutters and charcoal-burners would come past our camp. They were a ragged, ribald, noisy crew, who came jangling past on their tall mules, half a dozen boys on donkeys riding with them. Seeing them for the first time in the wavering moonlight, and roused from sleep by their loud conversation, we wondered who and what they could be, but they passed through amicably enough, with a shouted jest at Elias still half asleep with his *keffiyah* wrapped around his head. Then we would sleep again until the first rays of the sun striking over the eastern rim fell on to us and woke us to the calling of the flocks, the liquid flutings of the shepherds, and the shouts and cries of the opening day.

At last we decided we must go, as our stores were gradually getting depleted and we had no hope of replenishing them until we finished this portion of the journey. So early on the morning of 23rd August we packed up, abandoning a ball Elias had brought up from Beirut for the children, various tins, and a bottle of mercurochrome to our acquaintances among the shepherds. We had made a tentative arrangement by post with some friends in Beirut to meet them at Akkar, where there was a road-head, this weekend, and we were anxious to telephone to confirm the engagement. The *gendarmes* told us there was a telephone at Beino, a village below the escarpment on the north-western side of the plateau, so we struck off down the military road we had already pioneered. The donkeys were rested and fit, having had virtually no work to do for nearly eight days, beyond carrying the children around on their forays into the surrounding glens. The road itself was stony and neglected, and in places nibbled away by landslides and rockfalls, but it was perfectly negotiable by jeeps and even by buses, one of which had disgorged a party of sportsmen from Halba the day before, for a day's shooting in the forest. We made good time down the road, gradually leaving behind us the pines and spruce of the forest, and coming down on to a poor country of stony brown earth and yellow stubble, which changed in time into a richer cultivation of maize and vivid green tobacco plants. Water ran all about us, and the threshing-floors beside the occasional mud houses we passed were piled high with chaff. The stubble was speckled with goats wherever we looked, and little brown boys came running across the empty terraces to gape at us as we passed. Winding down into the foothills of the plateau, we met some of the charcoal-burners, their beasts laden with brushwood and logs, and further down the slow, sinister sound of drums told us that a burial was being prepared somewhere on the hillside below us. We came upon the mourners just as they emerged on to the road – sturdy, rough men in black, their headcloths fringed low on their foreheads, carrying iron-tipped staves in their hands. They replied to our greetings with reserve, but the grey-robed Sheikhs with their spotless white turbans, who had doubtless been conducting the ceremony, replied civilly and benignly, walking in a dignified group down the road. Just before we reached the foot of the hill we were overtaken by two of the *gendarmes* from Kammouha, who gave Miles and his mother lifts on their horses, but arrived at the bottom, our ways split, for we found that Bezbina had the only telephone, some two miles further on.

It was now approaching noon, and we were anxious to get our business done. We pushed on through the heat in the familiar rich orchard cultivation of the sheltered valleys of the lower range, and eventually, following a road which wound maddeningly through vineyards, came to a pleasant coffee shop beside a mosque, with a spring pouring out into a basin of icy green water at its entrance. This was Bezbina, and, tying up the donkeys, we left Elias with the children to order lunch at the coffee shop, while we went on to the telephone we were told we would find further down in the village.

Bezbina is a straggling village surrounded by fruit orchards, tucked under the wooded flank of the Kammouha plateau. Its population is a mixture of Moslem and Greek Orthodox Christians, each party being centred around its place of worship. We found the telephone in the village store, kept by a Christian. It was one of those old-fashioned affairs with a handle which one wound to summon the exchange, and the storekeeper's wife seemed to be in charge of the machine. She was a bustling, energetic woman, mother of several children, who popped out from her kitchen behind the shop to deal with our request. After a prodigious amount of handle-winding, she announced that the line seemed to be interrupted, and that she was unable to make the connection to Tripoli. After a few moments' pause, another violent attack began on the machine, this time to summon another exchange, which was cajoled and bullied into forwarding our call. We now had to wait until Beirut accepted our call, which could mean anything from ten minutes' to an hour's delay. The storekeeper's daughters started bringing him in his lunch on an assortment of small platters, which he, hospitable man, insisted on sharing with us. The whole family joined together in pressing food on us, in the intervals of assaulting the telephone and screaming down the wire in voluble Arabic. The minutes wore by as we consumed tomatoes and a white cheese flavoured with pepper, hot beans, bread, big bunches of grapes and little cups of coffee. Periodically Madame would appear from her kitchen, wind the handle and demand in excited tones what had happened to our call, which we had registered as 'Urgent' in the hope of speeding it. After over an hour's delay, the bell finally rang for us, and Beirut was on the line, but it was too late, our friend had already left his office and was out of touch for the rest of the day. This was a nuisance, but we were prepared by now for any disappointment. Not so Madame, who seized the telephone again and berated the unfortunate operator with unabated energy. We, however, made good our escape, hearing as we left some other unfortunate hallooing wildly down the line, vainly trying to ascertain when his expected call would come in.

This hold-up with the telephone, and our lunch, had brought us well into the afternoon, and instead of making for Akkar Atiha, as we had intended, we decided to remain in Bezbina and set off early the next day. A camp site was soon found for us by the Christians, a handsome young man who had been born in Honduras interesting himself greatly on our behalf. His uncle, Spiridon Hasim, was *Mukhtar* of the village, and a man of substance and education. We camped on a small terrace under some trees beside the little church of St George, a grey stone building full of icons and blue-and-white distemper. Our installation was not without incident, Big Stick nearly knocking a deaf woman off the three steps leading up to the terrace, and Little Stick for some reason best known to himself, attempting a flying leap at the terrace wall, got stuck halfway and had to be hauled back in considerable disorder. At last, however, we were all settled in, the tent up, various gifts of fruit and milk received, and supper prepared. The clouds had been gathering on the mountainside above us for some time, and a light damp mist interrupted with gusts of rainy wind settled about us as we prepared for bed. Elias had prudently negotiated a bottle of *arak* from the storekeeper, so we shared that amongst us, and went to sleep in the gusty wet night warm and uncaring in the shelter of the church wall.

Next morning was clear and sparkling and the mist and cloud had receded to the uppermost level of the mountain behind us. All around us the gardens spread over their containing walls, the grapes in trusses mixed with the rosy-red blush of the ripening pomegranates, while the figs on their broad-leaved branches hung enticingly over our heads. We were bidden a warm farewell by the *Mukhtar*'s family, who pressed further gifts of fruit on us, but this abundance did not prevent Big Stick from eating the wreaths off the family mausoleum when we were not looking. Concealing this as best we could, we shook hands all round, and set off once more, pausing to buy a torch and batteries from the hospitable storekeeper as we went. At first we retraced our route of the day before, until we reached the crossroads at Bourg, where a handsome, dilapidated Arab *serail* stands in the middle of the plain beside a white, domed mosque. Curious as to the identity of this imposing derelict, we approached the massive nail-studded doorway in its parti-coloured stone surround, with the elegant Arabic inscription above the lintel. Inside we found a peasant supervising the repair of a splendid vaulted window niche, while the small open courtyard presented a charming pattern of light and shade, as the sun penetrated the thick trellis of vine with which it was roofed, and flickered on to the lemon and tangerine trees growing around the open tank inside. 'You should go around and see the other side of the courtyard,' they told us. 'Its much bigger than this.' So we walked on around the flank of the building, and were surprised to come on a formal garden of cypresses occupied by two young men in European clothes. One of these, it transpired, was the owner of the *serail* and the land surrounding it. With his mother, his two young sisters and his bride, he had come up from Tripoli to supervise the fruit harvest.

He was a languid, fair young man, and the conversation did not go easily.

'What is your village?'

'I beg your pardon?'

'What is your village, London or America?'

'Oh, my village – London.'

Inside the house things were hardly better. Through a narrow passage in the thick walls one entered a marble courtyard, planted with orange and tangerine trees in the centre, around a stone water-tank. The pavement was prettily laid with narrow black lines of marble defining the entrances to the various rooms opening off the central court, and two little maidservants of twelve or thereabouts were busy washing the worn white stone. The place was crumbling and dilapidated, and had been patched here and there with concrete and plaster, no attempt being made to preserve the handsome seventeenth-century stonework of the original. Seated on upright chairs were the female members of the family: the mother, an energetic woman of fifty or so, with fine blue eyes, and her two anaemic-looking daughters, students at one of the European schools in Tripoli. Lounging in a deckchair was the bride of three weeks' standing, a pretty, dark-eyed creature as ripe as a split peach, her flesh bursting in warm abundance out of her nylon pink lace nightgown and negligee.

The young women were all very bored, and complained of the tedium of their life during this enforced summer exile on their estate.

'It's more than forty kilometres to Tripoli, we've no radio, there's no neighbours, this old house is falling to pieces about our heads, we never go out; what is there for us to do? Mama and our brother are busy with the peasants and business, and insist that we've got to stay here until the season is over. Tripoli is so hot, what else can we do?'

Coffee was brought, and a large box of chocolates, while a few sharp words were flung at the little maids – 'At least there's plenty of servants here, and cheap too, not like Tripoli' – and the bride yawned and stretched and showed her little pearly teeth. She was seventeen, and spoke French, and looked a good deal more full-blooded than the other members of her new family. They, wan and sallow and unenterprising, with their long, pale, manicured hands and colourless grey eyes, exuded an atmosphere of querulous *ennui* which accorded ill with their setting and made it weary work among the coffee cups.

Bidden farewell with amused incomprehension, we set off once more on a gradual traverse of the mountain flank towards Akkar, and the castle perched on a rocky spur of the mountain beside it. The road wound around the contours, rising slowly all the while and, leaving the fruit cultivation, led into a country of rich green maize, its tall fronds undulating in the light breeze. From the height of the road we could look on to a sweeping panorama of the coast from the olive-green smudge of Tripoli in its orange groves to the pallid curve of the plain up to Tortosa in Syria. Below us was the plain of Akkar, the great granary of northern Lebanon, which covers an area of some twelve thousand hectares and reaches inland towards the Homs gap and the pass into the Syrian plain. The closely cultivated plain on to which we were looking was one of the richest possessions of the Crusader Counts of Tripoli, but long before the Franks came the land had been colonised by Roman settlers under the Empire. The first town captured in Lebanon by the Crusaders was Arqa, the birthplace of one of the Emperors – Alexander Severus – which was already then a town of considerable antiquity, being mentioned as a Phoenician settlement in Egyptian and Assyrian tablets. Arqa today is a great mound of rubble, one of the many *tells* which dot the plain, and which indicate the sites of ancient settlements.

The importance of the castle of Akkar to whoever dominated the plain and the route into Syria is easily understandable. It was built by the Arabs in about the tenth century, perhaps earlier, and passing from the hands of the Fatimid sultans to the Seljuk Turks, who were already threatening Asia Minor and the Byzantine emperors, it yielded to the Crusaders on their capture of Tripoli in 1109. Thereafter, it remained mainly in the hands of the Franks, until its final capture by the Mamluk Sultan Baybars in 1271, who brought up siege engines and battered it into submission.

From Akkar the Crusaders were able to raid far inland to Syria, cutting the road from Homs to Baalbek, from whose Governor they were sometimes able to exact tribute. They could signal across the plain to Krak des Chevaliers, the great fortress dominating the Homs gap which belonged to the Hospitallers, and to Safita, the Chastel Blanc of the Templars, lower down in the foothills of the Nosairi mountains, both over the modern frontier in Syria. The Crusaders gone, and after them the Mamluks, the castle remained in use until 1618, when the Druze Emir Fakr-ed-Din, on his return from exile in Italy, stormed through northern Lebanon, demolished Akkar, dismantled the castle and removed some of the stones to his capital at Deir el Kamar in Southern Lebanon, thus fulfilling his promise that 'the stones of Akkar shall rebuild the homes of Deir'.

The shell of the castle, however, still remains, on a rocky crag isolated by the two torrents which join at its northern extremity to form the River Akkar. Where this crag was attached by a narrow neck to the mountain, a level space has been cleared and an artificial channel cut through the rock by hand, virtually making an island of the castle. A rock-cutting similar to this is to be seen on the coast near Tripoli, on the site of the castle of Nephin, to whose lord Akkar once belonged. We could see the plan of the castle quite clearly as we toiled up the steep flank of the western side of the gorge, led by two peasant women who assured us it was unsafe to camp anywhere in the vicinity of the castle. Wolves, jackals, evil spirits, we never discovered what it was so agitated them, but they were shrill in their denunciation of our chosen camping site, an old mill on the tree-shaded banks of the river below the junction of the two tributaries. Led by them, we came by a boulder-strewn mule track to Akkar village, hidden in a grove of walnut and chestnut trees, whose bulk was further enhanced by the vines growing all over them.

The houses of Akkar are stone-built, of a tawny colour, and fortress-like in their solidity. Traces of the former importance of the place, before its ruin by Fakhr-ed-Din, are to be seen in the mosque with its bands of black and white stone, and the tower with the Baybars' lion on it as a heraldic device. This lion was probably taken from the tower at the southern extremity of the castle rock, facing the rock-cut moat, which is decorated with bas reliefs of these lions, grinning like Cheshire cats, with a broken chain around their necks.

The shrouded atmosphere of this village, secreted in its shadowy groves of trees, was a little oppressive, and we determined to push on up the mountain to the spring of Sheikh Djenaid, a site, we were assured, which was bound to meet with our approval. Led by a ragged youth on a tiny donkey, we clambered on up the rocky path, now wading through the stream that rushed at intervals through it, now taking to the tops of the stone dykes that enclosed it in an attempt to find a level surface to walk on. Below us the hillside fell away to the lip of the gorge, and the castle and its plan lay like an architect's *maquette* on the tawny background. The hillside was most carefully terraced and irrigated, and the green maize rising in tiers to the forested rim of the amphitheatre was beautiful to see. This forest crowned the grey ramparts of rock at the head of the valley, and hung, a great dark barrier, across the last stretch of path.

Here, where a crystal-clear stream ran over the pebbles beside the track, we were fortunate enough to meet the Sheikh of the village, a noble-looking old man with a pale aristocratic face, accompanied by several notables. He was dressed in a spotless, cream-coloured silk robe, and had a most benign expression. He seemed of another race to the rough, black-clad mountaineers surrounding him. Elias hastened to greet him, and to explain our presence and identity. 'We have heard,' he said, 'that there is a famous spring here, and we have come to camp beside it, if the Sheikh permits us.' After a short consultation, the wish was granted. 'But take care,' the Sheikh added, 'and don't disturb the Wali's tomb.' Then, bidding us go in peace, the little procession moved off down the mountainside.

We now entered the dark grove of trees surrounding the track, and climbed in a gloomy hush to the clearing above us. It was a sombre, unexpected scene that met our eyes. The hillside came down in a smooth rock face, down which the innumerable trickles and cascades of an abundant spring fell into a shallow rectangular stone basin, some thirty feet wide. No sunlight penetrated this clearing, for the holly oaks and hornbeams of the forest grew tall and thick on either side. A few rough stones scattered among the trees indicated that this was a cemetery, and on the other side of the tank was a stone shrine, presumably the tomb of the Wali, or saint, of the place. Some men were standing about in the clearing, their guns slung over their shoulders, and their black clothes blended well with the forbidding atmosphere of the place. The Sheikh's acceptance of us having been noted, they greeted us without further comment, and we were free to gaze about us at will, and drink from the water gushing so freely from the rock. The face of the rock, we noticed, was tufted with primrose and violet leaves, and maidenhair fern grew from every crevice, shivering in the spray. It was a strange place, and the strangeness did not wear off, even though we spent all next day there, moving off on the third day.

We camped in a clearing a little way off from the cemetery, but close enough for us to be aware of the Wali and his spirit, which apparently haunted the grove. The children were very impressed by the Wali, and showed no enthusiasm for his tomb, which was just as well. We put our tent up beneath a big walnut tree, where a turbulent brook rushed downhill through a tangle of bramble and undergrowth, and a gap in the trees gave us a view over the amphitheatre of the River Akkar. Behind us the forest crowded steeply down, and the tall trees of the sacred grove hemmed us in on our left, their sombre darkness further intensified by the straggling vines that hung in lank tendrils in the sunless gloom. On our right, on the other side of the brook, we could see a small, low, wooden hut, made of logs like an American trapper's cabin. This was the nearest human habitation to us.

During the afternoon we received various visits, our callers eyeing our gear with curiosity, but as the evening drew in we were left to our own devices. As the night thickened, a mist rose up out of the hillside, and wrapped in snaky coils around the tree-tops, pressing in mysteriously on the circle of light and warmth about our fire. Sitting there drowsy and alone, listening to the noises of the night and the calling and hooting of what seemed to be owls on the cliff above us, we were startled by a sudden crash as something sprang over the brook, and the next moment a wild, shock-headed figure carrying a long stave loomed up in the flickering firelight. Too startled to move, we replied automatically to the man's greeting, bidding him join us in a cup of the hot tea we were sipping. He was perhaps disappointed that we had reacted so tamely to his sudden arrival, but settled himself down in friendly fashion to gossip and smoke for half an hour. He was a farmer, he explained, come to turn the irrigation water into his terraces. For so many hours of the night the water was his, then his neighbours would take their share in turns. The Lebanese mountain farming has one delightful characteristic – delightful, that is to say, to anyone who enjoys playing with water. Much of the work while waiting for the harvest to ripen consists in clearing channels, opening and closing small obstructions, turning the water this way and that as it is required. A long-handled hoe is the implement used, and very few of these peasants were ever without one. The use and sharing of the water is perhaps the most delicate matter to be decided by the village communities and their headmen, and one fraught with infinite possibilities for mischief-making and feuding. An unscrupulous peasant can take advantage of a neighbour's absence or illness to sneak out and steal his water under cover of night, or destroy the stone dykes and dams which control the flow. A greedy man may claim more than his share, and a weak man be powerless to resist him, and it is the duty of the headmen to prevent these disputes and adjudicate matters to the satisfaction of the majority. Our shaggy friend was out each night at this season, he said, looking to his own interests, for who would look to them if he didn't? There were others abroad in the dark night, and the hooting and calling we had thought were owls were the signals they passed to each other on the different levels of the hillside, as with their long-handled hoes they spread the water through the different sections of the crop.

With a cheerful goodnight, our visitor sprang off over the brook, using his hoe as a pole to help his jump. We sat on for a while, with the mist creeping around us and the jackals screaming and howling in the forest above. Then we bundled into our sleeping-bags and slept, ghosts, jackals and evil spirits forgotten, until the stir of people passing down through the trees awoke us, and we roused in time to see the wraith-like mists of the night dispersing in the warmth of the risen sun.

Our neighbour in the log cabin was a small, fine-boned old man, neatly clad in the black clothes of the mountaineer, a pleated, round-necked blouse the only note of colour in the sombre elegance of his dress. The Akkar people wore a black headcloth similar to those we had noticed coming up to Fnaidig – the big square of silk being surrounded by a fringe of chenille bobbles which, when wrapped and twisted around the head, fell low over the forehead, before being caught up in a jaunty twist at the back of the head, and falling in folds over the neck. This style of tying the *keffiyah* was characteristic of the mountaineers of the north, and looked gallant and dashing on the young men, who wore it tilted well forward over one eyebrow, so that the folds at the back had something of the graceful fall of a cock's plumage, and greatly enhanced their proud carriage and dandified appearance. Their silk shirts were finely gathered and smocked, round-necked, and closing on the shoulder; they were red and pink and lilac in colour, and were held into the tight-legged black jodhpurs by a black cummerbund. Their staves in hand, their guns slung over their shoulders, and their strong throats and ruddy faces framed by the black headcloth, the mountaineers were a handsome, wild lot, and had the air of belonging to another century than our own.

Abu Ali, as our neighbour was called, had a wife, Umm Ali, a nut-brown beauty considerably younger than himself, and mother of an only child, a fat little girl of three years or so, the indulged darling of her parents. Unlike the rest of the children we saw, this one was dressed in some semblance of European clothes, and had an incongruous straw sun-hat perched on her tangled chestnut curls. Umm Ali was strong-willed and temperamental, the reverse of her husband, who had a gentle and whimsical charm which matched his appearance, which resembled that of Max Beerbohm to a remarkable degree. She came early to our camp, and subjected Elias to a prolonged cross-questioning as to our status and intentions, which led to the children and their mother being bidden to the cabin to make use of the washing facilities there. Our dirty clothes were seized and carried away in a huge bundle by Umm Ali, while the family trailed up in gloomy anticipation bearing soap and towels and combs and brushes, ready for the promised bath.

The Abu Ali house at close quarters was very interesting. 'What a nice house,' remarked Miles, 'I would like one like this. There's a place for everything.' And so there was, each quarter of the low, dark, square room being reserved for a different use. There were no windows, and the light and air came in from the open doorway. The flat mud roof was held up by a massive centre beam supported on the smoke-blackened trunks of three young trees, roughly shaped with an axe. The left-hand back portion was piled with logs and charcoal and feed for the animals, for they were preparing, said Umm Ali, for the winter, when they would be snowbound for three months. Dividing this from the right-hand, was a barrier of sacks of flour and sugar, with here and there a cupboard or chest-of-drawers. The floor was of mud, and on the right-hand side spread with straw mats, and spotlessly clean. The bedding was all on the roof, where the family slept in summer, but what was not in use was folded tidily and put away on shelves. Beside the door were boxes for the pigeons, who cooed and gurgled soothingly about the rafters. There was a comfortably purring cat and a hound puppy, and hens scratched in the doorway. Spare shoes for the family, solid black leather slippers, soled with old tyres, hung on hooks from the ceiling, as did extra storm lanterns, bunches of herbs, strings of peppers and garlic, ropes and pieces of harness. As Miles remarked, there was a place for everything, and every necessity of life was thought of. Umm Ali showed with pride her store of cloth lengths, which she would make up into clothes during the long winter months; her medicine chest with its bottle of mercurochrome next to a box of dried mallow flowers, good for coughs. From one box she produced sticky nougat-like Arab sweets for the children, from a cupboard her packet of coffee, from a heap by the door a watermelon for everyone to eat. Meanwhile the bath was preparing outside, a great cauldron of water heating on a mud stove. By and by it was pronounced hot enough, and the first child was stripped and stood on a wooden stool beside the shallow drain near the door. First Umm Ali seized a loofah and soaped it lavishly, then, pouring a little water over her victim, attacked vigorously. Not content with scrubbing the child till it was almost raw, she kneaded and massaged its head till it cried for mercy, then, doused and half drowned with sluicings of hot water, it was lifted over to the straw mats, and dried and dressed and combed and trimmed, and finally expelled to the sunny yard cleaner than it had been for a long

while. Umm Ali was implacable, and the most piteous complaints
from her victims were only met with shrill chidings and indulgent
kissings, while the dreadful work of cleansing went on unabated.
The children's mother did not go unscathed from these operations.
Her turn came, her clothes were borne away, she was seated on the
stool, her long hair was loosened, water was poured, the loofah was
plied, the pain was excruciating. Umm Ali scrubbed with unabated
vigour, aided by another young woman and, worse still, prolonged
kneadings and rubbings of the head commenced. By the time the
longed-for sluicing down began, the water was so hot it turned the
flesh lobster pink. Worse was to follow. A terrible combing and
braiding of the hair commenced, which produced tears of pain in
the owner's eyes, while the unsympathetic children stood around
to watch their parent suffering their own agonies. Umm Ali and
her friend had a fine time, and having finished with their guests,
started on themselves. Various petticoats and jackets were flung
into the wash now bubbling in the cauldron, and a small girl of
about Sebastian's age was forced to undergo the ordeal of scrubbing
and braiding, which she bore with commendable fortitude. It was
interesting to note that the child's flowered jodhpurs were made
on a most practical model; there was no seat to them at all, and
the frilled legs were held up by string braces. The women wore a
shift or blouse similar to the men, tucked into their baggy jodhpurs,
which were held up by a pyjama cord. Over this they wore a frilled
petticoat, which was caught up and tied in a knot over their buttocks,
like a bustle. On top of this was a little frilled jacket, buttoning over
the bosom, and with long sleeves. All these garments were made of
flowered flannels and cottons of various colours, in which blue and
orange and pink predominated, all softened and faded by repeated
washings and dryings in the sun. Their long hair was braided in
two pigtails, and pinned closely around their heads, where it was
covered by a bright headcloth. This costume, with its tight-fitting
jacket and long, leggy look enhanced by the bulky folds of the
knotted petticoat, was not unbecoming to the young women, with
their lithe, springy walk and straight-backed natural carriage, and

on the little children, who wore a miniature version of it, it was amusing and charming.

Umm Ali was not content with her lot. 'Ah,' she would say, 'things were very different in my father's house. I am ashamed of the poor way we live here, offering you no hospitality, letting you lie out like that at night. At my father's house that would never be permitted. And then look at Abu Ali – poor and old, and only father of one child. Indeed, I would leave him tomorrow if I could – if I found someone who would take me away' – this with a meaning glance at Elias, who hastily changed the subject. It was obvious Umm Ali had taken a great fancy to Elias, now back in his character of Abu Talal, whose flashing eye and black moustaches had not been without effect at various stages of our journey. Whenever Abu Ali was absent in his fields, Umm Ali would confide to us her sorrows and disappointments, and tell us how unworthy her husband was of her. We basely abandoned Elias on these occasions, evading his anguished glances of appeal, and delighting to observe with what skilful plausibility he would find business to occupy him, or the children to chaperone him.

Umm Ali's interest in us had one good result: she provided us with an excellent guide.

'You want to get to Akroum? But of course Abu Ali shall lead you. He's an old man, and one thing he does know is the routes over all these mountains.'

'Do you really know the way to Akroum, Abu Ali,' we asked, 'and would you like to guide us?'

'This woman's family lives beyond Akroum,' he replied. 'When I was seeking a wife I often went over there, and know the way well. I will guide you tomorrow with pleasure, and show you where the Wadi Saba is, and take you to Sayyid Ali's house.' So the matter was arranged, and very satisfactory it proved.

Our plans made, we set off down the mountainside to explore the castle, and halfway down, to our surprise, we came upon our friends from Beirut who, faithful to their engagement, had contrived to reach Akkar by car. They had come bearing gifts of roast chicken and wine, but overcome by the steepness of the climb and the incertitude of our whereabouts, had given up, drunk the wine, eaten the chicken, and were now sprawled in comatose relaxation beside the track. We bore them back rejoicing to our camp, where they stayed an hour, and then accompanied them down to the village, where they started on their long journey back to Beirut. This visit impressed our local acquaintances very much. 'To come all that way and climb all that distance for a cup of coffee and an hour's conversation, that showed real friendship!' And they eyed us curiously to see what it was about us that inspired such devotion.

By now we had a number of acquaintances, and the circle around our campfire that night was a large one. People had come by during the day with wounds and complaints for which they begged treatment, and for which our limited first-aid kit was totally inadequate. One man had a deep cut in the palm of his hand plugged with tobacco, which is claimed to stop bleeding. Two young men turned up and tried to draw us on Arab politics – what did we think of British action in Muscat, and questions of a like nature, but we refused to be drawn, and the conversation passed off amiably into more harmless channels. Our shock-headed friend sprang like a jack-in-the-box into the circle again, and the talk droned back and forth, and the cloud and mist wrapped round again, and the trees rattled and sighed in the night wind. Ringed round the fire our guests sat swarthy and picturesque, while Elias plied the coffee-cups, and the talk meandered in paradox and parable, and the jackals shrieked in the cliffs, and the owls hooted in the trees. At last the fire died, our visitors departed and we sank untroubled into sleep, unmoved by Big Stick's brays or Elias' snores.

We were up early and prepared speedily for our departure with Abu Ali, who came frail and neat on a little mouse-like ass as diminutive as himself. Umm Ali engaged Elias in earnest conversation as she delivered our laundry, from which he escaped with rather a flustered air, and then we were off, following a grassy track up into the tree-grown cliffs above us. We climbed up very steeply through the white rocks, until we emerged on the top of the cliff, and could look down on to the rounded tops of the holly oaks around the Wali's tomb, and Umm Ali standing like a coloured toy on the flat roof of her house. We now turned into a splendid forest of pine and juniper and cypress, and our path wound its way gently upward through forest glades and shrub-grown outcrops of rock. We frequently lost sight of each other, but the accompanying music of thumps, thwacks, bells, snorts, oaths and exhortations as Elias and Abu Ali kept the donkeys on the desired track prevented us losing contact with each other. This was essentially high pine forest, and after about two hours of march, across the grain of numerous ridges, we emerged on the rim of another amphitheatre. Below us the denuded slopes of the valley stretched down in wide terraces golden with grain, and formed the foreground of a great sweeping view from the inland extremity of the plain of Akkar on our left, running up into the pale foothills of the Nosairi mountains, to the long, dark, shaggy hump of the mountain rising immediately across the valley from us. This forested mass looked forbidding enough, but it was nothing to the barren, treeless, tawny mountain rolling away in peaks and folds inland from the head of the valley. This, we now learned, was the Jaafar grazing area, and very desolate and uninviting it looked from our vantage point opposite it.

Abu Ali now led us off on a lateral path towards the head of the valley. There was a spring concealed in an outcrop of rock on this slope, but it was muddy and flat to the taste. The path grew steeper as we dropped down to the angle of the valley-head, and we came on to small terraces of fine-looking hashish, nearly ripe. Some sort of settlement seemed to exist at the top of the valley, for we could see a long, flat mud roof clinging to the curve of the hillside, half obscured in trees. The nearer we got, the more hashish we saw, until finally we came into the settlement, a few low cabins huddled against the cliff, the long, low building whose roof we had first seen being the largest building in the place. The path around the curve of the valley was very narrow, and the donkeys kept well to the outside edge. Little Stick, indeed, seemed to prefer to teeter along on the rough stone coping of the supporting terrace. Women and children began to stir curiously out of the houses, and a fat-bottomed boy in a baseball cap, carrying a muzzle-loading gun, shouted aggressively up to us to know whether we were Christian or Moslem. These youths and boys are undoubtedly the plague of the Arab world, and this one was quickly joined by another two, and a stir and excitement commenced in the gathering throng below us. Little Stick at this moment jogged his load against a tree-trunk, lost his balance and fell thump on to the mud roof of what must have been a hashish-drying shed ten feet below him. Emotion all round, and in the confusion which ensued the question of our identity was happily forgotten. The villagers' relief that the donkey had not gone through the roof of their shed, and our relief at Little Stick's recovery, apparently unharmed, from this fall, led to mutual congratulations, especially as a train of men with heavily laden donkeys arrived at this moment to add to the general clamour and confusion. We escaped from this entanglement with relief and, pausing only to water the animals and ourselves at the gushing spring in the angle of the incline, hastened up into the obscurity of the forested mountain which loomed before us.

This mountain, Abu Ali told us, had once belonged entirely to the people of Akroum, but in recent years the Jaafars had encroached on it and driven the Akroumis back towards the eastern end of the spur, towards which we were going. We were now not so far away from Kammouha, which lay westward along the forested wall of mountain we had already crossed, and we appeared to have unwittingly entered the very territory we had been anxious to avoid. However, there was nothing to be done about it now, so after a short pause for lunch we pushed on upwards through the pine forest.

The children were in very good spirits, and fortunately no one had been riding Little Stick at the time of his fall, Abu Ali's ass being more of a novelty. They amused themselves by chanting various jingles they invented as we went along: 'Dee-dumba, dee-dumba' being one, which finally reduced Abu Ali to silent laughter, for 'dumba' in Arabic means 'tail'.

We also carried with us various handsomely striped caterpillars, which we had nursed onwards from Kammouha; they appeared to be the caterpillar of the hawk-moth.

The track was steep, and the donkeys made heavy work of the ascent, but the sharp, piny air of the forest was stimulating and we crept slowly up the flank of the mountain in a long traverse, the valley falling out of sight below us, and the grain terraces we had crossed taking their place in the pattern of forest and cultivation tilting towards the distant plain of Akkar.

When we were clear of the forest, we found ourselves toiling up the stony slopes of poor-looking hashish terraces, which grew stunted and neglected among the boulders and spiny cushions and clumps of thorn that dotted the harsh soil. They looked as if they lacked sufficient irrigation, but so windswept and desolate was the area that their meagre appearance was not out of place.

Abu Ali plucked a head from one of these plants and, sniffing vigorously, indicated that we should do the same. 'It helps one get up the hills,' he said and, nothing loath, we each plucked a flower and, children and all, sniffed our way steadily up the hill. The dry, acrid smell was not unpleasant and, whether it was the actual properties of the plant or the novelty of the idea, we all continued with renewed energy.

So stony and inhospitable was the landscape that it was with surprise we saw a shepherd boy gazing in wide-eyed astonishment at us from a rocky hillock. Without waiting for our greeting, he bolted off, ahead of us, and disappeared around a bend of the track, which brought us out in a few minutes to a small plateau, with two or three stone huts crouched in the lee of an outcrop of rocks. A black-clad mountaineer stood on his roof-top, obviously watching out for us, but responded civilly enough when Abu Ali rode forward to enquire the possibilities of getting some chaff for his ass from him. We felt no inclination to linger, and passed on, while a pack of shaggy dogs rushed snarling out at us, and a rabble of children set up a shrill yelling and jeering which followed us long after we were out of sight.

It was now past mid-afternoon, and a bitter cold wind sprang up, strong enough to make us bend against its blast. We were walking down the backbone of what appeared an immense whaleback, high above the rest of the surrounding countryside. On our left the clouds were beating up from the sea-coast, and obscuring our view, but on our right we could look across the intervening valley to a barren tangle of bare mountain-tops, their clefts and declivities deeply shadowed in the soft evening sunlight. It was a desolate place, and the scudding rack of cloud and dead and mournful light did nothing to improve the appearance of the dark grove of stunted holly oaks that barred our path. From the circles of stones with their rough headstones we could see lying beside the path, we deduced this was an ancient cemetery, and a more important pile, ringed with boulders, confirmed our belief. 'This is a Wali's tomb,' said Abu Ali, 'and his ghost haunts the grove at night, so it doesn't do to linger here.' Little strips of cloth fluttered from the twisted, wind-racked trees above the shrine, and votive offerings in the shape of potsherds, broken combs, pieces of mirror, were laid on the tomb. With prudent forethought the children added a button, a piece of shirt and a handful of their hair to the pile, and we hastened away down the dark tunnel of trees, the wind wailing about us, and thoughts of Coleridge's 'savage place, as holy and enchanted as ere beneath a waning moon was haunted' running in our heads.

Abu Ali did not seem anxious to dwell on the subject of ghosts, and shortly afterwards, pointing to a steep, narrow gully descending on our right hand, said: 'That's the way down to the Wadi Saba, but you can't get a donkey down it.' The Wadi was now clearly visible below us, a great gash in the mountainside, running down beneath a tawny cliff-face some hundreds of feet high to the junction of two gorges, which carved their way through the knotted tangle of the mountains. The floor of the valley was hidden from us, but the rock-face, streaked with red and brown discolorations, had a curious archaic quality about it, and one could well fancy it carved with curious reliefs by a people using the valley as a trade route.

The day was beginning to fade, and the prospect of a night out in this howling wilderness was hardly alluring. We were so high up that we could see over into Syria without effort, and the Lake of Homs glittered far off in the ashy pallor of the plains. We were at the extremity of the long spur of mountain which we had first seen barring the horizon from the head of the military road at Kammouha, and very close to the frontier of Lebanon. 'Don't take us into Syria, Abu Ali,' we begged, for we could see the thin lines of road in the plain below, and the small clusters that denoted settlements and perhaps frontier posts. 'The Syrians aren't friends of ours, and they'll never believe we've come this way for pleasure.'

It was with some relief that we came on a very old man, bent beneath a load of maize that he carried slung across his back. 'Akroum is down there,' he said, pointing down to the valley, 'but there's nobody there now, as there's no water at this season, and everyone moves up the mountain.' The wind was so strong that we were crouched behind a hedge of thorn during this conversation, but even so the wind blew away half our words. 'Sayyid Ali, did you say? You want to see Sayyid Ali? He's my nephew by marriage, and he lives about half an hour's walk away over there,' and he pointed over to our left, where the cloud was swirling in among the rocks. Losing no time, we took hasty directions, and set off into the rocky desolation ahead. Just as we were beginning to despair of getting anywhere in daylight, we came on to a torrent of goats pouring out of the clefts of the rocks, and streaming off in the direction we were going. 'Yes, Sayyid Ali's place lies over there,' and pointing to a curious wind-eroded cliff, the goatherds moved off by various narrow paths and footholds after their beasts. In the gathering twilight we hastened on up the stony path, like rather inadequate Childe Harolds, till, turning the cliff, we came on to a cultivated terrace of maize. At first we did not notice a man who stood immobile on a boulder, some distance above the track, his rifle slung over his shoulder, his long US army coat blending well with the hillside, his close-wrapped *keffiyah* and white *shewals* glimmering in the twilight. He watched us in forbidding silence, and remained where he was until we came up to him and, after greeting him, asked the way to Sayyid Ali. Then, turning on his heel, he motioned us to follow him, and strode off ahead. This was hardly an encouraging welcome, but we were all too cold and tired to care very much, and our host himself, whom we encountered shortly afterwards, hastening up the rocky path to meet us, amply made up for his henchman's coldness. News of our coming had probably been relayed on by the goatherds, whose calls and halloos we had heard echoing about the cliffs after we had left them, and Sayyid Ali had hurried out to inspect the unexpected travellers. He appeared absolutely dumbfounded to see us, and his eyes rolled from the children to their mother, from their father to Elias, in undisguised astonishment, while the sweat poured down his plump forehead, and his breath came in short heaves. Various henchmen stood glowering around him, but Sayyid Ali never faltered in the courteous manner in which he greeted us and, having read the note from the foresters which we gave him, gazed at us with a glimmering of understanding. 'Where have you come from?' he asked, as we followed him down the mountainside. 'From Sheikh Djenaid? Why, you must be tired, for I don't suppose you're used to this sort of work, like us.' We were now approaching his house, a two-storey new stone building attached to an older, smoke-grimed cube of the familiar pattern. The new house had bright blue shutters, and was entered up a concrete stair, while underneath we guessed there were storerooms and stables for his animals. A well stood in one corner of the mud courtyard, and hens scratched in the dirt, and fierce-looking dogs came growling out from around the corners of outhouses. The house stood in a sheltered meadow surrounded by scrubby trees, and commanded a view of the path in both directions. A mud tomb with whitewashed patterns on it caught our eye as we approached: 'My father,' remarked our host, adding 'Sunni' with a sidelong glance to see if we took in the distinction. This was interesting to us, as it meant we were no longer among the Shia Metwali families of the Hermel area.

We now entered the house, and found ourselves in a room five paces by five, colour-washed in rudimentary patterns, and bare of all furniture except a portable iron hearth with a charcoal fire smouldering in it. Bright-coloured quilts were stacked tidily in an alcoved recess, and mats and cushions were spread on the floor around the walls. A youth, suffering from Asian flu, we were told, lay in one corner, but he was hastily removed by the women of the household, who now appeared for the first time. Sayyid Ali was himself a man of about thirty, stockily built and inclining to plumpness. He was plainly dressed in a loose grey gown belted with leather around his waist, a collarless shirt and white *shewals* completing his attire, while a woven skull-cap perched on the back of his pink, balding head. His complexion was fair and his brown eyes quick and lively, while his small toothbrush moustache gave a certain comical, egglike quality to his face. The women, on the other hand, were superb, very tall, with small, fine-boned faces set off by the long ringlets that dangled from under their enormous swathed turbans. Their costume was similar to that of the woman we had met at Kammouha, but the quality and colour of the materials were richer and more sumptuous. Their gowns flowed in a sweeping train from a small yoke set high between the shoulder-blades, while in front one could see their full-flowered pantaloons falling in folds about their ankles. On their breasts they wore chains of necklaces, and gold earrings and bangles testified to the prosperity of the household. More mattresses and cushions and rugs were quickly spread for us and, taking off our shoes, we sank gratefully back against the wall. Dusk had fallen outside, which made the sensation of shelter and repose even more delightful. Coffee was brewed for us on the hearth, which was quickly blown into activity. The roaring acetylene lamp was lit and hung on a hook in the ceiling, the radio blared popular Arab songs and long ranting polemics from Cairo. Our luggage was piled up on the balcony outside, and the donkeys led away to food and a stall for the night. Other guests arrived, a pair of mounted *gendarmes* tired from an eight-hour patrol, and two sheep-dealers come to do business with Sayyid Ali. We all sat around among the cushions, tired and worn, chatting desultorily among ourselves, until suddenly the women and henchmen appeared, laid a long cloth on the floor where we were sitting, and spread a splendid supper for us. There was grilled chicken and fried liver, three great plates of rice pilaff, fried eggs, salad, *hommos*, yoghurt, piles of round bread – several plates of each, so that the cloth was covered. Urged on hospitably by our host, we all fell to and, tearing off pieces of the bread, scooped into our mouths whatever caught our fancy. *Arak* was set for the Christian sheep-dealers, which they did not hesitate to use and share with us, and fruit and rice pudding followed in due course. When we were at last all sated, we drew back, and our host and his male retainers took our places and finished off what we had left, and then what little remained was taken off by the women, presumably to be eaten by them and the children in the kitchen next door.

Having eaten, everyone felt much more cheerful and more sociable and, bringing in some stools, our host invited us to sit, and a teasing cross-questioning of us began, much enjoyed by everyone present. A little girl ran out to nestle on her father's knee and be fondled affectionately by him, and the women gathered smiling in the background, sharing in the conversation and seeing to their guests' needs. One of the henchmen crouched over a big wooden coffee mortar, bound with brass around its narrow neck. With a long wooden pestle, almost as tall as himself, he began a rhythmic pounding of the coffee beans, which with its clicking sound was not unpleasant to the ear, and formed a soothing background to the hum of talk filling the room.

'In your country, is the stranger made as welcome as he is with us Arabs?'

'Yes,' we replied mendaciously, 'the English are warm to strangers.'

'When I come to Beirut, will you give me shelter in your house?'

'Listen, O Sayyid Ali,' we replied through Elias, 'in our house in Beirut – and mark its address well, so that you don't forget it – we have a room twice as big as this, where our two small children sleep. All that shall be for you, and for whoever you bring with you, for as long as you like, and you shall see yourself how the English treat their friends.'

This answer pleased our interrogators, and they laughed good-naturedly and fell to asking us why we tramped like this through the mountains. 'We travel with mules and donkeys because we have no roads in our mountains, but surely all foreigners ride about in cars?'

'This is wild country,' said Sayyid Ali, 'there are no doctors or hospitals should anything go wrong with you. When my father was sick, it took two men to carry him in relays down the mountain on their backs, to get him to Koubayat, so we could take him down to the doctor in Tripoli.'

'If you came to our country,' we replied, 'would you stay in one place, in London? No, you would go everywhere, to see all you could. So do we do, and where we can't go by car, we come by donkey.'

The children had long ago wrapped themselves in a quilt and lain down in a corner and drowsed into sleep. We longed to follow, but until the coffee and tea had circulated and the questioning had ceased, we had to take our share in the entertainment of the evening. At last Sayyid Ali took pity on us, and asked if we would like to sleep, to which we gladly assented, and left Elias and Abu Ali to do duty for us. The room was thick with cigarette smoke and loud with voices, while the radio wailed unceasingly in the background. Sleep came hard in such circumstances, especially when a loud and quarrelsome game of cards started on the other side of the room, and persisted until one a.m. At last the radio was cut off, the glaring lamp turned down and we settled down to sleep, seventeen of us stretched out on mattresses around the room. Abu Ali coughed as if he were in the last stages of tuberculosis, but swore it was the English cigarettes he had been smoking, the snores and teeth-grindings had to be experienced to be believed, the children scratched restlessly, but at last we sank into some semblance of sleep.

At dawn next day everyone got up, and we rose too, wan and hot-eyed. A long wait ensued while breakfast was prepared, and meanwhile three more guests arrived, a patrol of foot *gendarmes*.

Sayyid Ali's house appeared to be the ultimate point inland of these border patrols, and it was obvious he was not exaggerating when he said that coffee and tea were kept constantly prepared on his hearth for the incessant visits he received.

The two sheep-dealers now retired with our host to the comparative seclusion of the courtyard where, squatting under the shelter of a wall, they got down to business. They were Christians from Zghorta, and were buying on a large scale for a big butcher of Tripoli. Sayyid Ali's wealth was in his flocks, and hundreds of pounds' worth of business was done like this, squatting in the corner of courtyards, tramping over wild and inhospitable country. These buyers would be going on to the Jaafars, they told us, and didn't expect to be back in their homes for many weeks to come. Once the purchase is made, no money changes hand, for it is a rash man who travels these mountains carrying cash. Letters of credit are given to specified merchants and bankers in the city, and a complicated system of credit and assurance ensures the maximum satisfaction to everyone concerned. The purchased animals are brought down at agreed dates by drovers, such as Elias was in his youth, coming down through the mountains slowly, so that the animals can feed and keep in condition.

The business done, the question of our next move arose again. We had discussed our plans the night before, and though Sayyid Ali told us he would give us a man to take us through to the Hermel side of the range, he did not advise it. The people were uncivil, but that was nothing to the harshness and difficulty of the country. Water was the great problem. The springs were few and far apart, and were scant and unreliable at this, the driest season of the year. The Wadi Saba had one spring, halfway down its length, but the water was strongly tainted with minerals, and not considered very good. Of the rock-carving we received very clear descriptions – a panel some ten feet by six depicting a man with a spear attacking a lion, with a queen sitting near by on a chair or stool. A half-moon and three stars completed the carving. It was on the left-hand side a quarter of an hour's walk from the spring. We could, if we wanted, go down into the gorge to look at the carvings. It was three hours' march away, and would have to be done on foot, and without the children, as it was impossible to take donkeys down, and it would mean spending another night on our return at Sayyid Ali's house.

That clinched it. 'For God's sake, Elias, we couldn't face another night like the last. We'd better give up the Wadi Saba, get down to Koubayat, and decide what to do there.' Elias was quite content to do our bidding, and explained to Sayyid Ali that we feared the going would be too hard for our children, and that we could no longer impose on his hospitality, and would go down to Koubayat that day.

Breakfast was now served, more or less the same meal as we had had last night, and we all sat down and stuffed ourselves in silence, till, belching loudly, we sat back replete. Again the retainers and our host took our places, and again the women, stately and graceful in their rich robes, came quickly and silently to clear away the meal. The mounted *gendarmes* were the first off, swinging up on to their horses with a great clatter, and giving a cursory farewell all round. Sayyid Ali watched them go with a slight cloud on his usually cheerful face. 'He doesn't mind feeding their horses when they spend the night here,' explained Elias, 'but he objects to having feed commandeered to take away.' Next the foot *gendarmes* went off, their heavy rifles and ammunition belts swung across their backs. Another round of tea and coffee followed for us and the sheep-dealers, who had taken a great fancy to Sebastian, and then we were ready to be off. Persuading the children to abandon an enormous horned toad they had discovered squatting by the well, and which they proposed adding to our collection of livestock, we all lined up for a farewell photograph in front of the house. Then we took a formal photograph of Sayyid Ali, two great bandoliers slung across his chest, and a rifle in his hand, and finally another group of the women in their fine dresses, all mixed up anyhow with retainers, chickens, dealers, dogs and children and ourselves in the dusty, poky little yard. At last the gear was loaded and, accompanied by our host, we set off through the meadow in the direction of Koubayat. Sayyid Ali took us to the top of the ridge, and then we said goodbye, grateful to him for his generosity and good treatment of us. 'Don't forget, Sayyid Ali, and come to us in Beirut,' and then with a last handshake we turned up the track and set off towards the road-head.

SEVEN

Down to Tripoli

W E HAD NOW REACHED the limit of our journey along the northern range of the Lebanon, and we turned our back on the mountain without regret. Our plans were made, and we knew exactly what we wanted to do. We would get to Koubayat that day, part with Abu Ali, and next day start down the road to the plain. Somehow or other we would get to Tripoli, where we could consult a doctor about the children's skin complaint, which was becoming increasingly irritating. Then we would hire a lorry, load the donkeys, and transport ourselves up to the mountain pass above the Cedars, and start down into the Beka'a from there. It was all too easy, and the doubts and incertitudes of the last days being resolved, we stepped out gaily, and turned our minds forward to the next stage of our journey.

Soon we entered the pine forest again, and left behind the rocks and thorns and dizzy sweep of landscape, with Syria lying dusty white and brown beneath us. The trees screened us from the hot morning sun, and scrambling and slipping down the rough steep track we came to the base of the big mountain, and crossed the narrow valley at a ford, thickly grown with pink oleanders. As we splashed through the stream, we were challenged by three mounted *gendarmes*, who emerged from the screen of oleanders and demanded to see our papers. 'What do you have in your luggage?' they demanded to know, and showed signs of wanting us to unload and open it up; but fortunately our letter of recommendation from Beirut did its work, and they became very jovial and friendly. The children persuaded Abu Ali to cut them switches of the oleander with his knife, and wreathed themselves in the pink flowers, and decorated the donkeys as they rode along. Our way now led in a gently rising slope along the left-hand side of the valley, past streams and beds of oleander, and hawthorn trees bent shadily over the path. Before us we could see Andeket, where the road up from the coast ended, but on the outskirts we turned left, and over a rough stony path came finally to Koubayat, about four hours after leaving Sayyid Ali.

Now that we were back in civilisation, our hearts sank slightly as we looked about us. A wide, straggling main street, lined with poor-looking houses, two or three poky stores, a few youths lounging among the fly-blown debris of the shopfronts, and that was Koubayat. A coffee shop, however, soon caught our eye, and, tying up the donkeys, we settled ourselves down in the proprietor's upstairs room, while he rebuffed the curious citizens who came to look at us. Having eaten, we took advice on a camping site, and led by Abu Ali walked on to the Spring of the Lady (Ain el Sitt), under an immense plane tree, with a little stream curling pleasantly away through the orchards to the town. Here we finally parted with Abu Ali, paying him two pounds for all the services he had rendered us from our first arrival at the spring of Sheikh Djenaid. Before he left he taught Miles to tie his headcloth like a true mountaineer, then, staff in hand, slipping on to his little ass, rode off neatly up the flank of the valley, heading across country to the forest above Akkar.

Early the next day we were off, having repulsed an offer by two gypsies, dark, swarthy fellows who with lute in hand came and squatted under the plane tree, and sang us jingling Arab songs. They proposed buying Little Stick from us. Our road wound pleasantly through the rolling upland country, and gradually the great barrier of the forested mountain fell away behind us, and the view opened out on to the wide, shimmering plain beneath. Vineyards and fields of tobacco surrounded the occasional hamlets we passed through, and mulberry trees shaded each cottage, for this is a silk-making district, and the rearing of silkworms is an essential part of the village economy. As we swung down the folds of the foothills, we could look across the plain to the distant mauve mountains of Syria, and see Krak des Chevaliers white like a thimble, sticking up on the skyline and guarding the passage at its feet. We were walking down into Crusader country, and traces of their occupation were to be found all over the area we were passing through. At Biré, where the dilapidated ruin of a fine Arab palace now degenerated into an untidy farm faces a charming mosque and fountain, shady with trees, a track leads off to the gorge of the River el Kebir, some three or four miles away across the seamed and scarred landscape. Here one can still see the foundations and cisterns of the Chateau Felicium of the Crusaders, cut out of the black basalt of the local rock, and guarding the crossing of the river where its tributary, the Mendjez, joins it. This castle could signal to Safita, and possibly to Krak and to Akkar. Halba, towards which our road was leading us, was also the site of a castle, halfway between Tripoli and Felicium.

We marched fifteen miles down the road, the landscape growing more desolate and forlorn and empty the lower down we came, until we spied an empty lorry approaching us up the road. Flagged to a halt, a brisk exchange began between us. 'Sixty to Tripoli,' 'No, thirty,' 'Fifty,' 'We'd rather walk,' 'All right, forty,' and the bargain was struck. In next to no time the huge six-wheeler was turned and backed up against the side of the road, the donkeys shoved in, and we all clambered aboard and sped off down the twenty-odd miles to Tripoli. Soon we were out of the foothills, and bumping across the dusty plain, past the scattered tents of a wandering tribe of gypsies, past the big mud-hut settlement of Palestinian refugees, sprawled among the reeds like an Indian village, past the shoaly, pebbly rivers with their bright clumps of oleander, past the cactuses and bananas and date-palms of the plain. How we laughed to see 'Fnaidig' written on a signpost pointing up a narrow, rutted road, leading off into the desiccated flanks of the foothills; how we enjoyed the sight of the brilliant sea washing silkily on the white shore. Behind us lay the ardours and discomforts of the stony north, before us waited a brief enjoyment of the urban delights of Tripoli.

* * *

Tripoli is the chief town of northern Lebanon. It lies among the orange groves of the coastal plain, where the Abu Ah River, issuing from the Kadisha gorge, runs into the sea. Its name is derived from the Greek, and refers to the three 'towns' or quarters into which the city was divided in Phoenician times, when it was the chief city of the Phoenician Coastal Confederation. The merchants and citizens of Tyre, Sidon and the island of Rouad, off the Syrian coast, each occupied a sector of the town, surrounded by a wall.

The County of Tripoli was one of the three Latin states which owed nominal allegiance to the Kingdom of Jerusalem. Traces of the Crusader period are scattered in the courts and narrow alleyways of the old quarters of the town, on either bank of the river. The chief mosque is built on to the remains of the cathedral of Sainte-Marie de la Tour des Croisees; the charming mosque of Teylan, in the purest Arab style, rises on the site of a Carmelite church, and the tawny bulk of the castle, dominating the river from a mound in the centre of the city, bears in its name, Sandjil, the memory of the Provençal family of Saint-Gilles who were the first Counts of Tripoli. Another linguistic souvenir of the Franks is the name of the aqueduct which still brings water into Tripoli; it is called the Kanatir el Brins – the arches of the Prince – and was built by one of the Latin lords of Tripoli.

Provençal legend has it that it was to one of the daughters of the Count of Tripoli that Jaufre Rudel, the troubadour, addressed his poems. Which lady it was, Melisende or Hodierna, who was addressed as his 'Amor de Lohn' is not clear, nor is the accuracy of the tradition sure. Having for love of his distant lady determined to go on the Crusade, the poet was stricken with illness before he reached the Holy Land. Brought into the harbour of Tripoli, his friends sent word to the castle that Jaufre Rudel lay dying in the town. The Count's daughter hastened to him, and he blessed the fortune that had allowed him, even though dying, at last to set eyes on the face of the lady he had loved so long, and from so far away. The legend adds that she took the veil after his burial.

One curious survival of the more ancient past of the city is the spring rising up in a large circular stone basin in the courtyard of the Dervish convent of Koubbet el Beddawi. The basin seethes with fish, protected and fed by the people of the neighbourhood, and by pious visitors come to pray in the mosque. Certain fish were sacred to Astarte, the Phoenician love-goddess, whose cult was similar to that of Aphrodite, and sacred pools and wells were features of her worship. Indeed, she is said on one occasion to have changed herself into a fish, which, like the dove, was considered a symbol of fertility. With the coming of Christianity, many of her old shrines and practices were incorporated into the worship of the Virgin Mary, and it is interesting to record that among the Christian inhabitants of Tripoli there is a tradition that a church once stood where the Dervishes now have their mosque.

The inhabitants of Tripoli are predominately Moslem, of the orthodox Sunni persuasion, and known for their turbulence and disaffection. The town in many ways feels itself more in sympathy with its Syrian neighbours than with the central administration in Beirut, and, like Tyre in the south, would willingly opt out of the Lebanese Republic. The ranks of the swarming, vociferous poor of Tripoli are swelled by the Palestinian refugees, spilling out of their camps, and clustering in fly-blown squalor in old buildings and ramshackle tin shanties, and who, mixed with the floating population of a seaport and important road and rail junction, can make up on occasion a very formidable mob.

Our lorry driver, to our consternation, instead of bringing us into the centre of the modern town as we had hoped, now announced that he must put us off at the Bab Tabbane, at the entry to the old town, as he dared not be reported to his employer for wasting time and petrol, to say nothing of making some money on the side. So willy-nilly we were offloaded on to a bare patch of ground in the seething disorder of the poorest quarter of the town. Three donkeys being unloaded from a lorry was in itself nothing very remarkable, but our appearance, ragged and dusty though we were, soon caught the attention of the crowd. Losing no time, we put the children on the donkeys and started off quickly up the road, hoping to lose ourselves in the throng of donkeys, pack-mules, cab-horses and *fiacres* that cluttered the entrance to the town. The donkey, led or driven, has the least rights of any in the terrifying confusion of Lebanese town traffic: this we soon learned, as buses and cars pulled out in our faces, taxis honked, drivers cursed, cyclists swerved among us, and the inexorable murmur of comment and astonishment followed in our wake. As we shouldered our way through the gathering throng, for the only time on the whole trip the hope crossed our minds that we would meet no one we knew. Advice and enquiries now began to be shouted to us by the curious crowd, and when we explained that we were seeking a *khan* or stable for our donkeys, a great hullabaloo arose among the ragged porters and market men surrounding us, while the different merits of rival establishments were argued among them. With that readiness to enter into another's problems which is shared throughout the East, a man soon volunteered to lead us to what was described as a very good *khan*, while the *fiacre* drivers passing through the throng added their advice and admonitions as to place and price, and little boys peered and pressed, and the comments on our appearance, nationality, purpose and status circulated freely in the crowd. 'The Street of the Nut-sellers, the Street of the Nut-sellers, that's the place to go to, you'll find a *khan* there,' seemed the general burden of the advice, so, led by our new friend, we turned off into the narrow, winding alleyways of the *souk*. Here the houses grew so close together, their ramshackle balconies hung with washing, that little sunlight penetrated to the noisome gutters and vaulted warehouses of the merchants. Piles of nuts were laid on cloths, or spilled out of sacks and straw containers, in the quiet fustiness of the shop interiors – peanuts, pistachios, walnuts, almonds – while a busy rabble of curious onlookers rapidly crowded the balconies and courts of the street. We reached the *khan* in a throng of vociferous helpers, while the proprietor – a stout, moustached Moslem – gazed at us with surprise and suspicion. However, he unbarred his gate, and we moved into a tall, vaulted stable covered in almost medieval filth, where a few mules and donkeys were drooping sadly among the flies. The filth and stench were formidable, but we were in no position to be finicky about things, and would in any case be away within forty-eight hours. The baggage unloaded, the price agreed and a portion paid, the donkeys watered and a feed put down for them, and we were ready to go. Above our heads the call to prayer wavered deafeningly from a minaret wired for sound, while outside in the alley the crowd increased every second like a swarm of bees. The flies clung stickily to our clothes and faces, the sun was fierce in the yard, and the soft, moist air of the coast made us all stream with perspiration. Two ragged Syrians from Homs, their yellow gowns as dusty and stained as our own clothes, pointed out to Ralph that he had no fly-buttons left on his trousers, then eyed the broken shoes and ragged jeans of the children with cheerful commiseration. Friendly helpers now procured us a *fiacre*, and helped Elias load the gear, while others, perhaps unwisely, persuaded a taxi to force its way up to the neighbourhood of the *khan*. We took off in a wave of emotion, not unfriendly, but heightened and excited by the novelty and strangeness of our appearance and the ambiguity of our purpose.

The Hotel Hakim, an old-fashioned establishment just off the main square of the town, received us with commendable *sang-froid*. They placed a small room at our disposal for our gear, all broken and torn by rocks and thorns, the stores of porridge and sugar and tea hopelessly shaken together by Little Stick's fall. Our taxi-man was finally disposed of after an impassioned argument. He followed us into the hotel lobby demanding four times the normal fare, and flared with rage when it was refused. This battle of wills raged for something like ten minutes, the man refusing to be pacified with an extra shilling, which he ill deserved. But then, by one of those curious changes of front so often witnessed in Arab argument, the matter ended, the victim having at last risen in indignant wrath and denounced in fury the importunities of the Tripolitans. A point is always reached in these clashes when one or other party is goaded into an uprush of genuine rage: this condition reached, there is nothing further to be done, the matter goes by default and, purged by emotion, the contestants go about their business, the loser accepting the situation philosophically.

Our activities in Tripoli are easily followed from the items listed in the house-keeping book.

'Doctor, chemist', starts the page, then follows:

'Repairs camp-bed, duffle-bag, trousers, sandals'.

'Purchase shoes, kitchen-gear'.

Then comes 'Toys, games, ices etc', and a further entry of 'Beach', so it will be seen we were not entirely occupied by business.

The chief glory of Tripoli are the splendid orange groves and fruit gardens which surround it, stretching from the town itself to its harbour at el Mina, a mile or so away. Inside the city there are gardens too, sumptuous with green and bright with bougainvillea, and very charming cemeteries, shady with trees, the graves and mausoleums enclosed in cages of filigree ironwork, and the turbaned headstones tilting among the irises that grow around many of the tombs. But for the children it is the sweets and ices of Tripoli that are most memorable. The pastry-cooks and sweet-makers of Tripoli are famous, and rose-leaf jam, and orange-blossom jam, and pumpkin jam covered with bleached nuts, are among their specialities.

Very pleasant was it to stroll in the warm, soft evening, with the neon signs flaring in the arc-lit streets, the shop-interiors brilliantly lit, and the prosperous Levantine citizens passing ceaselessly up and down the pavements.

The cafes were all full of men reading newspapers, or playing tric-trac, talking together at the close-placed tables, watching the people moving about the street.

The cinemas flared, the radios blared and the taxis added their squealing tyres and plangent motor-horns to the cacophony of sound. The ice-cream parlours with their mirrored walls and marble counters swam like fish-tanks in the lurid green reflection of the street-lighting, and sitting at the small iron tables we ate mulberry ices and mango ices, stripy Neapolitans and delicate green pistachio ones. Pomegranate juice squirted cool and fresh into sherbet glasses was another joy, and the infinite variety of cakes and sweetmeats provoked agonies of indecision among the children. Spread out on the wide, shallow aluminium trays, these delicacies are variations of an essentially similar theme. A sweet syrup made by melting down sugar in water with a squeeze of lemon juice, and flavoured further by a teaspoon of rose-water or orange-water, is almost always an ingredient, and various stuffings of pounded pistachio, almond, walnut or pine kernel, mixed with fine sugar and rose-water, or powdered cinnamon or cardamom are extensively used. Pistachio cakes are delicious, and so are those filled with chopped dates, and honey-balls had been a favourite with us ever since our life in the Turkish quarter of Famagusta, where there had been a famous maker of these delicacies.

Our early visit to the doctor had led to an immediate diagnosis of the children's skin complaint. It was scabies, undoubtedly contracted at Kammouha. The treatment was simple and efficacious and, as the infection was only slight, it was mastered in twenty-four hours. By a curious coincidence, the chemist from whom we bought our medical stores was a nephew of the *chatelaine* of the crumbling *serail* at Bourg. 'I heard from my family that some foreigners had passed through, walking towards the north with donkeys and children. What an extraordinary idea! I hope you don't think all Lebanon is savage and backward like that!'

'No,' we replied, 'we know it isn't, but we know also it isn't all like this,' pointing around at his immaculate shop, the latest American, French, Swiss drugs lining the shelves, the imported baby-foods, the beauty preparations, the weighing machine, the big sponges, the white-coated assistants – all the appurtenances of a wealthy and indulgent society.

Through the agency of the British Bank in Tripoli, we contracted with a transport firm to haul ourselves, our luggage and our donkeys up to the Col des Cèdres on the watershed above the Cedars. We parted gratefully from the Hotel Hakim, which had been helpful and obliging, and very reasonable in its charges, and started loading up the lorry. The party being split into two, a friend of ours having brought Elias back from Beirut in his car, the children and their mother crowded into the car, while the men drove off into the *souks* to retrieve the donkeys. A long delay ensued, which was finally explained when we all met on the road out of the town. The *khan* keeper had refused to deliver the donkeys, had protested that we might well be spies, Jews, God knows what, had demanded to see papers of identification, and had finally compromised with his conscience for the matter of a sterling pound or so, yielded by an Elias grinning with rage and fury.

The donkeys appeared touchingly grateful to see us again, which led us to suspect the treatment they had received in the *khan*, and we ground on up the winding road, through the olive groves and fruit terraces, a united party again. We stopped in Ehden, smouldering and sulky under the occupation of the army, to buy fruit. The pretty little market square with its shady trees and fountain was deserted except for a few soldiers and glum-looking inhabitants. No tourists or holidaymakers were about to buy the beautiful fruit and vegetables displayed in the open-fronted shops. Even our bizarre emergence from a lorry was regarded as a hopeful indication of returning prosperity, and we did our best to satisfy everybody by buying something from each shop in the row. The pears and plums were delicious, and we filled two big baskets with assorted fruit and vegetables, all clean and fresh and in the peak of condition.

Our lorry-driver was a native of Ehden, and was much twitted on his new role of donkey-carrier, so we were quickly hurried away, passing on the outskirts of the town an armoured car parked sentinel-wise on a curve of the road. Soon we were entering Becharré, and we could look across the gaping canyon of the Kadisha at the weary way we had trudged a month ago. Then the lorry began the steep upward crawl up the wall of the amphitheatre, and looking out we could identify places we had sweated or rested at, the scenes of many little incidents which we could hardly have borne to repeat.

We whirled through the Cedars with no desire to stop, and swung up past the ski-lift towards the pass. Hardly had we got off the tarmac and started zigzagging up the rough stone road than our driver became restive. 'What sort of road is this to expect a man to drive on? I hadn't bargained for this when we left Tripoli.' This complaint was repeated at intervals during the slow, bumpy ascent, and exploded into a burst of temper and a demand for extra money when we reached the top. The price agreed in Tripoli was sixty lira, about seven pounds, and we were determined not to be bullied into paying more. Besides, during the first rumblings of the storm we had had the wit to unload the donkeys and gear, so had the distinct advantage of, as well as being numerically superior to our burly adversary, a huge, round-headed, blond fellow, strong as an ox. Having learnt that the man was an employee, not the owner of his own vehicle, we saw quickly what he was about and, stubbornly refusing to pay another piastre, offered to give him a note to the bank, with instructions to meet his demands should they be justifiable. The storm raged with much shouting and gesticulating for five minutes or so, but we were tired of the Tripolitans and their extortions and refused to budge. 'You're all going to kill yourselves anyway, so why hang on to your money?' was the parting shot. 'You can't take it with you where you're going, so why do you worry?' But as the lorry ground into gear, he waved to us quite good-humouredly, and we parted amicably enough on the windswept pass.

We were now 8,000 feet up, and the cold bit into us. North and south the barren, desiccated, bald-faced backbone of the mountain chain extended as far as we could see, and on the western flank the land fell away in the familiar giant's staircase to the sea-coast forty miles away. Before us, as we turned our back on the enormous amphitheatre of the Cedars, stretched an entirely new landscape. There rose the lesser chain of the Anti-Lebanon, swelling to the great bulk of Mount Hermon far to the south; between us, far below, stretched a wide, flat valley, patched brown and yellow with cultivation and continuing in each direction as far as we could see. This was the valley of the Beka'a, and this was where we were going.

PART TWO

EIGHT

The Col des Cèdres and the descent to the Beka'a

THE SUN WAS ALREADY SINKING WESTWARD towards the sea when we set out down the shadowed mountain. The wind bit sharply as we stepped out cheerfully, glad to be on the move again, the children racing and chasing along the rough, stony road, the donkeys jingling and clinking as they hastened their steps to the shouts and blows of Elias.

As we descended, the foothills, which had not been so apparent from on top of the pass, assumed a greater importance, and the Beka'a gradually disappeared from our sight. But the Anti-Lebanon itself remained clearly visible, its flanks bathed in the soft, warm sunlight, the valleys and folds of its surface already sunk in shadow. We were walking down towards the spring of Ain Ata, where we intended to sleep the night, but after two hours' descent we found ourselves still on the bare, shaly side of the mountain. We pressed on in the gathering dusk, the mountainside above us already dark and forbidding, while across the plain the Anti-Lebanon glimmered rosily in the fading light, its feet in darkness and swift-spreading shadow. The children no longer raced and chased, but rode the donkeys or, like Miles, picked their way silently and carefully down the loose, rubbly track.

Between us and the foothills there appeared to be a dry, sunbaked plateau, scored with vineyards, and as the night deepened, a few lights began to twinkle out of the gloom below. We stumbled on the spring by chance, a murmurous rush of sound indicating that we had reached our destination. In the dark we could dimly discern a great mass of boulders in an open space, covered with goat droppings. We seemed to have come down the side of an amphitheatre, but it was too dark to see where we were. While we busied ourselves with unloading the gear and preparing supper, the children explored the rocks and found the spring gushing from under the overhang of a huge boulder poised on two others, like a cromlech. The water from the spring-head was so tinglingly cold that it gave one a momentary sensation of intoxication.

The night was cold, and we prepared hastily for bed. With some difficulty we found a shelf on to which we could just fit the tent, and in the slowly increasing moonlight settled ourselves among the rocks and stones for the night, our heads wrapped tight in our *keffiyahs* against the cold. We seemed hardly to have settled into sleep when a scuffling and noise of men and beasts struggling among the rocks brought us into startled wakefulness. In the bright, cold moonlight we could see mules and donkeys heavily laden with huge sacks backing up confusedly on the ledge where we had pitched the children's tent. This was the only track up the rim of the amphitheatre, and we had effectively blocked it. The pack-drivers, muffled like ourselves in their *keffiyahs*, shouted gruffly to know what we were, but waited good-humouredly enough while we half-collapsed the tent, and edged the mule-train carefully past the still-sleeping children. They were a party of flour merchants from Becharré, come down across the mountain into the Beka'a to buy wheat, when the price was right at the end of the harvest. They were travelling by night, as we were to do later, to avoid the heat of the day, and had started on the final lap of their journey at midnight, hoping to reach Becharré early next day.

Next morning we awoke to find the goats already with us, an odorous black tide streaming over the lip of the amphitheatre, tucking themselves up tidily on the ledges and cavities of the rock, or clicking neatly along the track above us, shaking their ears and gazing blankly at us with their curious flat yellow eyes. The goatherds, an old man and two children, told us the village was only fifteen minutes' walk below us, and, having eaten a leisurely breakfast, we started off down the track.

The village of Ain Ata had little to recommend it. A dusty open space with a lorry jacked up for repair, a few stone houses and a church, for the people are Christians, a store where one could buy tins of sardines and corned beef, sweets and combs and razor-blades, and not much else except the fowls scratching in the rubbish heaps and the villagers themselves standing around waiting for the lorry to go. Our arrival provided a welcome diversion, and soon we were the centre of an amused and friendly crowd, who speculated freely on our appearance and motives. They were all ready to advise us on our next stage. 'Half an hour to Yammoune,' they said cheerfully, 'just keep going and you'll be there in half an hour.' So, having bought ten eggs and a hatful of pears, we passed through the shabby village and set out into the glare of the sun.

The mountains now rose up grey and heat-riven on our right-hand side, the jagged crest outlined against a sky pale with heat. On either side stretched the dusty vineyards, with only an occasional figure to be seen tending the vines far away up the hillside. An hour and a half later found us still plodding through the deserted landscape, victims once more of our own credulity and the mountain-dwellers' inability to estimate time by any other standard than their own. That at least is the only explanation we can give of the enormous gap between prognostication and performance which affected all our movements. We never got an accurate estimate in terms of hours for any stretch of the journey, partly because a mountaineer travelling alone will take all sorts of short cuts impossible for a laden donkey, partly because they seemed genuinely to feel that we would be disheartened by the truth. Haphazard though our system of marching might be, with long dawdlings interspersed with sudden bursts of speed when Big Stick thrust forward into the lead and went jingling off at a pace that left half of us hallooing forlornly for mercy, our general pace was not much slower than that of other travellers whom we encountered on the course of our journey. But we lacked the steady discipline of their progress, the long hours of unremitting slog, the uncomplaining acceptance of monotony and discomfort. We were for ever being distracted by things to see and things to eat, water to splash in and flowers and fossils and fir-cones to collect and hoard and haggle over, while Elias, Nelson-like, turned a blind eye to our signals, and pushed on ahead to some shady spot, where we would come upon him half an hour later, smoking a cigarette and idly chatting with whoever happened to be about.

On this occasion it was noon before we reached Yammoune, and it was only the increasing number of people that we encountered in the vineyards that encouraged us to go on. By and by we saw tall glades of poplars and other trees, and turned thankfully towards the blue- and whitewashed houses we could see among them. Arriving almost unnoticed in the noonday heat, we were greeted cordially by a young man whom Elias addressed and were led by him through various alleys where fine, ruddy-faced girls and women peered laughingly out at us, and finally emerged beside a great derelict mound of grey granite blocks, where cattle were grazing, and women hanging out their wash on the tumbled stones. This was all that remained of a Graeco-Roman temple, built, like Baalbek, on a Phoenician site. Beside it stretched a small, shallow lake, clear as the sky it reflected, with ducks and geese swimming domesticatedly upon it. Here, according to legend, was where Astarte, the Phoenician love-goddess, changed herself into a fish.

Led by our guide, we passed the temple mound and, pausing to drink from an icy spring emerging into a stone cup beside the road, came on to the most charming scene we were to see for a long time. Beside yet another lake, pebble bottomed and so clear that we could see the bubbles of the myriad small springs welling up to feed it, were gathered the elders and notables of the village. The lake was bordered with sward as green as any English lawn, and here grew weeping willows, alders, poplars, in an elegant naturalness that a landscape gardener might have envied. Seated in small groups and circles on the grass were the men of the village, enjoying the freshness and shade of the trees, their dark blue gowns of broadcloth contrasting with their white headdresses, and beyond them the village flocks of goats drank in the lake, or drowsed like their owners beneath the trees. These people were Shia Moslems, an isolated community of only some hundreds, the hereditary enemies of our friend the *Mukhtar* in Akoura, four or five hours' march away over the great hump of mountains cutting across the end of the valley where we now were. They greeted us kindly and with no unseemly mirth or curiosity, a contrast to the more familiar inquisitiveness of the Christians up the valley which we noticed throughout our travels.

On the far side of the lake – the ornamental water, one might call it – was an enormous willow tree, whose roots grew out of the water. Beneath it was a carefully levelled terrace, belonging to the house of one of the notables present. Here we were courteously invited to repose ourselves. Mats and cushions were hurriedly brought by the house owner, stools and a tray of fruit were provided for us, and we were encouraged to eat our lunch in peace and tranquillity. We had a delicious picnic, having with us some luxuries from Tripoli such as a salami sausage, and little cucumbers and plums which we cooled in the water of the lake beside us. Our hosts maintained a discreet reserve, and only when we had finished eating were we able to persuade them to join us in a cup of coffee and a round of cigarettes.

'Stay with us here,' they said. 'Why hasten away? Rest a few days – look how much water we have, and how fresh and cool it is here under the trees.' But we were hastening on to Baalbek, for we had calculated that we could reach there next day in time for the last night of the folkloric display inside the great Roman temple. 'Have you been to Baalbek?' we asked. 'Have you seen the dancers and singers who have come from all over the Lebanon to perform before President Chamoun?' But they only shrugged and looked vague and said, 'Why, as for *dabke* dancing, our shepherd boys could dance and sing all night if they wanted to, without going to Baalbek for it.'

After a little while we all sank into somnolence, but roused ourselves up at about three-thirty to load the donkeys once more, and to prepare to be on our way. Our hosts all stood up straight and serious in their long blue coats, which almost touch the ground: they are girdled around the middle with a big leather belt, which doesn't conceal the ammunition belt worn within the wrap, against their white shift. We shook hands all round, and murmured many words of thanks and obligation, the children following us around the circle of farewell, and shaking hands too, looking straight up into each man's face, then glancing modestly downwards, as they had learnt from Elias. He, meanwhile, was suavely exchanging handclasps and pious hopes for the further success of our journey, and thumping the donkeys and booting Middle Stick into line, and settling the differences between Sabrina and Sebastian as to who should have the rein, and who should have the stick as the wretched Little Stick was urged into motion.

So we turned away in the cool of the afternoon, leaving the tranquil water and trees behind us, and followed the track of what seemed a great irrigation ditch dug across the wide green meadows. These seemed to be the dried bed of a drained lake of considerable size. All over these meadows we could see herds grazing, and little boys running with their sticks, and hurling stones accurately to turn their charges in the direction they wanted. It was a scene of pastoral leisure and spaciousness such as we had not seen since we left Kammouha. From out of the rushy sides of the trench ducks and geese scuttered as we passed, and as we came to the end of the meadows, and started to follow a track up the barren, stony foothills, we saw below us a watermill, and the water from the irrigation ditches roaring as it rushed underground.

Our way now led onward through a deserted, scrubby wilderness, following a foot-track alleged by the elders of Yammoune to bring us out at Deir el Ahmar in two hours' time. We walked on briskly enough, up and down the folds of the foothills separating us from the Beka'a. The track meandered on over dusty red earth and stony troughs and depressions, now leading upward to what would seem a point of vantage, only to deceive, next leading down through thickets of thorn and scrub to further disappointment. We finally reached the crest in the late afternoon, and started a traverse across open hillside to what appeared a settlement some way below us, for we could see terraced fields, and trees, and evidence of cultivation. The day was beginning to fade as we came down through close-growing groves of hazels. Our track led past hashish terraces and then, encouragingly enough, bordered a rushing irrigation channel which indicated that a settlement was near.

We finally emerged on an open basin on the stony hillside. Two levelled places indicated the threshing floors and a few stunted may trees bent obliquely over the colour-washed stones of what we could see was a Moslem cemetery, whose graves were scattered haphazardly over the flank of the hill. As we stood debating whether to stay or go on, for it looked a barren, comfortless spot, a stout old man on a stout bay cob appeared. It was obvious his path would lead him close to us, so Elias stepped forward to intercept him. We watched the encounter with a certain interest, for we were aware that night was close at hand, and were anxious to get settled before it came. 'Peace be with you, O Sheikh,' called Elias, adroitly seizing the old man's hand and kissing it. 'We are travellers on our way to Baalbek, and ask leave to camp here for the night, for our children are tired and we don't know the way.' We had been sitting rather wearily on the ground while this encounter took place, but now we rose and exchanged formal greetings with the *Mukhtar*, for so he turned out to be. 'I am the headman of this village,' he said, 'and all these houses' – pointing to the scattered houses of the settlement behind him – 'belong to me and my sons. We are of the Jaafar family, and anything we can do for you, we shall be glad to do. Stay here tonight, and for longer if you like, and if anyone questions this, say I told you so.' With this he left us, riding off towards some houses beyond the threshing-floor. Hardly had we got the loads off the donkeys than willing help appeared in the shape of a small, bright-eyed man with a black toothbrush moustache and an old American GI jacket worn over the usual white jodhpurs. Soon all the nearby houses had sent their quota of onlookers, including several young women, bright and fresh-faced, who wore severe black wimples wrapped tight around their heads, so framing their faces that they looked rather like women in medieval wall-paintings. Their dresses were modern in style and black in colour, and underneath they wore long black stockings and neat little black patent-leather slippers which showed off their shapely legs very well. They marvelled to see the tent go up so quickly, and more so to see the Lilos blown up and the bedding laid out. They marvelled also to hear Elias conversing with their menfolk – 'One speaks Arabic quite well' – and they marvelled more to hear that we had come through Jaafar country further north. 'And so you saw Sheikh Ali himself – we are of the same family – ah, he's a fine man, so generous, so hospitable, no doubt he looked after you well.' Elias in full recital of what he thought fit to tell our hearers of our travels was not one to let a slight inaccuracy mar the flow of his narrative, and this confusion of Sayyid Ali with Sheikh Ali did much to enhance our status in the eyes of this Jaafar community. No countenance was given to some youths who from the outskirts of the crowd rudely cried out that we must be Jews, and the mature men turned away silently from them in disapproval of such odious manners. Dusk fell as the crowd gradually dispersed, not before a youth arrived bringing milk for us and our toothbrushed friend brought over some feed for the donkeys with the *Mukhtar*'s compliments. 'I am sorry I cannot offer you the hospitality of my house, but I am an outlaw, and live by the charity of these people myself. But take this anyway, as a token, and believe me when I wish it was more,' and with this he thrust a saucer full of chips fried with tomato juice into Elias' hand, and disappeared off into the darkness. We were rather pleased to receive this addition to our supper, and gobbled it up avidly along with a mess of noodles, beef tea and sliced sausages. The children were soon in bed and asleep and we three adults sat idly around the fire, talking over the day's events together. We noticed a lantern bobbing away below somewhere to our right, but were hardly prepared for the upsurge around us of a group of armed men, who seemed to rise up out of the surrounding night, their blue broadcloth gowns merging with the dark. We all three stood up instinctively, with fixed smiles of greeting wreathing our faces, as if we were silently saying 'Cheese', while the firelight flickered over their white *keffiyahs* and undershirts, and gleamed on their bandoliers and shining teeth. 'Be welcome,' we said, making hospitable gestures; 'let us have some coffee or tea,' to Elias, who immediately started clinking cups and mugs together, and putting on the kettle. 'No, no,' cried our guests politely, 'we have come to ask you to visit us. We are the sons of the *Mukhtar*, and really it embarrasses us that you should be sleeping out here like this, instead of in our father's house, or in one of our houses.' But we excused ourselves as best we could. 'Our children are asleep,' we said, 'and it is a pity to disturb them,' and turning the conversation as we settled down beside the flickering fire, enquired into the ramifications of the *Mukhtar's* family.

Personal questions are never taken amiss in these circumstances. Indeed, to be incurious of one's fellow men indicates a certain lack, as if some vital spring of human sympathy were missing, and is a condition to be remarked on and even pitied. So we plied the *Mukhtar's* stalwart sons with questions, and they responded readily enough, their golden eye-teeth gleaming in the firelight, their strong, swarthy faces turning attentively to each speaker, as the questions and responses flowed through Elias between us. Their father, the *Mukhtar*, was now nearly eighty, but he had four wives, and by these four wives he had ten sons now grown to manhood, and these were they who sat before us. There were others still children, and daughters too, but these men already had grown children of their own, and under their father were the elders of the settlement. Theirs was the hard life of goatherds and sheep-dealers, with the hashish grown around the settlement as a cash crop. The people of Yammoune were no friends of theirs, and they rarely went down into the Beka'a. Rough and ready and self-contained they seemed as they sat there in the cold night under the stars, their rifles by their sides, their cartridge-filled bandoliers crisscrossed over their gowns, their big, rough hands carefully cradling the cigarettes we all passed so politely among ourselves.

The coffee finished, they rose to bid us goodnight, and to extract from us a polite promise to come early next day to take coffee with the *Mukhtar* before we left, and then with many wishes of peace and repose for us disappeared into the night, their acetylene lantern roaring in the silence. Only a young, fair-haired man remained, and the outlaw, Mohammed Ali, who seemed glad to have news of the outside world. Nearly five years ago he shot a man – his second – 'Unfortunately he had friends in the police,' and since then had been living as an outlaw, under sentence of twenty-five years' imprisonment if caught. He was a cheerful, goodhearted fellow, not one to repine unnecessarily, but a shade of melancholy crossed his face as he explained the precariousness of his existence – no home except on the sufferance of his relatives, a constant vigilance, ever alert for the arrival of strangers or *gendarmes*, and a virtual imprisonment on the wild range of mountainside around us. 'I'm never happy unless I have my gun beside me,' he said, showing us with pride a gleaming, well-cared-for, modern rifle. 'I used to take the hashish down into Beirut sometimes, but it's an awfully tricky business, and anyway in the end someone denounced me, and I was lucky to get away. I used to walk down over these hills – we know all the ways, and it used to take about a week on foot – but it's too risky, so I just live here, and give a hand where I can. I daren't go down into Baalbek – far too many policemen about – and as for going into Syria, there's no point in that. I can't get work there, and they'd send me back if they caught me.' His cousin was a generation younger, and had no real sympathy, beyond the dictates of family feeling and hospitality, for the old warring spirit of his elders. 'Of course we fight if we have to, and of course there are blood feuds and inter-family quarrels' – mostly over grazing rights up here in these mountains – 'but what sort of life is it that Mohammed Ali here has to lead? I don't want to spend all my manhood living with the wolves and animals of the mountain. I'd rather grow hashish, or better still, apples, and have my children learn to read and write, rather than waste their lives in perpetuating old quarrels.'

This was an attitude we encountered many times among the younger men, both Christian and Moslem. The old world of blood-feuds, of warring raids and stubborn lawlessness had a romantic charm seen only from the perspective of the coffee shops and tric-trac boards of Beirut. Here was the reality in all its confining futility. Mohammed Ali accepted the disapproval of his cousin with good-humoured philosophy. His way of life was fixed, he would never escape from it. He could envisage no alternative; and he would live out his days an outlaw in these hills, a half-life, but his own.

Next day saw us coming down through terraces of hashish and over turfy pastures, past great irrigation works and at last on to the sunburnt expanse of the Beka'a plain. 'So you are walking through our country,' said a sack-suited young man who detached himself, agog, from a group by the village shop as we passed through Schlifa. 'Very good, very good; we ought all to do the same,' and primed with one of Elias' capsule accounts of our travels, stepped daintily back over the ruts into the shadowy inactivity of the coffee shop.

Meanwhile we set out down the straight, dusty track across the plain to Baalbek. It was nine o'clock and the sun struck down out of a pale blue sky. On either side stretched the fields of maize and corn, with here and there a dusty olive-green square of ripening hashish. Sometimes the strips of corn had been cut and cleared, and the burnt, dry stubble stretched away to the neighbouring boundary. Here and there were spindly, leaf-thatched watchtowers, from which the peasants overlooked their crops, to make sure no one filched them during the night. Sometimes we passed by acres of melon and marrow, but mostly it was grain cultivation.

Not for nothing was this the granary of Rome in the days of her Empire when Baalbek was a great garrison city, and her temples were raised for a rich and energetic merchant community. This was Goelesyria – hollow Syria – once a gift from Antony to Cleopatra, the great rift valley stretching from the steppe-land of northern Syria to the shores of the Red Sea, bounded on either side by the barren crests of the Lebanon and Anti-Lebanon mountains, and further down encompassing the lake of Tiberias, the Jordan Valley and the Dead Sea. The whole plain lies some 2,500 feet above sea-level, and the air is crisp and dry and invigorating. Now, however, the sky grew leaden pale with heat, the landscape lay bleached and quivering in the glare, and we trudged on, moving like ants across what seemed an endless open space.

We were in a different world from that of the mountain. Far away, across the chequerboard of cultivation, we could see other tiny figures busy with the occupations of the plain, loading camels with sacks of wheat and chaff, piling up melons into heaps for the lorry wreathed in its own dust-cloud to take away. Halfway over we diverged from our track and struck out over the dried red earth towards what we thought must be Baalbek, a dark green oasis with tall buildings rising in its trees, but a quarter of an hour later we realised that we were wrong, and that Baalbek lay to our left, straight down our original track.

This was a disheartening moment, for we were all feeling the heat, but we tacked back towards a tall group of poplars that we could see, and rested a while in the meagre shade they afforded. There was a muddy, frog-infested streamlet emerging from a rush-grown stretch of turf, enough for the donkeys to wet their feet in, and to snatch a mouthful before Elias led them to the shelter of the trees, but not clean enough for us to drink. We all flopped out on the turf in exhaustion but, after a while, nibbling the few plums we had left, we set off once more into the blinding heat of the plain.

We marched steadily on, and eventually saw the unmistakable tall columns of the Temple of Jupiter rising airily out of a great spreading mass of greenery far ahead. This was the oasis of Baalbek, a little town of some nine thousand inhabitants, surrounding the great Roman temple towards which we were heading.

Back now on our right track, and with our destination in sight, our spirits rose and we recovered some of the gaiety of the early morning. 'To Baalbek, to Baalbek, upon a white horse,' sang the children merrily, and, 'Baalbek walls are tumbled down, all its columns on the ground,' improvising words and rhymes and alliterations and laughing delightedly at their own ingenuity.

Anthea in particular delighted in this form of amusement, and was ably abetted by Elias: 'Ya Anthea, ya Anthea,' he would sing, and 'Bezbina, Bezbina, Sabrina, Bezbina,' she would chant back, her shrill voice taking the sharp Arabic pitch, her hands clapping automatically to the clearly defined beat.

In this way we came to Baalbek, entering through the scattered groves and orchards of the outskirts in company with an elderly peasant riding a white horse, who had joined us on the plain. We seemed to come in through some sort of ancient necropolis, then by winding lanes, with tempting glimpses on either hand of shady green orchards and glinting irrigation channels. Water was all about; it ran out of crevices, it seeped through the turf, it flashed in streamlets beside our track. We entered the town by the back way, passing through dirty, nondescript alleys motionless in the noonday heat. It was now after twelve, and three hours since we had come down on to the plain at Ghlifa, seven miles away. Our hearts gladdened at the prospect of rest and refreshment before us, we hurried on eagerly, till turning a corner the father and mother of all smells hit us, literally bringing us to a halt. Before us rose a great barrack-like building, festooned with laundry, some ancient vestige of the town's past now converted to present needs. A rabble of dirty children and a few seedy men in shabby suits clearly indicated that this was a settlement of Palestinian refugees. Wrapping our headcloths tight around our faces and ignoring the curious looks thrown at us, we urged the flagging donkeys forward, anxious to escape the noisome stench which enveloped us, and in a few minutes emerged on to the open space before the entrance to the great temple enclosure, and paused thankfully in the deep shade of the walnut trees there. There was a municipal water-point in the square, and we were eagerly filling and draining our water-bottles when a curious sighing sound from Little Stick caused us to look round at him, in time to see him capsizing slowly to the ground, Sabrina and Sebastian still on board, too surprised even to cry out.

This new development was something of a facer, but so tired were we all that at first we felt no emotion of surprise or regret.

'Thank God he lasted till here,' was the unsentimental reaction of us all, as we regarded him prone on the shady ground. Before us the square stretched bare and deserted in the noonday sun, except for a little knot of curious Palestinians peering from the deep shadows of a shopfront on the far side. Elias, his head dripping from the tap where he had been sousing himself, brought a can of water over, and gently trickled it on Little Stick's head, who after a few minutes opened his eyes and started to get up.

As soon as Little Stick seemed somewhat recovered, and all the donkeys had drunk their fill, we moved off slowly around the walls of the temple enclosure, huge, tawny, sandstone blocks which dwarfed the fruit trees clustering in the gardens beneath them. Little Stick's unfortunate collapse had made us pause long enough to attract attention, and we were followed by a straggle of nasty children shrieking abuse and throwing stones, until we turned sharply on them, brandishing our sticks and roaring threats to summon the police. Except for two or three scraggy little girls who followed at a distance, we were left in peace, and we entered a world of cool and quiet and soft, dusty silence. The great solid walls rose above us, with an occasional fragment of inscription or ornamentation set at random into the fortification, the fruit trees and shady walnuts only allowing an occasional shaft of light to pierce the green gloom. The trail of little girls being dispersed by a few sharp blasts of unmistakable Arabic from Elias, we offloaded the donkeys and left him settling himself comfortably amid the gear for a sleep, while around him the flies droned gently in the still air, and the sunlight fell in golden shafts on the tawny walls.

Baalbek is in the curious position of having a new identity thrust upon its ancient agglomeration of temple, fortress, marketplace and dusty, deserted provincial town. Like all places of strategic importance in this great compost heap of succeeding cultures, Baalbek, with its abundant water, and its position at the head of the Beka'a, was inhabited from the beginning of history onwards. Originally a Canaanite settlement (Ba'al Beka: the God of the Beka'a), evolving into a Phoenician trade centre, conquered and settled by Alexander and his Greeks, a Roman colony under Augustus, the centre of a fashionable rite under the Empire, a Christian town under the Byzantines, conquered by Moslems, raided by Crusaders, ravaged by Mongols, fortified by Arabs, neglected by Turks, excavated by Germans, restored by French, visited by intrepid European travellers from the twelfth century onwards, the great temple enclosure contains memorials to them all, from the bas-relief of Heliopolitan Jupiter himself, with his ancient Phoenician attributes of lightning flash and whip, to the names of lady travellers of the 1880s, boldly inscribed high up on the then unexcavated walls of the Bacchus temple.

Temples were raised here to the Heliopolitan Triumvirate: Jupiter, Venus and Mercury, who absorbed and continued the traditions of the more ancient Semitic gods Hadad, Atargatis and Simios. So popular did this become that Heliopolitan Jupiter was worshipped as far away as Rome. It was for him that the great sixty-foot-high columns were raised on their rectangular platform 260 feet by 140 feet, dominating the surrounding courtyards and temples, and forty feet above the gardens of the oasis. Of the original fifty-four columns only six remain, still linked together by a fragment of entablature. Earthquake, and the rapacity of a turbulent populace eager for the lead and bronze riveting the sections of the columns together – which they used to manufacture bullets – has brought down the rest. What remains can be seen in the open space beside the better-preserved so-called Temple of Bacchus, in reality dedicated to Venus. Here on the huge, tumbled blocks of the entablature are the beautifully incised garlands of flowers, the gaping lions' heads, the bulls, the acanthus leaves, the beading, all the profusion of ornament which made Baalbek a great triumphant assertion of the wealth and power of the Roman Empire. Around the vast courtyards the architects are still labouring to bring order to the tumbled wreck of the past, hoisting pillars into position, clearing and uncovering and tidying away into the huge underground vaults and tunnels which honeycomb the substructure of the three-and-a-half-acre main courtyard. A Byzantine church dedicated to St

Barbara (whose day is still celebrated by the Christian inhabitants of Baalbek) has been cleared to reveal the central altar, a big solid structure fifty feet high whose ingeniously constructed stairways and corridors enabled a ceaselessly moving throng of the pious to participate for a few seconds in the mysteries of sacrifice. Of the two big basins of water, charmingly decorated with cupids and nereids and other fancies, one is well-preserved, but the other, built over by the Arabs, seems mutilated beyond repair. An Arab mosque, constructed out of materials taken from the ruins, occupies one angle of the enclosure; a tower of the Mameluke period is accessible from the eastern end of the Bacchus temple. Sir Richard Burton, during his Consulship at Damascus in 1870, was responsible for clearing away a screen in front of the Bacchus temple entry, thus allowing its exquisite doorway to be seen. The door-lintel, decorated with an eagle holding a garland in its beak, is badly cracked, and was propped up by Burton to prevent its falling. The German archaeological expedition of 1901 later secured it more firmly.

Outside the massive fortified walls, a charming small circular temple dedicated to Venus, and once used by the Christians as a shrine, has been completely restored, and stands by a muddy ditch as a miracle of good taste and restraint in comparison with the overpowering splendour of the temples within. There the scale is so large, the area of the enclosure so vast, that it is with surprise that one recognises motifs and devices familiar to the student of English mansions and country houses of the late eighteenth century. Robert Woods visited Baalbek during his tour of the Levant in 1751. When he made his drawings nine columns still stood in the temple of Jupiter, but by 1784, when Volney visited the ruins, only six remained – those which stand to this day.

These six columns are now displayed on posters distributed far and wide abroad by the Lebanese Tourist Office. For the past two years the Lebanese Government, anxious to exploit the tourist resources of its beautiful country, has organised a cultural festival in the temple enclosure, modelled on those popular in Europe and America. Aided by an enthusiastic band of wealthy Beirut society women, it has brought in dancers, actors and musicians from the leading European troupes and orchestras. Throughout July and August the two small hotels of the town, the Palmyre (built on the site of the ancient amphitheatre) and the Hotel de la Source, are packed out, and ballet-boys from London posture among the ruins, and toga'd Frenchmen trumpet out Racine on the steps of the temples. The performances themselves are held at night, and the audience, packing the shadowy *cella* of the ornate Bacchus temple, is the cosmopolitan society of Beirut, motored in from its summer villas at Aley and Sofar and neighbouring summer resorts, huddling in furs and glittering with diamonds, and the volatile students of the American and French schools and universities of Beirut.

Today everything was different. This, the last night of the 1957 Festival, was to be devoted to a display of Lebanese folk dancing and entertainment. Some two hundred dancers and entertainers had been assembled, largely at the instigation of the President's wife, Mme Chamoun, and an immense crowd was beginning to pack into the town. We walked slowly through the heat to the Hotel Palmyre, hoping to have some news of friends there, but found instead a horde of teenage youths and girls, clad in peasant skirts and T-shirts and toreador pants and jeans, busy practising dance steps to the sounds of the jukebox and their own clapped hands. Pushing our way through the throng of Coca-Cola drinkers and square-dancers, we attempted to explain our situation to the harassed management, but it was only when we saw ourselves in the mirrors of his smart contemporary-style vestibule that we realised how utterly out of place we looked. Our faces thick with tawny dust, our clothes crumpled from sleeping in them, our shoes torn, we seemed like creatures from another world and, hurriedly retreating, we crossed over the road to an empty-looking bar, where a Palestinian youth brought us beer, but could produce nothing to eat.

Flinching from the heat and the curious stares we now knew we were likely to attract, we decided to take a taxi to the Hotel de la Source, at the other end of the town. We drove half a mile or so through the seedy centre of the town to where the hotel stood secluded in its own stand of trees, separated from the public road by a good long driveway. This seemed just the place for us, and our hopes were pleasurably fulfilled.

The wife of the proprietor was a pleasant-faced young Irishwoman, who dispensed something of the calm efficiency of the hospital matron. The hotel itself was a stone-built Lebanese house, cool, old-fashioned, its marble floors scrupulously clean, its extensive grounds shady with trees and shrubs, with water trickling gently into stone basins, and fragments of Corinthian capitals doing duty as garden tables. Here we were most kindly received, permission was given us to camp in a secluded corner of the grounds, and we sat down under the trees to a delicious meal of salad, cold ham, sour milk, sardines and great wedges of juicy pink watermelons.

NINE

Baalbek, and the journey down the Beka'a

W E SPENT FOUR DAYS IN BAALBEK, camping in the gardens of the Hotel de la Source, resting ourselves and the donkeys, and sending Elias off to Beirut to see his family and to replenish our supplies. The town was slowly sinking back into its habitual inertia after the artificial excitements of the festival, and the narrow souk behind the main crossroads presented its ordinary air of aimless commercial activity, shabby men in headcloths conversing in the fly-blown interiors of the merchants' booths, and serious family parties from the outlying country districts discussing the purchase of a pair of patent-leather slippers.

Throughout these days we did little but enjoy the quiet and privacy of the gardens, and the baths and laundry and sanitation of the hotel. In the evenings we strolled down the drive to the coffee shops of the Ras Al Ain, where an abundant spring gushes out of the Anti-Lebanon in a park-like setting, shady with trees and green with lawns, and is channelled into pools and cascades before being taken down into the town in a small roadside canal. Here in the cool of the afternoon and evening the burgesses of the town stroll with their families and sit in the waterside coffee shops drinking *gazoozas* and coffee, and smoking their hubble-bubbles. The family parties of women sit in groups on the grass, their babies being cradled or suckled or staggering around within the safe confines of the admiring circle. Flocks of geese and ducks hiss and flutter in the streams, and sheep and goats and cattle file home in the soft sunset light. From the coffee shops come the tinny ululations of the radios blaring out popular Arab song-hits and the laughter and shouts of some jovial party of Christians sitting over their bottles of *arak*, while the little children run in and out of their legs, and the young men play football on the green. Then the soft dusk comes down, the fairylights in the cafés begin to twinkle in the cool night air, the stout young matrons in their western clothes push their perambulators homewards down the tree-lined road, and the francophile coffee shop owner whom we patronised would sigh gently for the past, and reach for another bottle of beer from the cool depths of his water-basin.

This is the easy, unpretentious life of the Levant, whose charm pervades all our recollections of our life there. Sitting under the vine-trellis, watching the melons spinning in the tiled basin, is no great thing in itself, but the acceptance of life that it implies is an attitude common to all members of the community. The pleasures of life are cheap in a simple society: shade when the sun is hot, sun when the air is cold. The jasmine trained to grow beside the door, the rose and carnation planted in an old tin, the pleasure and interest in the stranger's company, the repose after hard and exacting toil, are things shared by rich and poor alike, and give coherence to a society often split apart by religious and economic differences.

The children enjoyed themselves in Baalbek. In the mornings they used to take Big Stick out for exploring rambles up the stony slopes of the Anti-Lebanon. Half a mile or so from the hotel they found a charming three-berth Roman tomb in a shallow cave in the open ground. Here they used to spend hours in the heat of the day, sheltered from the sun by the overhang of the cave, which one entered down a sort of tunnel. They would lounge there playing cards and reading their favourite French comic, tucking up against the cool stone of the coffin niches, oblivious of the spiders and ants and lizards which shared their refuge with them. They also provoked a minor flood in the gutters of the town, by inadvertently letting out the plug of the water tank in a coffee shop beside the mosque – a particularly charming small, shady courtyard barely visible from the road – but the indulgence of the East towards small children saved us from undue recriminations.

Very lovely is it in spring to stand on the terrace in the south-west corner of the Jupiter temple, and to look across the wide expanse of the Beka'a. Beneath one are the gardens and cultivation of the oasis, with the fruit-blossom pink and white on the trees, and the new yellow leaves of the poplars and plane trees rustling in the breeze. Around and above are the massive stones of the fortified walls, with daisies and dandelions and anemones in the turfy crevices. As far as one can see down the valley, the iridescent green of the young wheat fills the plain, only interrupted occasionally by a clump of trees indicating a settlement, and the cloud-shadows move like cats' paws on the sea, until they fall purple on the snowy crests of the Lebanon. The wind bites sharp and chill, and down below in the gardens the peasants work huddled up in their winter gowns. Not so now, at the end of summer, when the sun beat down remorselessly out of a cloudless sky, and the distant mountains grew pale and unreal and indistinct in the noonday heat.

Our road lay straight down the Beka'a for fifty miles or more, and for the first time we would have to travel on a main road. We were anxious to get this leg of the journey over as quickly as possible, and to avoid the heat and the heavy traffic (for this was the main road from Homs and northern Syria) we decided to travel as much as possible by night.

We left Baalbek at four o'clock in the afternoon, and coming out of the town fell in with the only travellers of our own kind we met on the entire journey. These were three young Germans, who had been studying at Salamanca University and had made their way across Tunisia and Libya to Egypt, and were now on their way to Damascus and Jerusalem. We walked a mile or so together, exchanging impressions, but they were hitch-hiking, so we left them at a convenient stand, and later in the evening they passed us, waving cheerfully from the back of a workmen's lorry. We, in the meantime, found our own pace on the dusty track beside the tarmac road, and walked steadily on as the flanks of the Anti-

Lebanon went through their familiar gradations of colour, rather as the Dolomites do, and the dark came welling up from the floor of the valley.

Just before the light went we turned off and rested in the rubbly furrows of a ploughed-up strip, eating the supper Elias had prepared before leaving Baalbek, and then set off in a determined effort to cover as much ground as we could at one go. The traffic, which we all found very disturbing and alarming, slackened off, the donkeys were rested and in good fettle, and the children were excited and impressed by the darkness of the night, the emptiness of the plain and the always stimulating sensation of being on the move again. We walked fourteen miles that night, and hardly met a soul, until we came on a peasant creaking along in his cart with a load of melons for the market at Chtaura. We kept company with him in the bright moonlight until we came to where the road crosses the Litani River in a thick belt of trees and rushes. It was now after nine at night, and we decided to sleep here in the shadow of the trees, on a flat stretch of ground some little way off the road. We slept anyhow on the ground, not bothering to put the tent up, our *keffiyahs* wrapped tight around our heads to keep the dew off, the donkeys tethered to tree-stumps at the side of the stream.

We seemed persistently unlucky in our choice of night camping spots. This time a train of camels nearly trod on us as they padded silently along, each camel bulging with great sacks of wheat balanced on either side.

'In God's name, who are you?' cried the startled drover, peering through the shadows at us, lying like so many enormous caterpillars on the ground, 'and what are you doing, lying here across my track?'

'Smelling the breezes,' answered Elias sleepily but literally, employing the Arabic phrase for an outing or picnic, but this incongruous answer seemed to satisfy the man, who strode on gigantic through the misty night air and disappeared with his beasts into the bright, moonlit plain.

We all slept soundly enough after this interruption and awoke very early the next morning before the sun was up. The plain lay grey and formless in the pre-dawn light, the dew thickly pearled on our blankets and on every web and leaf of the thickets. This heavy dew of the Beka'a has been noticed by all travellers, and we were frequently warned of it. We wasted no time in getting on our way, our morning drowsiness dispersed by a frantic commotion on the nearby road, where two peasant women were engaged in a violent quarrel with the conductor of one of the village buses, as they attempted to load three goats and a bundle of hens into his already heavily laden bus.

Stimulated by many a hearty wisecrack from Elias on this subject, we set off down the road, confident that we had broken the back of this particular stretch the night before. Our road was no longer the main trunk road, but a slightly longer, older one which skirted the flanks of the mountain. We started to draw away from the flat, open expanses of the plain, and vineyards and fruit cultivation began to appear on the chalky hillside. As the sun rose, the Beka'a spread below us in a glittering pattern of reds and browns and ochres, which were soon lost, however, in the universal pallor of heat. All along the flank of the mountain we could see villages terraced up the steep sides of small abrupt valleys leading down to the road we were on. Above them swelled the tawny inhospitalities of the Sannin massif. All these villages, Qasr Neba, Temnin, Niha, contain traces of the Roman occupation, in some rock-cut sepulchres, in others, like Niha and Qasr Neba, small Roman temples. There is one, some distance above the Niha temples themselves, that one reaches by a road cut by the Romans out of the face of a cliff. Half an hour's walk brings one to where it stands, empty and rather forbidding on the deserted mountainside, its Corinthian capitals and columns all jumbled down by the shock of earthquakes, and the grape hyacinths in spring growing among its stones.

We had left the savage poverty of the north behind us, and from now onwards our road was never to take us far from the amenities of village store and wayside coffee shop. At Abla we stopped, hot and sweaty and rather fagged, at a store kept by an elderly, moustachio'd Druze. Here we had a second breakfast of cream cheese rolled up in the thin, papery mountain bread, and a delicious honeydew melon, three and a half kilos in weight, which we devoured in a matter of minutes. There were also pears, and bunches of grapes dripping from the tap, and stimulating cups of coffee for us all. The whole bill came to three and a half lira – about a shilling a head. In this village we also saw some brilliant yellow-and-black birds, strung on a string with an indiscriminate bag of hoopoes, fig-eaters, sparrows and other little brown birds and offered for sale by the village grocer: they were weavers, migrating southwards.

As the glare of noon increased, we sought about for some shady spot in which to rest and while away the worst of the heat. This was to become increasingly difficult as we went down the valley, as we were now passing through an area of intensive fruit cultivation, and we were not anxious to expose ourselves to the threats and abuse of some angry peasant, seeing in us strangers come to filch or destroy his crop. At last, near Fourzol, we found a meagre grove of mulberry trees standing in an empty field, and here, undisturbed, we dozed away the hot afternoon.

The village of Fourzol itself lay some little distance away off the road, terraced up the steep sides of the Wadi Habis (the solitary, the one alone). This settlement was old before the Romans came and, above the village, cut in the rock face of the cliff sealing off the valley, are innumerable cells and sepulchres. On one bank of the Wadi are two curious courtyards, cut out of the rock, connected by four steps. They lie open to the sky, empty, enigmatic, perhaps the site of some ancient sanctuary to Baal and Astarte. This theory is in some sort supported by the dimly discernible relief of a cone in one of the sepulchres, a symbol common to many early cult centres of this region. Further up the hillside one can scramble to a disfigured, weather-worn *ulrif* of a mounted figure picking a fruit from a tree, while another figure holds up an enormous bunch of grapes. These neglected, half-effaced survivals are to be found in several places in the Lebanon, where every tree and stream and high place had its *baʾal* and *ashtoreth*. A primitive belief in sympathetic magic encouraged the worshippers to practise ritual sexual intercourse, in the hope that, as like produces like, so their flocks and fields and springs and fruits would seed and increase. These practices were absorbed and glossed over and decently dressed up in the ritual and allegory of Graeco-Roman times, but persisted at various cult-centres into the Christian era, and were the object of many of the condemnations of the early Christian writers, and repressive measures by the Emperors.

A village bride in Lebanon still pelts her husband with an orange on entering her new home, and crushes a pomegranate beneath her heel, the multitudinous seeds of the fruit being a symbol of fertility. Both fruits, along with doves and fish, were attributes of the Semitic love-goddess, and the orange-blossom of the European bride is a relic of this ancient superstition. Some see in the modern practice of kissing the bride a survival of the pre-nuptial prostitution exacted from all female devotees of the cult. This was later commuted to a symbolic shearing off of the bride's hair, a practice maintained by Christian nuns on their dedication to the Divine Bridegroom.

The whole of this section of the valley down which we were now passing is particularly rich in architectural monuments of every age, for we were approaching Chtaura, which lies in the valley on the main Damascus–Beirut road where it comes down from the 5,000-foot Dahr el Baidar pass over the Lebanon range. This pass is kept open in winter by snowploughs, and is the only one usable from the Homs gap in the north to the southern gap by Merdjayoun, where the Litani River turns sharp right to the sea, through the gorges under the ruined Crusader Castle of Beaufort. Where the Damascus road doubles behind a jutting spur of the mountain, as it starts its climb to the pass through the Anti-Lebanon into Syria, a Roman temple stands on the crest looking like a small fort from far below on the plain. Opposite is a smaller eminence, on which is the domed shrine of Nebi Zair, a legend-enshrouded holy man whose memory is kept alive by the villagers of Mejdel Anjar, the village sprawling on the eastern slopes of the temple spur. Here an elegant stone Ummayed minaret rises out of the flyblown poverty of its mud houses. All along the foothills of the Anti-Lebanon are traces of ancient occupation, old shrines, and tumbled Roman temples, swampy thickets where the yellow irises grow, which were lakes until drained by the Arab governors of the fourteenth century. The Ummayed sultans of Damascus had a pleasure palace here, where they would come to hunt and enjoy the delicious air of the Beka'a, and not far away are the toy blocks of a model village built to house refugees from the Armenian massacres of the 1920s, and now inhabited by Palestinian refugees.

* * *

Chtaura, apart from being an important road junction, is also an increasingly popular summer resort, especially with wealthy Arabs from the Persian Gulf. As we plodded on in the afternoon an imposing cortege of black Cadillacs swept past us, each filled with sunglassed Arabs in spotless white robes. These were some of the Sheikh of Kuwait's household, enjoying an outing from the Hollywood style villa he has in Chtaura.

We avoided Zahle, famous for its *arak*, and a favourite resort of well-to-do Beirutis, who like to spend the summer evenings drinking and eating in its open-air restaurants beside a rushing stream, being anxious to get through this rather sophisticated area as quickly as possible. We were walking through beautifully kept vineyards most of the time, the grapes hanging in enormous purple bunches from their trellises; many belong to the Jesuit Mission and are made into a wine which is sold all over Lebanon.

The Jesuits have a very fine farm just outside Chtaura, at Tanail, and here we were affably received by the Father Superior, and given permission to camp for a night in the grounds. In 1860 the French Government, at the time of the Druze and Maronite troubles, obtained from the Ottoman Government a grant of land in recompense for the murder of five Jesuit missionaries. This land was given to the Order. It was at that time mainly marshland, malarial and unhealthy. Despite a heavy death toll from illness, the fathers succeeded in draining the land, some two hundred hectares in extent, and now, with the trees and vineyards, vegetable gardens and hay fields, it looks like a farm in France. We camped behind a hedge in a grove of silvery poplars, close to a limpid brook welling clear and cold from a little spring-house. We were in a French *parc* full of tall, shady trees and carefully swept paths decorously winding amid the shrubberies. Occasionally a black-clad figure would be seen pacing silently down the deserted *allées*, immersed in a book, for as well as a farm, Tanail is a rest centre for Jesuits in all the Missions of the Middle East.

We slept soon and soundly that night, going to bed at dusk, for we had covered thirty miles in the last twenty-four hours. We were awoken early the next morning by the bells of the chapel and very soon were startled by bursts of hymn-singing, interrupted Ave Marias and loud atmospheric cracklings from the surrounding shrubbery. Investigation disclosed that the grounds were being prepared for a celebration in connection with the Virgin Mary's birthday, which was to be celebrated tomorrow; red and white bunting was being hung from tree to tree, an outside altar with an amplifier system was being tested and a triumphal archway of palms was being erected over the main gateway. Thousands of worshippers were expected from an early hour the next day, and the whole grounds were to be given over to parties from all the schools and organisations under the Jesuit control.

We prepared ourselves for our departure that afternoon by going into Chtaura to do some shopping. It is nothing but an extended agglomeration of grocery stores, with an occasional restaurant or petrol pump intervening.

'All Syria shops here,' said the plump, multi-lingual Armenian grocer, pocketing our cheque with commendable commercial willingness to take a risk, despite our rather travel-worn appearance; 'they buy here all the things they can't get in Damascus.' And so it seemed, for the taxis and cars with Syrian number-plates, and a good few with diplomatic plates, were constantly coming and going outside the doors, and the stores with their clean, Americanised interiors, all deep-freeze and soft-drink advertisements, were full of people buying canned goods of every description. The shelves were piled high with tins, dehydrated soups of which we bought a quantity, cheeses, face-cream, paper tissues, soap, toothpaste, detergents, drink, everything you could think of – a modern treasure-house which did much to add to the comfort of our journey.

The children meanwhile were enjoying the sophisticated delights of a children's playground, a small pen where for about two and sixpence a time sallow, smartly dressed little children could squabble peevishly over brightly painted swings and see-saws, while their maids and attendants gossiped on the roadside. Retrieving them, we returned to the more rustic atmosphere of the farm.

Here all was bustle and earnest endeavour on the part of the numerous lay-helpers, the amplifier squawked incessantly, excited suggestions in Franco-Arabic exploded unexpectedly from among the tranquil graves. The Jesuits themselves seemed in the main detached from these proceedings. An occasional figure would be seen strolling in the distance, or returning from the icy-cold, tree-fringed swimming-pool deep in the grounds. An elderly American priest from the Mission to Iraq engaged us in conversation across the stream, while we were tidying up our gear: 'Jealousy is the besetting sin of the Arab world,' he said; 'the masses haven't the mental equipment to understand Communism, but they do understand keeping up with the Joneses. They can't bear to think of someone getting something which they don't have, and will get themselves involved in the most compromising political situations just in order to keep up with and outdo their neighbours.'

While we prepared and packed, after the children had had a brief swim in the pool they enjoyed the run of the farm. It is unexpectedly European, a cart entry through a solid door, a cobbled yard, and fowls and turkeys scratching about in one corner. A huge grange held the hay, and below were the stalls where big, large-uddered Friesian cows were eating at their mangers. There was a dairy, where we drank long, creamy draughts of milk fresh from the cows, and where we bought butter, made that day, and the creamy-white cheese that was lying out on the cool marble slabs.

In the season one can buy superb Argenteuil asparagus, grown in the gardens, and strawberries, and there are big pots of honey, and packets of lime tea to be had. On one side of the courtyard we could peer through a passageway into a charming secluded garden, shady with lime trees, where dahlias and sunflowers and zinnias were growing; on the other was a pen with a few gazelles in it, and a peacock lived among the turkeys.

* * *

We left Tanail at dusk, and passed through Chtaura blazing with lights like a Wild West honky-tonk town. Just where the road starts to climb upwards to its pass over the Lebanon, we turned left, and under the full moon started walking southwards down the Beka'a. We walked on slowly through the tranquil night, the shadows black and enormous under the trees, the plain below flooded with silvery light. We were all thankful to have left the busy, popular main roads behind us. We were walking towards the Druze country and towards Israel, and intended to cross over to the seaward side of the mountains near Jezzine, using secondary roads and tracks where we could.

After a few miles we passed through a large village climbing up the steep side of a hill. Just beyond the village outskirts stretched a large flat piece of common land, dotted with threshing-floors and mounds of chaff. We camped on the far side of this, beside a stream which ran between the common land and the orchards and gardens of the village. Hardly had we settled than voices hailed us from the orchards, and men with torches and staves came over to inspect us. These were the *naturs* or village watchmen, who guard the crops at night. They were a jovial, friendly crew, who made us very welcome, fetched fruit for the children from their orchards, helped Elias with the baggage, and accepted our cigarettes and coffee with easy good manners.

'Wrap your heads up well,' they said, 'the dew here is very heavy,' and indeed it was, for when we woke in the morning our blankets and belongings were all furred with moisture, and a white mist was rising all along the course of the stream. The watchmen came early to help us load up. They brought more fruit for us, and feed for the donkeys. All around us cattle were being driven down to drink at the stream, and strings of camels were moving across the open expanse of the threshing-field. We now saw that the village lay on the slope below a ruined castle, which perched on a crag commanding a clear view over the Beka'a, guarding a secondary small valley running up behind it. This was a Druze castle. Further along from it, cut out of a rock face on the mountainside, was a large shallow relief of a temple, with what seemed a tomb opening below it. The watchmen said that up the subsidiary valley were many more caves and tombs, but they appeared to have no name or tradition attached to them.

We left Qab Elias, for this was the name of the village, rather late, and dawdled down a long, tree-lined road running just above the level of the plain. After our big push down from Baalbek, we none of us felt like hurrying, and were content with very mediocre stages. There was no real inducement to hurry. Water abounded, the springs came down from the mountainside at very easy distances, the area was intensely cultivated, and people were working all about us. The Beka'a stretched out rich and abundant below, with a meandering, tree-fringed line down the middle indicating the course of the Litani River. Looking back up the valley, we could still see clearly the little white temple of Mejdel Anjar glimmering on its mountain spur, while far away in front of us, on the other side of the valley, the great swelling mass of Mount Hermon began to dominate the landscape.

This was all once Druze country, and the French monument on the outskirts of Qab Elias: 'Here lie in peace the remains of the French soldiers of the 5th, 27th and 105th Infantry Divisions, killed in the Lebanon 1860' is a record of their ferocity. The whole area was the scene of bitter fighting with the French, first in the 1860s, then again in 1925, during the Druze revolt in the time of the French Mandate.

'Druzes very good people,' said Elias, as we walked along, 'very clean, very kind, not like Metwalis. Those very dirty people. Druzes not like that: they speak you straight, friend all man. Before big *afreet*, now very good man, no like trouble, plenty *aklam wa saklam*. Me many friend Druze people.'

In a land still slowly emerging from a welter of sectional jealousies and antagonisms it is rare to hear one sect or race speak well of another, and Elias was unusual in his tolerance of other communities. 'I am a Lebanese,' he would say, if the subject were raised, and he had none of the rancorous bigotry so often found in the Christian communities. A free-born Maronite from the Metn, the descendant of generations of stubborn, independent, fiercely self-contained peasant farmers, their own masters despite the flood of succeeding conquests which beat against the flanks of the Mountain, Elias could not escape a certain feeling of superiority towards the more insecure Shia Moslems who make up the Metwali community. Yet he was tolerant and good-natured towards those with whom he came in contact. Many Christians would not work alongside Moslems, but in our Beirut house we had a Metwali cleaning woman – pretty, docile, downtrodden creatures, completely in the power of their fathers and husbands – an unusual combination which none the less worked very well. 'Metwali woman poor thing (*meskeen*),' Elias would say. 'Father say marry, she marry, no *shufti* husband, no say nothing. He dirty man, maybe he patch-patch, maybe he have other woman, no say nothing. Father take money, sheep, goat, he very happy give girl. All Metwali same, girl she do all work, man do nothing, smoke it cigarette, make it plenty baby, plenty trouble ...'

Despite this, he came with us to the wedding party of Zeinab, our first girl, a pretty, round, grey-eyed creature of sixteen who had cried over the coffee-cups in our kitchen for two days when told by her father that she was to marry a bridegroom of his choice. Her father, Abu Moussa, was far too formidable a man to be gainsaid, and then there were her brothers also to enforce the family wish. Abu Moussa was the headman of a road-repair gang – a government employee, in fact. He lived in a hovel in the courtyard of a festering slum tenement on the outskirts of Beirut, a gimcrack edifice run up among the dusty cactuses and refuse-littered rubble of a municipal road-extension plan.

When we went to the wedding celebration, the main room of his two-room mud hut, about fifteen feet by twelve feet, was packed with all the women and children of the family. The only men present were the fierce-eyed brothers and cousins, and Abu Moussa himself, a tall, gaunt and moustachio'd old man in black-braided baggy pants and jacket. Zeinab herself was so changed that we were reduced to awestruck wonder. Dressed in a long dress of brilliant pink satin, motionless on a chair on a dais at the end of the room, thin gold bracelets on her arms (her dowry), her long waving locks cut and frizzed in a permanent wave, her face heavily rouged and mascara'd and lipsticked, she looked like some idol perched up there for all to see. The children could hardly recognise her, so changed was she from the artless village beauty we had known, and could not take their eyes off her as we sat on little stools drinking coffee and eating sweets, while a filmy-eyed old woman quavered a song of praise and rejoicing, and skinny little girls of seven and eight clicked their fingers and wriggled and spun in the traditional Arab dances. The bridegroom, a young policeman, was not present. He was awaiting his bride down at his family home in the south, where she would be conveyed by her family next day.

* * *

Ignorance is the mother of suspicion as well as of superstition, and the Druzes, by the secrecy surrounding their rites, have exposed themselves to both. Neither Moslem nor Christian, they are permitted by their religion to conform to either should such a course be necessary or convenient, while the privacy of their own rite is jealously guarded.

In manner grave, calm and dignified, the elders, with their full beards and woven *caftans*, a spotless white band encircling their fezzes, present an imposing appearance, reminiscent of nineteenth-century Bible illustrations. The women wear full-skirted dresses of various colours and materials, and all have a long, gauzy white scarf draped over their heads and wrapped back over their shoulders, which gives a certain classical grace to the turn of their heads. The young men nowadays are mostly clean-shaven and westernised; many emigrate to America to seek their fortunes.

They are a handsome people, often fair-skinned, frequently blue or grey eyed.

Traditionally, they emerged as a distinctive political element in the ninth century; as a formulated creed their religion is about a thousand years old. Not much is known about their beliefs. They are Unitarians who believe in one God, supreme, indefinable, incomprehensible, who has manifested himself to mankind in successive incarnations. The last was the Caliph Hakim, of the Fatimid dynasty, who reigned in Cairo at the beginning of the eleventh century. Caliph Hakim seems to have been mad. It is the only explanation of the cruelties and abuses he practised in the twenty-five years of his reign, until murdered at his sister's instigation. He believed himself to be the incarnation of God, and had himself proclaimed as such in the mosques, his statement being confirmed by one Ismael Darazi. This was so ill-received by the populace that Darazi was forced to flee, and took refuge in the Lebanon, where he converted some of the mountain people to the new religion. Meanwhile, in Cairo, Caliph Hakim's claims were being supported by a mystical Persian felt-maker, who succeeded in winning over a substantial group of adherents to the cult. On the Caliph's assassination, it was given out that he had only temporarily withdrawn from the world, and would return triumphantly at a later date.

The unfortunate Darazi was condemned as a heretic by his rival the felt-maker, and is still considered so by present-day Druzes, a curious anomaly in a people who are identified by his name.

The Druzes are first mentioned by name in the chronicle of Benjamin of Tudela (c. AD1170), a pious Spanish Jew who travelled extensively in the Near East, visiting the various synagogues and places of Hebrew interest. Of the Druzes he says:

They are called heathens and unbelievers, because they confess no religion. Their dwellings are on the summits of the mountains and in the ridges of the rocks, and they are subject to no king or prince. Mount Hermon, a distance of three days' journey, is the boundary of their territory. This people live incestuously; a father cohabits with his own daughter, and once every year all men and women assemble to celebrate a festival, upon which occasion, after eating and drinking, they hold promiscuous intercourse. They say that the soul of a virtuous man is transferred to a new-born child; whereas that of the wicked transmigrates into a dog or some other animal. This their way is their folly . . . The Druzes are friendly towards the Jews; they are so nimble in climbing hills and mountains that nobody can successfully carry on war against them.

There seems little doubt that the old pagan traditions of nature-worship and sympathetic magic died hard in the isolated mountain areas of the Lebanon.

Local Christian tradition has it that the Druzes worship the golden calf, but there is no tangible evidence for this belief. Worship of the male and female principle has also been suspected, but there is no authoritative record of these practices. It seems likely that the refugee Ismael Darazi found a sympathetic hearing among the south Lebanese mountaineers living in the vicinity of Mount Hermon because his message defined and gave form to ideas long current in this part of the world. Various other minorities inhabiting the Lebanese Syrian mountain system share a belief in the incarnation of the Deity and his successive appearances on earth: the Nosairis, the Isma'ilis (the descendants of those Assassins made familiar to Europe through the stories of the Crusaders), the Shia Metwalis, all have certain beliefs in common, at variance with orthodox Sunni Islam, and seemingly inherited from some long-distant pre-Christian, pre-Islamic pagan past. In the Eastern Hauran, on the other side of the Syrian frontier, hilltop shrines containing a black stone, and hung with rugs and other offerings, seem definitely to indicate some connection with the ancient Semitic cults, but in the Lebanon there are no shrines of this nature, only gathering places centred on a plain, unadorned meeting-house or *khalwa*. Here on Thursday evenings, the start of the weekly day of rest, the elders of the community meet to read their sacred books and to arrange the affairs of their community. The Druzes are not polygamous, and are faithful and attached to their wives, who enjoy more independence and respect than most Moslem women. They too attend the meeting-houses, and sit separate from the men in a space fenced off by a muslin veil. Much of their religious literature has found its way to Europe, carried there after 1860, and is stored in the libraries of the Vatican, Oxford, Munich and Upsala. No reference is to be found in it to the pagan survivals in the popular practices of remote Druze communities, but instead the books contain moral teaching of a high order.

TEN

Over the Jebel Niha to Jezzine

GERTRUDE BELL COMPLAINS SOMEWHERE in her letters of the tedium of riding down the Beka'a, but she travelled in considerably greater state than we did, with servants and escorts and canteens of silver, and presumably had more time for boredom. Our leisurely walk down the southern Beka'a exposed us to many pleasant encounters, and as the going was easy, and the area well-populated, we never lacked company or social encounters along the route.

The people were friendly and open-minded, and had a cheerful generosity which accorded well with the lavish productivity of their plain. Instead of the black headcloths of the northern mountaineers, or the flowing white of the Baalbek district, they wore blue-and-white-checked *keffiyahs*, rather like dusters, which, bleached by the sun, set off their sunburnt faces and light-coloured eyes very well. They laughed good-naturedly to see us walking along with our donkeys, and pressed offerings of fruit and vegetables on us from the abundance of their crop.

We passed through property belonging to a relative of our landlord in Beirut, and having convinced the *natur* that we were not a band of gypsies come to rob the melon crop, drowsed away the hot noontide in the shade of some mulberry trees. The distant pop of the guns of the Sunday sportsmen and the occasional cheep of a bird were the only sounds that broke the stillness. After an hour or so the *natur* reappeared with another man, who had worked as a gardener at the town house in Beirut. This coincidence was the occasion for much self-congratulation on all sides, and was worth two delicious honeydew melons from the fields stretching out on either side of the glade we were in. The gardener sliced up the fruit with his penknife and we all shared the fragrant, warm, melting melon flesh, while the juice ran down our faces and over our hands.

As the afternoon cooled we started off down the road once more, passing as we did so the proprietor's villa, and the proprietor herself standing trim and tweedy and reminiscent of continental country-house parties, watching her peasants winnowing the corn with long-handled forks. We did not pause to identify ourselves, but kept on down the undulating road, with the orchards and melon-fields extending on either side, and the great bulk of Mount Hermon changing colour in the sunset.

Dusk found us slowly climbing over rather barren moorland and, borrowing a bucket from an isolated farmstead, we drew fresh cold water from a deep, concrete-lined well, watered the donkeys and ourselves, and camped for the night in a stand of pines, on a grassy knoll some way above the road. This was one of the few solitary and undisturbed camps we were able to make in the course of the trip, and after a good supper, we all sank effortlessly into a sleep under the light of a nearly full moon.

We awoke to the delicious freshness and clearness and sweetness of a cloudless day. All around stretched an undulating, tawny landscape, with very little sign of human activity. Elias was already busy about his familiar tasks: pumping the primus, making the porridge, bringing us all hot cups of *cafe au lait*. The morning routine of putting on trousers, brushing hair, swabbing faces, cleaning teeth, began, and folding up the bedding into neat rolls, ready to shove into the duffle-bags. Shoes and sandals were fixed, the kitchen stores packed away, the donkeys brought up one by one for loading. A monotonous quaver from the road below indicated that the crazed blind beggar who had passed while we were resting the day before was once more on his way. Grotesque, misshapen, he was a familiar figure from Beirut, where he had a pitch outside Miles' school. He tapped erratically down the road and disappeared from view around the next bend. Presumably he was given a lift by some lorry, for we did not catch up with him on the road, and so were never able to ask him what brought him so far from his usual place.

Our road was gradually deserting the smooth valley floor and wound sluggishly through indeterminate foothills to some point as yet beyond our range of vision. We had left the meticulous fruit cultivation of the Chtaura area behind us, and now we were leaving the great wide, grain-growing plain as well. A peasant we met carrying two big baskets of ripe yellow figs, while his little daughter staggered along with another beside him, pressed handfuls of the fruit into Elias' hat. 'Aren't they good?' he said proudly, watching us eat the soft, sweet fruit, which tasted like bags of honey. As the sun had not yet struck on to his trees, they still had the freshness of early morning on them, which gave a delicious emphasis to their flavour. People greeted us cheerfully as we went along, hearty salutations in the conventional phrases of courtesy. They began with, 'The day be praised!' to which we would reply, 'The light be praised!' Then would come enquiries as to each party's health and wellbeing, and pious acknowledgments to God. At last we would bid each other go in peace, and cheered and stimulated by the brief human exchange, would pass on to new encounters.

We were passing just above the *col* of Faloudj, the scene of fierce fighting during the Druze insurrection against the French in 1925. It grew very hot, and below us we could see the thick poplar-shaded line of the Litani River, tempting us with its promise of deep pools and cool, rushing water. But the prospect of the scramble up again to the road was sufficient to deter us, and we continued on, under the rocky escarpments thickly covered with scrub oak, and past leafy green rows of mulberry trees, carefully spaced out on their terraces.

'These will make you cool,' called a lean brown old man, suddenly stepping through a screen of Indian corn, and piling a dozen or so large cucumbers into our hands. Behind him we could see acres of cucumbers alternating with rows of Indian corn, and laughing young women packing the cucumbers into crates for carriage to the city markets. He was quite right and, peeling the skin off with Elias' knife, we strolled down the road eating the cucumbers like bananas, and pushing the stumps into the mouths of the donkeys.

The morning wore on as we meandered in this way along the flank of the mountain. As the road gradually mounted, the terracing grew more shaggy and interrupted, and springs ran down into reed-tufted glades and groves of poplars and plane trees, while the blackberries and old man's beard hung in wreaths and festoons from the rocks, and the hillside above us began to bake and quiver in the heat. Rounding a bend, we suddenly came on a coffee shop built on the hillside below the road. This was Ain el Kerazi, the spring of the cherries. Abundant water ran down the neighbouring fruit terraces, and a clear, swift stream was led through the entire length of the coffee shop terrace, with small footbridges over it at intervals.

By unanimous consent we decided to stop and lunch here. We brought the donkeys down the steps on to the terrace, and unloaded them, and left them flicking their tails contentedly under the shade of some trees. It was a very long terrace, shaded with awnings and straw mats, the main part roofed with ancient corrugated iron. Sounds of merriment came at intervals from the farther end, but we were busily engaged in washing and shaving as best we could in the stream. The children were stripped, soaped and dowsed, and then put into clean clothes. We were all thick with dust and the grime of several days without proper washing, and it was a relief to wade and splash in the icy-cold water, and to shed our sweat-stained, crumpled clothes.

Arab food has not a great deal of variety, depending as it does on a few staple dishes and whatever fruit and vegetables are in season. But at this coffee shop we had an unexpected addition to the *hors-d'oeuvres*, fried chicken and piles of bread, which made up the usual menu. This was a dish of trout, taken from the Litani by the expedient of dropping a charge of dynamite, or creasing the surface of a pool with a rifle-shot.

As we were sitting in rather somnolent repletion amidst the debris of the meal, with the flies buzzing about us in their battalions,

213

a confused sound of music and cries and calls from the sportsmen at the other end of the coffee shop attracted our attention.

'Come and join us, come and drink with us,' they called. 'You're in Lebanon now, and we're all friends here.' They were motor salesmen from Beirut, young men spending a day shooting over the countryside in which they grew up. Their long trestle table was littered with empty dishes, glasses, bottles of beer and *arak*, with cartridge belts and gamebags adding to the confusion.

'This is our sixth bottle of *arak*,' they said cheerfully. 'We must have a new one for you. Madam, you will drink beer. Mister, you want *arak*. O brother' – this to Elias – 'let there be no hesitation, we are friends, we are Christians, we are Lebanese, and we must drink together.' The landlord, a stocky, red-faced man in shirt and pants, had obviously been following these recommendations for a considerable time, and now amid cries of encouragement began to undulate gracefully around the table in an Arab dance. Seizing a drum, Elias, a skilful operator on this instrument, began to beat out a *dabke* rhythm, and the children stood around in delighted amazement, and clapped their hands and twirled around in time to the music. The landlord was an excellent dancer, and sang happily to himself as he circled the table, while the audience joined in the song, and occasionally lurched to their feet to take his hand and twine giddily around in clumsy imitation of his neat footwork and languid hip movements. As the afternoon wore on, the noise and good humour became intensified. 'Bang, bang, bang,' went the heavily moustachio'd young man, seizing his gun and sending a volley through the roof, and bringing down a flutter of torn straw. This was great fun, and delighted everyone. The children applauded vigorously, and demanded more, and, nothing loath, the tall one in high boots took a pot-shot at some sparrows ill-advised enough to perch on a nearby branch. Taking Miles to the edge of the terrace, he encouraged him to shoot off wildly into the treetops, while all the men present shouted advice. Whenever we showed signs of moving on we would be hospitably thrust back into our chairs, and further supplies of *arak* yelled for from the kitchen. 'We Lebanese belong the West,' confided the weedy, bespectacled one, 'we must stick together in each other's interests,' and so, taking him at his word, we stuck together through the long, hot afternoon, the guns going off at intervals, the landlord dancing and the bottles piling up underneath the table.

The shadows were lengthening by the time we scrambled back on to the road. We were seen off affectionately and enthusiastically by all the party – 'Come and see us when you want a new car,' 'Come back tomorrow and we'll have another party' – and for a long time wild salvoes of gunfire and the beat of the drum followed us along the winding road.

Twilight was falling as we came up a deserted stretch of road, and stepping carefully over a dead snake we rounded a corner to find a group of priests and country-folk talking quietly on the steps of what appeared to be a large building of some age. This was the Greek Catholic convent of St Thekla, a farm and summer retreat belonging to the parent Convent of St Sauveur, a very large establishment on the seaward side of the mountain, which once had the eccentric Lady Hester Stanhope for tenant.

The priests were interested and concerned for us: 'But of course you must stay here. We can't let these pretty little children go away so soon. All this land around here belongs to our Order, and there's lots of water, for we have a big spring just above us on the mountainside.' A messenger was sent hastily to fetch the Father Superior, a thin, intellectual-looking man with a sparse beard and piercing glance, who spoke fluent French. Once we had satisfied him as to our identity, for we were nearing the Israeli frontier, everything was done for us. Willing guides showed us the way up the steep path to a small meadow underneath beetling limestone crags. All around fruit trees and walnuts grew in wild profusion. We camped beneath an enormous holly oak, fitting our bedding in between the spreading roots of the tree. A friendly, curious, good-natured group of priests and villagers came to visit us from the spring-house, where they had been enjoying the cool of the evening and watching the last light fade over the Beka'a. A pail of milk fresh from that evening's milking for the children, a basket each of apples and delicious firm grapes were brought by one of the farm servants, and we were begged to make known any wants we had. We hung our lantern on a branch of the vast, shadowy tree above us and in the soft, dark night prepared for bed. On another level of the meadow the farm's goats were settling for the night, and the subdued sounds of their movements, the tinkling of bells, and the occasional voices of the sleepy goatherds mingled with the sounds of the night around us, the bumping of moths against the lantern and the stir and stamp of the donkeys.

The dew was still wet on the ground when we awoke next morning, and the trees and vegetation were shining and fresh in the cool morning air. Going to wash at the spring, we found the Father Superior in his long black *soutane* supervising some peasant women as they straddled bare-legged in the stone channel of the spring, washing the wheat which was brought up by their menfolk on donkey-back in great sacks of coarse-woven black goat-hair. This was a scene we were to witness with variations along all the next stage of our journey, for after the wheat has been harvested, thrashed and winnowed, it is washed by the sack-load in streams and fountains by the women, then dried on the flat roofs of the houses.

'These people are our tenants,' explained the Father Superior, 'and we have a right to a proportion of their services. This is a big farm, and we sell our produce in Sidon, and also supply our schools at St Sauveur. This work is hard' – and indeed the women were hot and dishevelled as they heaved and turned the heavy grain contained by a barricade of sacks – 'but it is all in the service of God. In our Church every aspect of man's life is legislated for; there is not a single action for which there is not an appropriate prayer. Your children must not forget this simple yet severe life of the peasants when they go to Europe, and turn a tap to get the water they need to drink, and everything about them seems man-made and contrived. It is good that you take them like this among us, so that they may see how dependent we are on God's bounty and how by labour and application we must make the best use of those gifts which He has given us.'

Before we left we went to take formal farewell of these amiable priests. They were sitting in the sunny, whitewashed courtyard of their convent, half a dozen black-robed men with smiling, good-humoured faces. Gaily coloured cushioned benches supplied the seats, and from the graceful pillared ogive windows there was a splendid view over the terraced orchards, rocks and bluffs of the escarpment to the wooded course of the Litani, and the distant bulk of Mount Hermon beyond. Tric-trac boards and packs of cards and newspapers lay around on small tables, and a large box of chocolates, of which handfuls were pressed on the children. 'You must fill your pockets,' the Father Superior told them. 'Don't be modest. Here, let me put some more in,' and amid delighted smiles we drank coffee and then posed for an exchange of photographs. Long after we had wound around the curve of the mountain, we could see them standing on their terrace watching us as we waved back, until at last we turned around a bend and they were lost to sight.

Elias, who had presented a very pious, butter-wouldn't-melt-in-his-mouth appearance during our stay with the monks, humbly kissing the Superior's hand when we left, now regained his customary swagger, and exchanged hearty and complacent greetings with the various people we met on the road.

'Druzes big friend English peoples,' he told us as we went along, idly munching the apples given us at the farm. 'He no like French, plenty trouble, big war many French he killed. French plenty angry English peoples, no stop Druze go into Jordan; Druze happy, say English friend.'

We were now high up the side of the mountain, and the Litani had already begun to diverge from the main line of the Beka'a, starting to cut a channel which would later become the spectacular gorges of its rightward bend to the sea beneath Chateau Beaufort. The districts which we were approaching had all suffered from the earthquake of March 1956, when three successive shocks had put all Beirut in an uproar, and had damaged a considerably greater area than we had up till now realised. The long, straggling village of Saghbine, where we stopped to buy cigarettes, had obviously been severely shaken. Piles of rubble were still filling up the interiors of houses, here and there the solid stone fronts of houses had been patched up with concrete additions, or their old stones incorporated in new concrete houses. What appeared to be a house of some size and importance stood on the main street with its roof fallen in, the elegant iron tracery of its balconies sagging across its facade, and its green-washed rooms, frescoed in the Ottoman style of the last century, open to the sky. The whole place seemed rubbly and decayed, and we hastened on, despite the importunities of an old woman, who, finding that Elias, like herself, came from the Metn, begged that we should stay and make what remained of her home our own.

We were anxious to push on, for we hoped to cross over the mountain that day, and reach Jezzine on the seaward side by nightfall. The road was deteriorating, and as we threaded our way through the outskirts of Machghara, all fallen in and smelling of dirt and decay, it turned into a stone road which zigzagged its way up the steep sides of the mountain. Beneath us we could see the flat, square roofs of the village with the circular woven trays spread with raisins and plums drying in the sun, and piles of grain being spread and turned by the women. The slope beneath us was very steep, and each house looked down on that of its neighbour, with here and there a tree or a vine trellis to break the intricate pattern of cubes and rectangles. A riot appeared to be in progress down in the main street of the place; a crowd of people was assembling from every direction, and a confused shouting and arguing came clearly up to us where we stood on the edge of the road above, watching the scene below. Distribution of earthquake relief appeared to be the cause of the uproar, and it served its purpose for us, as everyone's attention was concentrated on the drama going on below, and hardly anyone spared a glance for the strangers who hastened through, anxious not to be detained amid the smells and disorder of this shattered settlement.

A whitewashed, vine-trellised coffee shop on a spur some way up the road provided us with shelter at lunchtime, even though its owner had left it to go down to the village. Some men working in the vineyards gave us water, sending a boy scrambling down the dusty white hillside to a hidden spring, from where he toiled up with a large earthenware pitcher full of cool water for us. We had with us at this time a charming small chameleon, about a finger in length, which we had picked up some days before. He used to travel in a porridge tin filled with vine leaves, but occasionally one of the children would have him out to while away the time on donkey-back. On this occasion he was travelling in a bowl of grapes, which by an unfortunate chance tipped off the donkey as we left the coffee shop, and in a matter of seconds he was lost. We searched the pebbles and stones and thistles and dried bents of the roadside without avail, for he was gone, and after a quarter of an hour's delay and regret we abandoned the search. Elias and the donkeys were now several bends of the road above us, so we decided to take a short, steep track up to him. This was a lung-splitting effort, made the more mortifying by the jeers and exhortations of the donkey party above, who were watching our progress with the greatest glee. We emerged breathless by a stone parapet, to find Elias eating sweets with the children, and slyly suggesting that we try Mount Hermon next time. Near by on the roadside was a small tablet commemorating the 1st, 6th and 8th Regiments of the Chasseurs d'Afrique, who built this road over the pass to Jezzine at the time of the Druze troubles.

Mount Hermon behind us was flushed purple and violet as we toiled up the road. This was the Jebel Niha, and we were crossing it at a pass some 4,500 feet high. The landscape grew very wild and desolate, bare, barren hills and slabs of ice-eroded rock, with every now and then some crag or spur dominating the road as it pushed its way across the forlorn and deserted landscape. Somewhere to our right we could see what appeared to be a flag and a trophy on a spur of the mountain, but it was too far off to identify it. It was easy to imagine Druze ambushes and the Beau Geste activities of the

French colonial achievement in such a setting, but we met no one except an old shepherd driving his flocks down towards Machghara. 'Watch out for wolves,' he told us, after we had exchanged greetings, and sure enough not very far on we noticed the large pug-marks of a wolf in the tawny dust of the road. We had been assured by the shepherd that Ain el Hor'ch – the spring of the plums – was only ten minutes away, but as the twilight closed in on us, it was obvious that this was only a well-meant desire to encourage us. A trickle of muddy water oozing out of the side of the road, and a scattering of sour-looking rushes, indicated that there were small springs along this road in more favourable seasons, but now, at the end of the long, hot summer, everything was dried out.

As the moon rose, the road started to descend. It went down in meticulous gradients, now white in the moonlight, now in deepest shadow as we passed under the lee of a cliff. After an hour or so of this it became obvious that we would reach nowhere that night, so we began casting about for some flat space on which to sleep. This was no easy task, but we finally decided on a strip of ploughed land below the road. Clearing off the worst of the stones, we quickly threw down our bedding, ate and settled to sleep. It was a wildly romantic site, the mountains all around rearing up against the starry sky, and a great riven precipice facing us across the steep, narrow channel of a dried-up watercourse. As we settled we could hear the jackals yelling and hallooing somewhere up the cliff opposite us, and we drifted to sleep to the accompaniment of their cries.

We awoke in the middle of the night to the sound of a strange dry rustling on the road above us. The clouds were gathering in the sky and long, mysterious wraiths of mist were reaching up the valleys and passing swiftly under the stars. It was an engrossing sight to see the cloud swirling around us, and the bright moonlight being swallowed up, then reappearing as the cloud dissolved and reformed elsewhere. The sound on the road turned out to be one of the sheets of our newspaper caught in an eddy of wind and swirling erratically up the road; a prosaic enough explanation, but one not arrived at until thoughts of *djinns*, ghosts and other unpleasant things had flashed through our minds. Some time later a troop of muleteers passed by on their way over the pass. 'What's this?' they said, as they spied us lying cocoon-like below the road, but pushed on to disappear up the road in the swirling mist. We woke finally as a young woman came stepping down the road bearing a jar of clarified butter on her head, which she was taking down to sell in the town below. It was then that we realised that opposite us, on the other side of the road, were about thirty white beehives, whose inhabitants were making sinister buzzing noises as they too prepared themselves for their day's task. We made one of the promptest starts of our whole trip, nobody being anxious to be present when the sun struck over the mountain on to the hives, and summoned the bees to come out.

Our road led down into a vast natural amphitheatre of grey stone, and wind-eroded blocks similar to the better-known Houses of the Ghosts in the Kesrouan. We picked our way down a stony track between rough stone walls and poor, isolated homesteads and quite unexpectedly, it seemed, emerged suddenly on a cliff just above the town of Jezzine, which was tucked on a ledge between the mountain slopes, on the lip of a precipice. Our greengrocer Nedim in Beirut was a native of Jezzine, and it was towards his home that we enquired our way. His mother and uncle and children greeted us cordially and were loud in suggestions and advice as to what we should do next. All their neighbourhood had been shaken by the earthquake, and half the house had fallen in on the family, fortunately without any serious injury to them. Most of their neighbours appeared in similar plight, and the familiar smell of dirt and decay hung around the place.

The day was sunny and warm, but the clouds of the night had not entirely dispersed, and hung broodingly above the line of the horizon, obscuring a sight of the sea. For several days past Elias had been prophesying rain – 'Eed el Saleeb make it rain; every year same time, no much, but finish hot. Another month, no more sleep outside.' The Eed el Saleeb is St Helena's day, and falls on the 14th of September. It commemorates her finding of the True Cross, and the bonfires with which she signalled her success from Jerusalem to Constantinople are repeated in all the Christian villages of the Lebanon.

We decided to go down into the centre of the town and see what we could do about finding lunch and a bath; we had also promised to buy Miles a knife for his birthday in two days' time, on the eve of the feast.

Jezzine is a pleasant little red-roofed town of some three thousand inhabitants, mainly Maronite Christians. It derives its name from the *Gezin* of the Crusaders, and was ceded to the Order of the Teutonic Knights in 1256, by the lord of Sayette, in whose fief it was. Its houses are mostly in the old-fashioned style of solid hand-cut stone, with terraces and archways, and the charming ogive windows which are such a distinctive feature of Lebanese architecture. Like much of southern Lebanon, it was economically orientated towards Palestine, and its altitude of nearly 2,500 feet made it a favoured summer resort for the wealthier citizens of Haifa. This summer traffic is now at an end because of the Arab–Israeli dispute, and nothing has come to replace it.

The town stagnates quietly among its fruit-trees, receiving a few visitors from the coast towns, and an occasional foreign tourist. It has one industry, which is pursued in little bothies and workshops all over the town. This is the making of Jezzine knives which have been famous in the Levant for many hundreds of years, and which even now are exported as curios to America. The yards and doorways of the workshops are littered with goat horns, which are used to make the handles of the knives. The horn is polished and decorated with various-coloured inlays, usually red or blue spots, and the knives have a characteristic bird-shaped haft. Elias and the children had all set their hearts on having some of these, and we decided to bathe and lunch and spend the afternoon sightseeing before moving out to find a camp site.

We directed our steps towards the Hotel Kanaan, described in the guidebooks as a first-class establishment. This turned out to be a tall ramshackle building four storeys high, set near the edge of the precipice in a grove of pine trees. Each floor had a magnificent tiled terrace, as big as a ballroom, the floor above being supported by very graceful marble pillared arches. On the balustrades grew pots of begonias and carnations, and an occasional tin of roses. A few cretonne-covered benches stood against the walls, otherwise the terrace was bare, deliciously light and airy, with magnificent views across the blue void below to the pine-covered slopes of the foothills, and the fleecy line of cloud hanging above the heat-haze of the plain and sea-coast below.

Our arrival had obviously thrown the household into a certain amount of consternation. The Hotel Kanaan, like many other similar establishments in Lebanon, was also the family home of the Kanaan family, wealthy citizens and landowners of the district, and Parliamentary candidates at the elections. This arrangement was a hang-over of the old days when the notable members of a community were expected to give hospitality to important and distinguished persons travelling through the area. The Kanaans were an enormously hearty, robust family, the men gross, energetic, shrewd, with their tarbushes perched on the back of their big round heads. The brothers had married sisters, each larger and fatter than the other – 'They must weigh at least a hundred kilos each,' muttered Elias, eyeing them with amazement.

A great activity began with kerosene and kindling wood, and a fire was lit under a dangerous-looking stove in a bathroom and, after some time, we were summoned to the bath. There was no plug, and the waste-hole was stuffed up with a rag; the bath had obviously not been cleaned for a long time, but the water was wonderfully hot and abundant. Soap was procured, and a bottle of hair-wash, and two by two we started on the great clean-up. These operations always took a long time; over an hour elapsed before we all seven emerged shining and shaven, in clean clothes, and keenly anticipating the large lunch we had ordered.

Observing the size and bulk of our hosts, we had reasoned that they kept a good table. We were not disappointed. Mme Kanaan, flushed and perspiring in her pink silk *peignoir*, had been busy in her kitchen ever since our arrival, and through the bathroom walls we had caught many shrill chidings and upbraidings and a clattering of pots from the kitchen next door. We lunched alone in a vast deserted dining-room, sparsely furnished with an elaborate sideboard and a chandelier. The spotless tablecloth was covered with a multitude of *hors d'oeuvres*, the characteristic *Meze* of the Levant. This alone was the equivalent of an entire coffee shop lunch. Next came a favourite dish: a great platter of snowy rice, accompanied by another platter of French beans in a gravy of braised tomatoes and titbits of tender lamb. A smiling maid encouraged us all to have second helpings, and, this done, we were then presented with a steak each, chips and a large bowl of salad. A certain glaze began to appear over the eyes of the party and the two men had recourse to the small bottles of *arak* to stimulate their appetite. A rice pudding next appeared, sweetened with rosewater, as a treat for the children, Elias rashly having informed our hostess that the children were very fond of this Arab sweet. Then came watermelons, grapes and enormous apples, and hot, sweet cups of coffee, and at last we were done.

It was only the promise to buy the knives that finally got us up from the table and into the street outside. We spent a happy time choosing one for each of us at a shop with the sign 'Nives and Potery' over the door, and for a hard-won concession in the matter of price (negotiated by Elias), we wrote out a corrected version of his sign for the proprietor. Wandering up through the shabby little town, we were disconcerted by a sharp shower of rain, and took refuge under the awning of a general store. An enormous American car with American licence plates was pulled up at the kerb, and its owner, a tall, slick, baggy-eyed man in a wide-brimmed Texan hat, was inside talking to the store-keeper. 'Say, what have you folks got there?' he said, coming out and casting a glance of surprise at Little Stick, who was looking particularly sodden and dejected in the rain. We had brought him with us as we wanted to buy donkey-feed, and also hoped to find some ornaments for his harness. 'What have you got there?' we said in reply, pointing to his car, and to his hat. 'Guess you can see I've been in Texas,' he replied, 'but I come from Tampa, Florida. This is my hometown, though, and I'm back on a project here. I'm a water-driller, and I want to get the water out of those mountains back there. There's no reason for anywhere to be short of water here. These mountains are all made of limestone, and if you go deep enough in, you'll get the water out. But you've got to use modern methods, and think big. I got teams out all over Syria, and down in Saudi Arabia, and way down on the Gulf. Get the water going in this part of the world, and you've got everything else.'

It seemed as if Elias' predictions about the rain were true, and the news from a *service* taxi man that Beirut had had an enormous rainstorm that day did nothing to encourage us to look for a camp site outside the town, for we were quite unequipped for wet-weather camping. We returned to the hotel, where all the Mesdames Kanaan were loud in their recommendations that we should stay until the weather settled again. Spectacular purple clouds were piling up from the sea-coast below, and there was a grumble of thunder in the air. The donkeys and gear were led into the big stables below the house, and settled more comfortably than they usually fared. We divided three rooms up between ourselves. Elias did best out of this, for he got a room to himself; the children had to double up in two single beds. Before we put them to bed, we were given what was lightly described as 'a tea'. The same table was again loaded with dishes, this time of sour milk, rice pudding, various jams and preserves, olives, cheese, a large pot of weak tea, bread, buns and a dish of fried eggs. Sodden with sleep and food, we went early to bed, while the thunder rolled about delightfully outside, and the vast, cavernous interior of the hotel echoed to the conversational exchanges of various worthies come to pass the evening with our hosts.

At four o'clock the next morning a tremendous roaring and stamping of boots on the marble corridors indicated that the master was up and preparing to go to inspect his orchards. The western-style lavatory opposite our door was then cleaned out by the expedient of pouring buckets of water down it. The plug, like the door-locks, had long ceased to function. We breakfasted and prepared to leave. Everything in the Kanaan household was on a large scale, including the bill: this came to something over eight pounds sterling, a rather severe increase in our usual standard of living. It was apparently calculated on the Tourist Department's standard list of charges for first-class hotels, but charming though the Hotel Kanaan might be, with its derelict grandeur and splendid situation, its best friend could hardly describe its accommodation as first-class. However, a cheque on the English bank in Beirut was received with the utmost confidence, and we bade an amicable farewell to everyone. The sisters were assembled like three graces on a turn of the stair to the garden, at ease in their *peignoirs*, and enjoying the freshness of the morning as they puffed their hubble-bubbles and drank little cups of Turkish coffee. We all posed together for a final photograph, and parted with many expressions of goodwill and esteem on both sides.

ELEVEN

Mouktara and the Druze Country

W E WERE NOW WALKING into the heart of the Druze country, and heading for Mouktara, where the leading Druze family, the Jumblats, have their splendid palace. The country all around was the scene of innumerable romantic adventures and exploits in the time of the Ottoman Empire, when the Druzes fought and intrigued implacably to control the Mountain and remain independent of the Turks.

The character of the country had changed. Dramatic river valleys cut through the great hump of the hills, and the eye was drawn insensibly to the shimmer of light under the cloud far below, that indicated the sea. We were walking along the edge of the Wadi Jezzine, traversing the flank of the mountain, while below us the shaggy, wooded bluffs tumbled down into the wild luxuriance of the valley bottom. The scale was immense, and we crept along the face of the mountain like so many insects, while below us the great sprawling mass of hill and forest, glinting river and blue-shadowed chasm slid imperceptibly towards the sea. The emphasis was all to the west. The mountains reared up behind us, gaunt, barren, neglected, while our road ran on between the gentle groves of olives and our eyes, godlike, roved over the landscape beneath us.

This was the country in which the famous Druze leader, the Emir Fakr-ud-Din Maan II, played hide-and-seek with the Turks for many seasons, until he was finally caught in 1633 in his cave hideout near the waterfall of Djezzin, and sent with his two sons to Constantinople, to be strangled there two years later.

Under him the Druze power extended from Antioch to Acre in Palestine, from the sea-coast as far inland as Palmyra in the deserts of eastern Syria. Controlling the sea-coast, he early saw the advantage of good relations with the West, and he encouraged the Italian and French merchants trading in the Mediterranean to make use of his ports. The *khan* or warehouses he built for them in Sidon still stand, a great courtyard surrounding a fountain and little tangle of garden, with rooms on two floors off an arcaded terrace. It is now an orphanage for girls, under the care of nuns.

Having been fostered by a Christian family as a boy, after the death of his father, Fakr-ud-Din was always on the friendliest terms with the Maronites, a fact commented on by many of the Europeans who travelled through his territory. It was his intrigue with them against their Ottoman overlord that brought the wrath of the Sultan down on him, and in 1614 the Pasha of Damascus defeated him severely and forced him to flee to Italy for safety. Five years later he landed in Lebanon once more, and recovered his position, which he held for another fourteen years, when, again incurring the distrust and displeasure of the Sultan, he was captured and sent to his death in Constantinople.

A typical figure of the Renaissance, Fakr-ud-Din had an acuteness and breadth of imagination which enabled him to see that it was by contact with the West that Lebanon could best exploit the liberty that its physical situation and the temper of its people had always enjoyed. Always friendly to the Italians, for it was at the Tuscan Court that he had spent the five years of his exile, he encouraged their merchants and engineers to trade, visit and advise on the improvement of Lebanese agriculture, architecture and fortification. Roman Catholic missions were permitted to settle; diplomatic agents were kept in Italy. His attention was not only devoted to commerce and the building up of his military power. The English traveller Maundrell, passing through Lebanon on his way to the Holy Land, comments on the beauty of the gardens he had laid out in Beirut, orange groves and fountains, and spacious terraces symmetrically planned. He exchanged Arab horses for imported hunting dogs, developed a carrier-pigeon post, improved the breed of local cattle.

Himself physically a small man, much mocked by his enemies for the shortness of his stature, he was none the less capable of enormous endurance. The road we were walking along led under the cliffs where he had hidden from the Turks for two months, in a retreat carved out of the rocks, known as Kalat Niha. This was where his own father, Qurqumaz, had died in 1585, probably of starvation or poison, like his son a fugitive from the Turks. Driven from there, he took final refuge in the cave by the Jezzine waterfall, where he was at last captured.

We had made a bad start from Jezzine, for getting clear of the town Big Stick had lost his balance on a steep slope, and had fallen sickeningly in a series of somersaults. Seen from above, the fall had the nightmare inevitability of a screen disaster. One waited to hear the crack of his neck breaking with a sort of stunned apprehension. Imagine our surprise and relief when we got to him, jammed once more against a rock, and freed him of his load. In a matter of seconds he was on his feet and idly browsing at a thistle-head, apparently uninjured except for a slight graze on his shoulder. His load of duffle-bags stuffed with clothes and quilts had obviously saved him again.

However, this *contretemps* had delayed us, and had made us not anxious to push on any great distance that day. We lunched at a coffee shop under the overhang of a tall stone cliff, where a spring fell in small cascades out of the mountainside, and dropped down the steep hillside to join the Nahr Barouk in the valley below. The coffee shop was in the charge of a small girl of ten years old, who made us coffee and served us cold drinks with businesslike efficiency. The children picked up a friendship with a Druze boy from Beirut, the son of an army officer, who was holidaying here at his grandparents' house. Scrambling among the rocks and pools of the stream, Miles slipped and ran a splinter of glass into the fleshy heel of his hand. This later became inflamed, and gave us our only cause for worry from the health point of view in the entire trip.

The villages we passed through were all constructed of heavy stone blocks, roughly bossed in the centre, which gave the houses an appearance of fortification well in keeping with the character of the country. They stood back from the road in their terraces of olive and fruit trees, occasionally forming up enough to make a street, more often scattered in a straggle on the hillside. From a distance they looked intact enough, but as one approached, it was obvious that the earthquake had damaged them extensively. At Bater, part of the town had slid down the mountainside and over the road into the ravine below, killing several inhabitants as it did so. Here we saw more signs of reconstruction than we had seen on the other side of the mountain. Skimpy little concrete houses were being built along the roadside and among the olive groves. Still windowless and doorless, they appeared a poor substitute for the massive buildings the people were being compelled to abandon.

We slept that night on the roadside, beneath some olive trees belonging to an elderly Druze who was painstakingly engaged in building himself a new house of concrete, with materials provided by the Government. The new home was rather like a house of cards – a concrete platform jutting out from the fall of the land, and supported on four concrete stilts, and a flat-roofed single room on the top, with open apertures for windows and door. The family were distressed that we should sleep like this in the open, and felt the humiliation of their position deeply, for the Druzes are a notably hospitable people in a land known for its hospitality. But we were worn and tired and glad to sleep anywhere, and after a little desultory conversation and some figs shared with the old man, stretched out our bedding and went to sleep with the sunset still colouring the horizon above the line of the sea.

Early the next morning the groves were astir with people walking down to their work in the terraces below. An invitation to breakfast came from our host's wife to the children and their mother, and they set off while the bedding was packed and the donkeys loaded. Inside the house everything was as spotless and immaculate as the hand of woman could make it. Straw mats covered the floor, a curtain of army issue blanket covered the door, others the windows. There was no furniture, one sat on a mattress with cushions against one's back. On pegs in the bare concrete walls, here and there cracked and holed, hung the clothes of the family. In one corner were the shining aluminium cooking-pans, and a primus. The family bedding was rolled up tidily in another. Sour milk was served, and delicious thin mountain bread, and plums and grapes and apples, and sweets for the children, and coffee and tea for the grown-ups. The children, sitting barefooted on the floor, were encouraged hospitably to eat. Each crumb they dropped was immediately seized by the quick-eyed woman or her daughter, and tidied away out of the window. The woman was of the Atrash family of the Hauran in Syria – 'He is of my family,' she said proudly, pointing to a newspaper cutting of Farid el Atrash, the famous Arabic film-star and singer – and she still wore her greying hair bobbed short and waxed forward on her cheeks in a sharp curl, under her spotless white veil. She was a severely handsome woman of about forty, with intelligent grey eyes. Her manner assured and courteous, she expressed no unseemly surprise at finding a party of foreigners camping in her gardens, only regretted that their situation was such that they could offer no better hospitality. Around the waist of her long black gown she wore a splendid silver-inlaid belt – 'From the Hauran,' she said, 'and it's a pity that we don't still wear the clothes our mothers used to wear.' She was referring to the tall horned headdress which the Druze women used to wear, and which is still worn by a bride in the Hauran. After breakfast she suggested a visit to see their old home, which to their distress had been condemned by the Government experts as unsafe, and which was due to be demolished very soon. We walked up through the olive groves to where we could see a great, dark, castle-like complex of buildings looming above us. Steps on to a terrace led to an inner courtyard, which in turn led into a vaulted arcade and through it into a series of marble-floored rooms, their vaulted ceilings cracked and split in an alarming manner, their narrow windows looking down on to the tops of the fruit trees outside. A few plush chairs stood against the wall, an ornate wardrobe and sideboard occupied what space was left. The walls were decorated with photographs of fiercely moustachio'd Druze notables of the Ottoman and French Mandate period. Criss-crossed with bandoliers and cartridge belts, they glared at us from behind a screen of hair. Among them was a photo of a closely veiled woman, only her brilliant dark eyes showing above the concealed lower half of her face. This was Sitt Nazli, the mother of the present Jumblat chieftain, and a famous personality in the days of the French Mandate. A great lady by any standards, she kept open house at the Jumblat palace further along the valley, and is credited with having been one of the models from whom the French novelist Pierre Benoit took his 'Chatelaine du Liban'.

We continued at a leisurely pace, our road clinging to the flank of the mountain, below us the deep valley of the Barouk river. The great sprawl of the landscape reduced all our efforts to minute proportions. It was with surprise that we could look back and see that Jezzine was now hidden from us by a bulge in the mountain wall and that a new vista of plunging chasms and shaggy hillside was opening before us.

We could see where the valleys of the Jezzine and Barouk Rivers joined as clearly as if we were looking down at a contour map. The white, pebbly shoals of their confluence were spattered with pink oleanders, and we could see the river, now known as the Awali, glinting among the thick, feathery vegetation of the gardens it irrigated. Hidden in these gardens are some antique columns of Egyptian granite, and up and down the valley are sepulchral grottoes, tombs, fragments of capitals, traces of construction, all indicating that this valley was worked and settled from a very early period onwards. Further down the valley, out of our sight, was the big Convent of St Sauveur, the parent foundation of St Thekla, on the other side of the mountain. It was on their property that Lady Hester Stanhope spent the last twenty-one years of her turbulent existence, dying mad, neglected and alone in the old Convent farm on a hilltop at Djoun which she rented from the monks. The farm, crumbled and overgrown as it is, its courtyard waist-high in bents and thistles, its ceilings fallen in on to the cell-like rooms which make up the living space, is not without a melancholy distinction of its own. Perched on its little hilltop in the foothills, only a few miles from the coast, it looks out over the wide, sun-struck, desiccated landscape of the Chouf, immensities of sky and pale stony land all around, with the faraway line of the sea accentuating the loneliness, the grandeur and the emptiness of it all. There is nothing extravagant or luxurious about Lady Hester's choice, any more than there is about her tomb, a simple slab of stone inscribed:

LADY HESTER LUCY STANHOPE,
BORN 12 MARCH 1776, DIED 23RD JUNE 1833

which one can find on a terrace near the house, set down casually among the pomegranates and the fig trees. The monks at St Thekla told us their Convent had once entered into correspondence with the British Embassy in Beirut, with a view to giving Lady Hester a more imposing tomb, but had received the answer that the present one would do very well, Lady Hester not having been one to care too much for the outward appearance of things.

Yet this was the imperious, strong-willed woman whose innate political acumen – not for nothing was she Lord Chatham's granddaughter and William Pitt's niece – led her to badger the British Government incessantly on the necessity of protecting and extending British interests in the Levant; whose belief in conspicuous expenditure was to harass banker, Consul and Treasury official alike, and eventually ruin her; and whose fearless self-confidence and disdain of the conventions impressed Turkish Pasha and Druze chieftain alike, and has caused the name of *El Sitt* – the Lady – to be recalled even today. Various accounts of her last years have come down to us; she was visited by Kinglake, of *Eothen* fame, and the French writer Lamartine, who also visited her powerful neighbour and enemy, the Druze Emir Bechir, and her private physician, Dr Meryon, published a lengthy account of his years in her retinue. The end is all madness, fury and embitteredness, a terrible falling-in of a personality built on pride, impatience and a vigour of mind that could take the ferocious intrigues of the mountain in its stride, but was for ever at odds with the sleeker self-sufficiencies of established government practice.

* * *

The apple harvest was at its height. All along the road one came upon groups of men stacking up cases of fruit for the lorries to pick up, and in every orchard men and women were busy plucking the fruit. Occasionally we would pass a Druze burying ground, the stone family mausoleums in which the dead are put, sheltered under spreading ilex trees. Sometimes even the mausoleums had been split and shaken by the earthquake.

The people we met greeted us with dignified cordiality; the men with their bushy beards and tall headdresses looked very little different from the pictures of their ancestors in the time of the Ottomans. The collapse and disorder in the villages were depressing, especially when one considered that eighteen months had already elapsed since the earthquake, and that another winter was soon to cover the mountain with snow. There seemed little evidence of a concerted effort to rebuild; piles of sand and cement bricks occasionally lay about the roadside, people had patched up fallen-in roofs, some were living in the flimsy new houses, most of which had a distressingly makeshift air. Possibly the new constructions would withstand another earthquake shock better than the thick-walled, organic growth of the old feudal villages, but their thin walls, unplastered interiors and generally gimcrack appearance promised ill for the cold and rain of the season now approaching. Many of the older houses were almost castles, so high and forbidding were their outer walls, with perhaps a pair of crude lions carved over the main doorway, or a charming fringe of stone roses and lilies decorating the walls of an inner court. One great mansion's upper storeys had sagged open, so that from the street below one could peer up at ceilings decorated in the Ottoman manner with formalised flowers and arabesques. At another we were given water drawn up by an antiquated pulley from a marble well-head in a charming parti-coloured stone courtyard. There seemed little attempt to conserve these handsome houses, often several hundred years old. What had fallen in was left, or cleared away to allow a concrete structure to take its place.

An exception was the enormous Jumblat mansion, a splendid honey-coloured house terraced up the hillside around a large central court. With its graceful double staircases, its enormous cypress trees and its commanding position on a hillside above the steep fall of the valley, it had all the romantic interest of a fortress mingled with the grace and lightness of a Renaissance Italian villa. We planned to spend a few days in Mouktara, for we had arranged to meet friends from Beirut there over the weekend. Miles' hand, in the meantime, had begun to be inflamed, and as we were in reach of civilisation we decided to have it looked at by a doctor.

We camped a mile below the village, where the road wound down to a bridge over the Barouk river. We pitched our tent in an orchard belonging to the young schoolmaster of the village, beneath some mulberry trees and just above the rushing stream. It was a charming spot. The river, golden brown like some Scottish trout stream, tumbled over boulders or spread out into pools deep enough to swim in. Overhead a tunnel of green made by the interlacing boughs of the plane trees and alders that lined its banks kept off the sun in the heat of the day. On either side the narrow terracing, sometimes only twelve or fifteen feet wide, rose in tiers, each level held by a solid drystone wall covered in ferns, until the rock walls of the cliff took over, and by tilting one's head, one could see the trees fringing its lip. In spring, all the terraces would be covered with wild flowers: cyclamens growing out of the crevices of the walls, anemones, orchises, little blue irises, ixions, ranunculus, while seen from above the fruit trees would appear like puffs of pink and white smoke. Now, except for dandelions and an occasional scarlet pimpernel, there were hardly any flowers left, but the hedges were full of blackberries and hazel nuts, the vines hung down heavy with grapes and an atmosphere of mellow fruitfulness pervaded the whole valley.

We were at first regarded with a certain reserve by the villagers when we went up to shop at the village store, but the young schoolmaster, who spoke French and English, was kindness itself. He was a 'scoot', he informed us, and had often camped with his company, so could comprehend there was no ulterior motive in our presence. The reason for the villagers' reserve soon became apparent. The Druzes were engaged in a quarrel with the Government, which had already exploded into violence, and at present an uneasy truce prevailed. Unclassifiable strangers like us were naturally suspect, but when they heard we were English, their confidence returned, and they harked back with pleasure to the traditional friendship of the British and the Druzes. This was a subject which often came up.

Napoleon's Egyptian adventure, with its threat to the overland route to India, aroused in Britain an interest in the Levant which had been more or less in abeyance since the time of the Crusades. A company of British merchants, it is true, had operated the Levant Company from a base in Aleppo; travellers like Lithgow, Mandeville and Maundrell had kept alive a certain interest in these parts which found an echo in the works of the poets and playwrights of their period. But until the eighteenth century the realm of the Grand Signior – 'the shadow of God upon earth' – was as far away and exotic to the average Englishman as the court of Kubla Khan was to Marco Polo's compatriots. France was more consistent in her interests. From the time of St Louis' Crusade the *amitié traditionnelle* of the Maronites and French was maintained, however tenuously, by trade, missionaries and diplomatic exchange. The Renaissance period, with its expanding intellectual horizons, saw Maronite scholars and agents settled in Paris and Rome; in 1616 the first French Consul was established in Sidon. By 1740 a treaty had been signed between Turkey and France putting all Christians visiting the Ottoman Empire under the protection of the French flag.

Meanwhile, as the theory of 'spheres of interest' gained ground, the other European Powers began to show interest in the Turkish possessions. Russia's ambition to amputate some of the limbs of the 'sick man of Europe' led to that deterioration of relations with the

West which culminated in the Crimean War. Britain, anxious for the lines of communication to her great Indian possessions, was at all costs anxious to prop up the sprawling bulk of the Turkish Empire. France, jealous for her privileges, supported the rebel Viceroy of Egypt, Mohammed Ali, ancestor of King Farouk, engaged in snatching independence from his master, the Turkish Sultan. Each Power, in a sort of macabre game of oranges and lemons, chose its favourite from among the different groups inhabiting the Empire. France, the Maronites, Russia, the Greek Orthodox, Britain, the Druzes. This interference played havoc with the delicate balance of relations on the mountain, and the hitherto friendly relations of the Maronites and Druzes deteriorated into the eventual dreadful massacres of the 1840s and 1860.

Like all communal upheavals, a period of tension and various petty incidents led to the outbreak of strife. The shooting of a partridge set off the first incident, in which the Druzes were worsted; two boys quarrelling in a village of the Metn precipitated a disaster of which the effects can be seen even today in ruined and deserted settlements in remote valleys, and the Christians of the district can still point out where their immediate ancestors were slaughtered or starved out by the Druzes and Turks. In three months, and within a space of a few miles, an estimated twelve thousand people were killed; many thousands more were ruined. In 1860 the European Powers at last intervened, and the French dispatched a force of seven thousand men to restore order. A new autonomous province, guaranteed by the Western Powers, and under a Christian Governor-General, evolved from the wreckage, but a legacy of inter-communal bitterness and suspicion has survived to the present day.

The Jumblats, in the midst of whose feudal territory we were now residing, had been prominent among the leaders of the Druzes. Their chief was sentenced to death for his complicity in the massacres, but his sentence was eventually commuted. Many Druzes fled to the Syrian Hauran, others emigrated. The present chieftain, Kamel Bey, is a Tolstoyan figure, a convinced socialist, yet the prisoner of his name and inheritance. Educated abroad, a

237

tall, thin, ascetic figure, a Parliamentary deputy, an enlightened landlord, he has attempted to put his convictions into practice by giving away portions of his estates, to the mortification and annoyance of his immediate family. The recent elections had stirred up emotions all over the country. Bombs had been thrown and an attempt made on the life of the President. Armed men had flocked to the assistance of their notables in every community. A party of five young men from the Hermon district arrived at the Jumblat house to offer their services; their chieftain was in Beirut, and after a few days they started back across the mountains. Intercepted by *gendarmes*, a gun-battle ensued, and the Druzes returned to Mouktara to seek shelter in the traditionally sacrosanct stronghold of their chieftain.

'How can the Government say these were armed intruders from Syria?' asked the schoolmaster. 'Everyone in Lebanon carries arms, and nobody can pretend they don't.'

'What right has the Government to interfere with our family relations? Everyone knows we all have cousins and relations in the Hauran. Half of Hermon in any case is in Syria. Why shouldn't our people stick together, and help each other as they've always done?' were the indignant questions flung at us when we called at the great house with a request to see over the property. So splendid did the house seem from outside that we were consumed with interest to see its interior, but little expected to find ourselves caught up in the heat and passion of partisan politics.

A chieftain or notable in the East has no private life; at any time people can descend on him, sit, stay, eat, sleep, all in the name of family and partisanship. Inhospitality or ungraciousness, the desire for privacy, interests outside the range of local problems are not understood by people who still believe in the old feudal equation of blind loyalty to automatic protection.

We were received with some suspicion at the doorway by a shabby-looking retainer, but on explaining our identity were ushered in while a hurried consultation took place upstairs. We were standing in a charming small court, entirely roofed by a fine trellis of vines. Stairways and terraces led off in all directions, for the house is constructed against the hillside in a series of ramps. Everything had an air of neglect and decrepitude, which did nothing to detract from its intense romanticism and beauty. On the highest level a spring gushed out under a vaulted stone canopy, to be channelled in a series of runs and cascades through terraces and gazebos down every level of the property, to emerge finally in the village square below the mansion as a public fountain. Great, stalwart cypresses lined the terraces, and vines and bougainvillea and sprays of roses and jasmine straggled and fell in swags over the walls and roofs of the buildings. After a walk around the gardens, we were invited into the main building. Here, in a vast, dusty, marble-floored reception-room, we were introduced to a small, hard-bitten group of middle-aged men. They appeared to be in possession of the place. Coffee was served, and we sat in a carpeted alcove listening to the now-familiar grievances, worries and regrets of the older generation. From our conversations with the schoolmaster, we had learnt that the younger generation of Druzes, like the younger Jaafars, were wearying of the feuds and rivalries and bloodshed of the older generation. 'Of course, we'll all fight if the Druzes are attacked,' he had said only the other evening. 'Kamel Beg has only to say the word, and the whole countryside will rise up in arms. But growing apples is better than killing men, and as more people are educated, they'll find other ways of settling their quarrels.'

The older generation of Wicked Uncles, as we nicknamed them, still clings nostalgically to the past. Men who were young and untamed at the time of the last Druze revolt against the French Mandate, in the 1920s, relive their youth in the feverish atmosphere of plot and intrigue, surmise and suspicion which dogs all Eastern politics. Their eyes flashing, our hosts passionately proclaimed their right to freedom from Government interference: 'Surrender a guest who has taken shelter in this house? Never! We will fight to the last man rather than put up with such an insult. Chamoun [the President] will soon see he can't get away with such impertinences. To think that we helped put him into power! Look how all those *gendarmes* ran away the other day from a handful of us Druzes; he needn't think we're not prepared for more trouble.'

After our coffee, we walked through the faded, carpet-hung reception-rooms out into the broad central courtyard. A double flight of stairs led down to the terrace below, and a splendid view across the valley and hills to the blue distance beyond spread out below us. Our hosts accepted our admiration of the building rather perfunctorily; they were more interested in impressing us with their ability to withstand a siege. First-aid equipment, ammunition, a bren-gun – 'We have twenty-five of these' – were of more importance than ceilings of frescoed roses and faded photographs of the Jumblat family. Shelves of French and English books, a signed photo of Nehru, some charming prints, were indicated as exotic testimonials to their chieftain's brilliance and erudition, but their idealised concept of a feudal Druze chieftain was irrevocably imposed on the intellectual whose simple and civilised tastes were almost submerged in the ramshackle splendour of this great mansion.

* * *

We stayed a total of five days in Mouktara, during which we took Miles down to Beirut by *service* taxi to have his hand treated at the American Hospital. We shared a taxi down with a man from Homs and his niece, who had come to visit her father, who was imprisoned for murder in Baaklin jail. The journey down was enlivened by a discussion of the merits of different jails, in which all the passengers took part. Travelling jam-packed in these taxis is not so disagreeable as might be imagined; everyone talks, life-histories are exchanged, a wayside bargain is never spurned, news circulates rapidly throughout the remotest districts. We were down in Beirut in little over an hour, passing from the dry, crisp air of the mountain into the soft air of the coast as we came down the precipitous curves of the Damour valley. We passed on our way the palace of Beit-ed-Din, now the summer home of the President of the Lebanese Republic, but once the stronghold of the last of the great independent Druze princes of the Mountain. Descended in the female line from Fakr-ud-Din II, the Emir Bechir Chehab II resembled in many ways his great ancestor; a notable intriguer, a doughty warrior, he survived four different periods of exile, and in 1850 he ended his days an unofficial prisoner in Constantinople at the age of eighty-four. Like Fakr-ud-Din, he saw the West as the pulley needed to haul the Lebanon out of the slough of dependence to which the Turks condemned all their conquests. Scholars were sent to Europe, foreign schools encouraged to open, roads and bridges were built, commerce was encouraged. The Egyptian campaign in 1831 to add Syria to Mohammed Ali's domain brought Bechir to his ruin: allied to the Egyptians against his Turkish suzerain, he came in conflict with the British, who opposed any threat to their route to India. The Druzes, stirred up by the threat of conscription to the Egyptian armies, rebelled against him, and the aged Emir was finally forced to surrender to the British. His strong and beautiful palace, built on the edge of a ravine, took forty years to build. The most skilful masons were imported from Syria, and nothing was spared to make it the most splendid edifice of its kind. Today the Service of Antiquities has lovingly restored the mosaic and marble of the entrances and halls. The vast open courtyard, above its giddy drop into the ravine below, is swept clear, and a museum inhabits the stables where once five hundred horses were accommodated. The painted wooden interiors of Damascene origin, gilded and worked with charming scenes and stylised representations of fruit and flowers, the sombre cypresses of the gardens, the magnificent sweep of the landscape, the marble bath-houses, the courts and fountains make Beit-ed-Din one of the show-places of the Lebanon.

TWELVE

The cedars of Maaser Chouf and the descent to Barouk

A PAIR OF HUGE SILKY BROWN OXEN attended by a cheerful youth, ploughing the narrow strip of terrace below us, was the signal for us to pack up our camp and start on the last stage of our journey. The end of summer was upon us; it was only a matter of a few weeks before it would be too cold to camp out in the haphazard way to which we were accustomed. It was hot enough, however, as we picked our way through a wilderness of rock and scrub on to the bluffs overlooking the narrow valley in which we had been camping. A massive shoulder of mountain cut off Mouktara from the uplands dominating the whole sweep of the plateau where the Barouk had its source, and it was across this that we forced ourselves upwards throughout a hot and exhausting morning. As we got up higher, the big tawny landscape, slashed through with blue-shadowed rifts and valleys, fell into perspective, and we could see the mountain coming down in great steps and ripples for as far as the eye could see.

We had in our street in Beirut a shopkeeper called George Chaker. We bought all our buttons, needles and thread from him, and occasionally apples, which he told us he grew up at his village in the mountains. Like many Lebanese, he had emigrated as a young man to America, and now, middle-aged, had returned to marry a sturdy young village wife, and to set up a little business in Beirut. 'You sure ought to visit our town,' he told us earnestly, in his creaky old-fashioned American voice. 'I'll tell my family you'll be coming that way, and they'll look out for you.'

'Chaker he go mad you not see his village,' confided Elias to us. 'He like *majnun* about his place; says Maaser Chouf best village in all Lebanon.' So to Maaser Chouf we were going, intending to go up from there to the forests which can be seen speckling the flanks of the mountain above Barouk. We had no idea of what we were coming to, we only knew from our map that we ought eventually to strike a road which would lead us to the village. We reached the road about lunchtime, a fine tarmac affair that wound enigmatically through a deserted landscape. It never seemed to end, but went winding on through acres and acres of vines, stretched out in tidy lines all over the rolling hillside. Occasionally in the distance a tall, leafy contraption standing on stilts on some prominent hilltop would show there were *naturs* about to guard the vines, but otherwise we hardly saw any trace of human occupation. It was late afternoon before we rounded a bend and suddenly saw before us a small red-roofed, stone-built town, set in the shallow curve of the head of the valley, with a thick smudge of cedars on the mountain just above it. We were all astonished to see such an established-looking township where we had expected to see only a lonely straggle of village, and made our way into the town with a certain amount of curiosity. As we were passing the tall, prosperous-looking church, a man detached himself from a group outside a store and came up to us.

'Are you the folks from Beirut my brother told me of? Welcome to Maaser Chouf. We was just wondering when you'd be through.' This was Michael Chaker, with whom we were to spend the next two days. His gentle New England voice, acquired in twenty-five years spent travelling as a biscuit salesman through the eastern states of America, fell soothingly on our ear as, chatting amiably, he led us through the town to the family house. This turned out to be a typical stone-built Lebanese house, set on a terrace with a vine over the porch, and a fine view out across the valley to the sunset. The household was rather macabre: an old, wandering mother all dressed in black, who had a passion for aspirins, and who roamed restlessly around the house at night; a brother who lived in a rough sort of shelter on the roof; a neat young wife and a lumpish nephew. We enjoyed a rather

Spartan communal supper by lamplight, each party contributing to the general store, and, being tired, retired early to bed on the terrace. Next morning, very early, the old lady came to wake us. She seemed distressed to find us sleeping outside, and hastily borrowed some aspirins to set herself up for the day. Elias went off with Anthea on donkey-back to do some shopping and, accompanied by our host, we set out to see the sights of the neighbourhood. First we went on a long walk to the top of a neighbouring hill, where there had once been a Roman fort; then down a declivity to see some tombs; then up another slope to see where a man had once found a gold treasure (this was very stimulating to Miles); back down a valley to where a derelict watermill slowly crumbled into nothing; up past some terraces which were being meticulously faced with cut stone; under a big chestnut tree where Michael Chaker remembered a bridegroom should by tradition be bathed by his friends on his wedding day. It was very hot, and we were quite glad to be taken to call on the priest – 'Father John' – a youngish man, trained at St Sauveur. Maaser Chouf has some two thousand inhabitants, two-thirds of whom are Greek Catholics, the remainder Druzes, and all living together in apparent amity. The town is famous for the quality of its *arak*, and for the number of its sons who have migrated and returned to settle in their prosperous old age.

The expanding population, and the disabilities from which Christians suffered under Ottoman rule, turned people's thoughts towards the New World opening up across the sea in the nineteenth century. The first Lebanese emigrant landed in America in 1854. Now the community numbers in the region of a quarter of a million. A third of a million Lebanese live in Brazil. Canada, Mexico, Australia, New Zealand, Egypt, Senegal, Nigeria, all have their communities, setting up grocers' shops and general stores wherever they go. Between 1900 and 1914 it is estimated that a quarter of the mountain population of Lebanon emigrated overseas, and there is hardly a family that has not relations or friends settled abroad.

The remittances sent home by these expatriate Lebanese play an important part in the economy of the country. Like the summer tourist trade, they are one of the country's major resources. Many, having made their fortunes overseas, return to their native villages. Others take the nationality of the country of their adoption, but retain their links with families and friends in their home country. Industrious, energetic, unobtrusive, they adapt themselves quickly to their new life, and by hard and unremitting toil make considerable fortunes for themselves and their families.

Father John had just written a pamphlet in Arabic proving that it was from the cedars of Maaser Chouf that Hiram of Tyre supplied the timber needed for the building of King Solomon's temple, and not from the cedars of Becharré, as is generally assumed. In support of his theory he pointed out that the Maaser cedars are very near the crest of the mountain, and it is not difficult to suppose that in ancient times the whole mountain was forested. The Litani River flows down the Beka'a close under the eastward side of the mountain, and makes its sudden bend to come out to the sea a few miles above Tyre. Why shouldn't the ancient woodmen have cut their timber on the mountain ridge, rolled it down to the Litani, and brought it by river to the sea? Interest in this ingenious theory is further sustained within the Greek community by the fact that the Becharré cedars are the property of the Maronite Church; a certain sectarian rivalry underlies the antiquarian enthusiasm.

All that day and half the next was spent visiting the prominent citizens of the community. Our host was indefatigable in leading us from one neat, prosperous house to another, where elderly couples, the man twisted and worn by long years of toil, the woman prim and neat like a Sunday-school teacher, lived out their retirement in the atmosphere of a small American town.

'Mighty pleased to meet you, Mr Izzard.'

'Come right in, folks.'

'How d'you like our town, Miz Izzard?' said the twangy, American voices, and the stuffed chairs were moved about in the polished parlours, and the housewife produced cookies from the modern kitchen, and we all talked about the weather, and the Church, and how things were over in the States, and the worn-out old men sat awkwardly about, fumbling for cigarettes with their knuckly hands and listening with a certain sheepish pride to the social fluency of their wives. A small town atmosphere of sedate prosperity hung over the place. 'A real nice neighbourhood' is how the citizens described it to us. We were taken to visit the doctor, who had served in the Sudan, the Judge's wife, a plump, comfortable club-woman, whose daughter had just passed her barrister's examinations and hoped to be appointed to the juvenile delinquency courts, an official of the Judiciary, and two old millionaires.

The official, in common with everyone else in the place, was growing apples. Being a wealthy man, he was investing thousands of pounds in the terraces he owned just above the village. Escorted by a small group of people who wanted something from him, he took us up to look over his property. The trees were in splendid condition, pruned and sprayed with expert attention, each terrace irrigated from the big concrete reservoirs he had constructed at the top, each level faced and cemented with carefully fitted stones. More terraces were being levelled further down, and over the steps leading to the different levels a shady pergola of vines had been erected. The apples all belonged to the two categories grown commercially by the Lebanese, both of American origin, one white and one red. It is only in the Kesrouan that one still finds a sharp local apple, similar to our Worcester Permains; everywhere else has been converted to the big American variety. We were given more than we could carry, for some of the fruit were over a pound in weight. When fresh, they can be delicious, but most are refrigerated for sale later in the season, and they tend to become cotton-woolly in taste.

The apple-growing business has developed in Lebanon with some of the dangerous hysteria of the South Sea Bubble.

'Everybody's in it,' said Michael Chaker gloomily, 'every fool who has an acre of land has planted apples, including me. These terraces used once to have mulberries, vines, figs, everything one needed for the house. Now they've all been ripped out, and there's a glut of apples on the market. There's no canning industry in the country, no commercial jam-making, fruit-drying or anything like that. People put their apples in store, and hope the price will pick up later on, for it's already fallen below an economic level of production. Rich men, like the Judge and the official, can ride it out, but us poor fellows with only a little family property are hit real hard.'

The apple growers, like the hashish growers of the north, are suffering from the political pressures of the Arab world. Egypt has always been the chief customer for Lebanese apples; the boom started at the end of the war, and as the apple prices rose, more and more people started to grow apples. It takes five years for a tree to reach full productivity, but as long as prices remained high, the original investment was recouped in a matter of a few years. Egypt started putting serious economic pressure on the Lebanon in 1956, by being difficult about import regulations; this year (1957) she was not buying in any appreciable quantity, and the growers were being very hard hit. To date, the Lebanese Government has helped out, but the full impact of the situation has hardly hit the country. Next season, when more orchards come into production, the glut will be much worse, and thousands of small growers will find themselves in difficulties unless an alternative market is found for them.

After a day and a half we began to feel we had 'done' Maaser Chouf pretty thoroughly, and we dreaded the approach of Sunday, when, we were told, the 'church parade' rivalled Beirut for elegance. It seemed hardly likely that we would rise to the sartorial standards of the ladies of the community, and we were determined to break loose from the round of social visits before that day arrived. Elias, in particular, was almost disgruntled:

'Old woman she gur-gur all day: all the time "aspirin, aspirin", not possible me do anything, she come *shufti*, and bring other old woman too.' Indeed, old Mme Chaker haunted her own home like an uneasy ghost. Events had long moved past her. Her husband dead, her brisk, competent daughters-in-law occupying most of the house, her sons, with the exception of the youngest, returned after many years with an alien standard of life, she had retreated into a world of shadows. Conscious of the traditional demands of hospitality, she was eager to do us the slightest services. At dawn she would come with a basket of dew-wet grapes; at noon she would heat washing water; at night she would rove distractedly about, sleepless in the shadowy, lamp-lit house. Her youngest son, too, haunted the back premises and the flat roof where the raisins and sultanas were drying in the sun and only Elias and the children ever saw him. We ourselves were caught up in the sober matter-of-fact complacency of a small and prosperous community.

It was with a certain feeling of relief that we started off up the steep mountain road behind the town. The donkeys, well-fed and rested, and carrying three days' supply of feed, stepped out briskly; ourselves cheerful and carefree, laughing as Elias, with ghoulish relish, described his experiences with Mme Chaker and her elderly sisters, who, like three Furies, had dogged his every step. The sun shone not too fiercely and, with every turn of the road, the feeling of ease and carelessness and delight in existence increased, that concentration in the moment which is the reward of the wandering life. The landscape fell away beneath us in great sweeps, and soon Maaser Chouf was nothing but a huddle of red roofs immediately beneath us. It was wonderful to be free again. Indeed, these next few days were the last we were to enjoy of that spaciousness and freedom from mundane worries which had sustained us so long, and unconsciously we knew it, and determined to enjoy every moment to the full.

We were a little disconcerted to round a bend and come upon a group of men sitting under the shade of a carob tree, on the extreme edge of the road. Were these the bandits who were rumoured below to have frightened off a gang of road-makers? No, these were the road-makers themselves, enjoying their lunch in the shade of the tree. A handsome youth sprang up, and ran to meet us; his was the bird-gun we had spied as we first sighted the group. Then we detected the Mayor's son, a lantern-jawed redhead, who raised bees, then an enormously fat man, a checked headcloth set nonchalantly on the side of his massive head.

'Welcome, welcome,' they all shouted merrily; 'come and join us, and share our lunch.' They were sitting on what seemed the edge of a precipice, so steeply did the mountainside fall away beneath them, and an enormous panorama of mountain, valley, upland and plateau spread out below, so that we seemed to be standing on the rim of the world. We all settled down in the patch of shadow, and shared grapes and figs, and nuts and slices of salami, while the donkeys shook their tasselled harness behind us, and the wandering breezes cooled our sweating brows.

The road-menders were in high spirits: the tale of the bandits had enabled them to establish the practice of returning to Maaser each evening, as they found it uncomfortably cold to sleep up on the mountainside at night. The road so far led only to the cedars. It had been cut and bulldozed out of the mountainside in a series of carefully calculated gradients. It was hoped later to run it right over the top and down into the Beka'a, providing an alternative route to the long roundabout detour through Merdjayoun, near the Israeli frontier. The progressive citizens of Maaser Chouf were naturally very anxious to extend a first-class tarmac road through their district, but were being sorely harassed by the citizens of Jezzine, who also saw the advantage of being on the connecting route, and were lobbying as hard as they could to acquire the advantage for themselves.

The cedars of Maaser number about four hundred trees, clustering on the slopes of a steep ravine over 5,000 feet up, just below a *col* from which one can see right across the Beka'a to Mount Hermon, and down the valley to Israel. A small spring seeps into a little stone basin, and a rough altar has been built against one of the bigger trees. We ensconced ourselves here very comfortably, camping beneath the shade of one of the biggest trees, while Elias impiously used the altar for his kitchen gear, and the children gathered branches and cedar-cones for a bonfire.

The site was superb, and as the sun sank all red and gold into the sea below us, the lights of the mountain villages began to twinkle out into the cool night air. As the darkness thickened, all the range of hills below us was diamonded with lights for as far as the eye could reach. We stood entranced, identifying now this, now that village or township, from the Druze country we had left to the faraway glitter of Sofar and Bhamdoun. The night air grew cold, and the great trees around us sighed and murmured in the wind. We sat huddled up in blankets and sheepskins around our fire, while the donkeys kicked and stamped among themselves, and Elias fed us with hot soup and meatballs which he had prepared down below in Maaser Chouf. The stars hung over us very close, Orion and Betelgeuse and Charles' Wain, so that what with the villages below and the stars above, we seemed to be going to bed in a blaze and glitter of diamonds.

All the next day and the next we idled away in blissful indolence. Once a pair of sportsmen appeared partridge shooting. They were wealthy young men in smart Italian suede jackets, whose parents had returned from Chile to look into their family properties in Barouk. They produced some *arak* for breakfast, in return for our coffee, and took Elias off with them on an unsuccessful beat across the crest of the mountain. We explored across the other side of the ravine, past an enormous ancient cedar whose bulk we could not girdle with our arms, and put up coveys of partridges which sped across the ravine with a whistle and flurry of wings. The farther side of the ravine was topped by huge, splintered outcrops of grey rock, with trees in among them. Here the children discovered a splendid natural fort, a big cedar growing out of the middle of a jumble of stones, and with its drooping boughs making a sort of tent over the turf beneath. Only at one place was the circle open, and from there one looked out over a dizzy fall of scree to the immense landscape below.

On the afternoon of the second day the water in the spring began to fail, and we knew we would have to move on. With Sabrina, we took Little Stick over the *col* to watch the sunset dyeing Mount Hermon pink and violet, and the darkness welling up from the floor of the valley. The whole great bare waterless hump of the mountain, 9,200 feet high, rose up straight across the valley from us, and we could distinguish the tiny excrescence on the southern summit which indicates the site of a Roman temple.

The mountain has been holy since earliest times. It was an ancient Semitic High Place, and on the top can still be seen traces of the funnelled basin used in the ceremonies of renewing the source. This was a rite much practised by the ancient inhabitants of this area, and consisted in ceremoniously carrying up offerings of water from the springs below, and pouring them out on the mountain-top. The flow of the water on the summit was presumed to stimulate the flow of the springs below. The Romans adapted and incorporated these old usages into their own rites, and small temples of their period are scattered on the slopes of the mighty mountain, on both sides of the Anti-Lebanon.

Next day we awoke early to a superb dawn – first a faint greenish gleam in the soft dark grey of the pre-dawn, then mother-of-pearl, then rose, then gold, then the pale, clear-washed radiance of a new day. Lying there on our shelf beneath the great trees, we heard the forest slowly stirring to life: first the isolated chirps and cawings of the birds, then the stir of their wings as they moved about in the boughs overhead. As the sun strengthened, the big tawny butterflies fluttered about in the shafts of light striking through the drooping boughs, and the hum of the insects and cicadas began to make itself heard.

We packed up with regret, for had it not been for the shortage of water, we would have been tempted to stay on for as long as our supplies lasted. Elias and Anthea had already pioneered a route for the donkeys across the head of the ravine and through the tumbled rocks to the crest of the mountain. We proposed to go along this till we could drop down through the forest to the spring of Barouk, thus postponing the return to civilisation for another day. We set off very carefully, each adult leading a donkey, the children straggling along behind on foot. To get clear on to the mountain, we had to traverse a steep, shaly slope, covered with loose round stones, hard going for everyone, but after half an hour's painstaking progress, each donkey being brought up to the others before another awkward stretch was negotiated, we emerged into firm going. We paused gratefully in the shade of the last of the Maaser cedars, a rather scrubby, wind-bent new growth, while a faint wailing in the distance indicated that Sebastian and Sabrina were finding the stony slopes harder work than they had anticipated. Before they appeared in sight, we could hear a long, angry complaint from Sebastian. Finally two small panting objects appeared in view, tears streaming down the face of one, so we relented and went back to meet them, and with encouragement and flattery and a certain amount of carrying, got them up to the donkeys. Once established there, their spirits rose, and we set off along the mountain in high good humour.

We followed what appeared to be a charcoal-burner's track, but it was overgrown and disused; there seemed to be no goat grazing on the mountain, for we encountered no shepherds, and it is probably this which has allowed a certain natural regeneration among the trees. It was pleasant walking along the airy ridge, the fall of the land masking our immediate surroundings from view, so that we seemed to be walking detached from everything, just ourselves among the yellow bents, and the partridges whirring away over the brow of the hill. After an hour we started entering trees again, and now we followed the track through glades of cedar and fir, which covered all the flank of the mountain, and extended into the hollows and declivities of the crest. This was by far the most splendid, natural and undisturbed cedar forest we had yet seen, and except for the occasional traces of the charcoal-burners, it seemed untrodden by the foot of man. The path started tilting downwards, and oaks and ashes began to mingle with the darker mass of the cedars. We paused for lunch in a park-like glade and, having rested, addressed ourselves to the business of getting down to Barouk, far below us.

This was indeed for us the end of the high mountains. The track became narrow and precipitous, and the donkeys had to pirouette neatly on a postage-stamp-sized platform before each turn. The fine sylvan scenery gave place to a scrubby undergrowth of burnet and cistus and then we emerged into a bare, shaly, burned-out hillside. The descent was steep and interminable, and we were all soon covered in a fine, reddish dust. Above us, looking up, we could see the last outposts of the forest we had left; below, the familiar arid fall of mountain led to the small pine-covered knolls and willow-hung stream of the source of the River Barouk.

THIRTEEN
The end of the journey

WE SLEPT THAT NIGHT on a pine-covered hillock a little way off from the spring and coffee shops of Barouk. Beside us was a sand quarry, manned by three small boys, presumably the sons of the owner. At irregular intervals they would seize picks and crowbars and lever off another mass of crumbling sandstone. The work was heavy for boys of their size, the oldest being perhaps fourteen, but they worked at their own speed. They slept huddled up in their quarry, but we stretched out under the trees, and woke next morning with stiff limbs and aching shoulders, for the ground was sloping and uneven, and we had all slept uncomfortably. One of the coffee shop proprietors being a friend of Elias, we were invited to take breakfast with him before we set off, so, leading the donkeys, we walked down to the spring.

The spring surges up abundantly into a concrete reservoir, then is drawn off through the trees and groves of the summer coffee shops in a series of streams and rivulets, so that one sits in a characteristic shady gloom at the small tables islanded in the midst of the rushing water. Despite the early hour, there were plenty of people about, and our ragged appearance aroused considerable comment. 'Are you rich people, or are you poor people?' enquired a schoolmaster, in careful English, gazing at us in unaffected curiosity. Like the Roman matron of old, we pointed to the children, stuffing themselves with bread and olives, and replied that though we were not rich in the material sense, we could hardly consider ourselves poor as long as we had our children. The sentiment was immediately understood by our audience, who began to regard us with kindly indulgence as one of themselves. Before we left, we posed for a photograph outside the coffee shop, taken by an itinerant photographer – one of those men who drape a black cloth over their heads, and after elaborate washings and manipulations produce a postcard to take away. This was a great success. There we all stand saying 'Cheese', except Anthea, whose toothless grin was so hideous that we begged her to keep her mouth closed. Our clothes were ragged and torn, and our toes stuck out of our shoes, but we all felt as happy and hilarious as we look, and we set out on the last stage of our journey with a light-hearted optimism only tempered by the regret that it would soon be over.

There were only a few days of September left to us, and we were working our way back towards our starting point. Behind us lay our last experience of the wild and lonely high mountains. From now on we were increasingly in contact with people, and only occasionally regained any of our former freedom and anonymity. The villages and resorts we passed through were all frequented by townspeople and tourists escaping from the heat and humidity of the coast, and had little of interest about them.

It was pleasant enough walking quietly up through the pines and rhododendrons on our way to Ain Zahalta, the sunlight coming in shafts through the trees, the mountain air sharp and sweet in our nostrils, uncontaminated as yet by petrol fumes. Once clear of the pines, we were in fruit orchards again, and the familiar crates of fruit waited at every corner, while the heat beat down fiercely on the quivering tarmac road, and our early morning pace slowed perceptibly. A large black American station wagon, its luggage rack loaded with trays of ripe tomatoes, screeched to a stop on a bend of the road, and to our surprise we were greeted cheerfully by two of the monks from St Thekla. This unexpected encounter was very pleasant, and served to distract our minds from the climb ahead of us. We had not far to go, and by lunchtime had reached our destination for the day, the Hotel Victoria at Ain Zahalta.

The Victoria is an old-fashioned establishment founded by the present proprietors' mother about fifty years ago, and has retained much of the flavour of its period. It has a solid, unpretentious comfort, and an atmosphere of quiet and seclusion very rare in the summer resorts of the Lebanon. Its visitors' book dates from the days when guests came up on donkey-back from the railway station some seven miles away and side-saddles had to be supplied by the hotel for the use of its female clients.

We were fortunate enough to encounter some friends from Beirut on the terrace of the hotel, who vouched for us, as our appearance was hardly likely to commend us to the owners. We were given an excellent camping site in the hotel grounds, and spent the next twenty-four hours getting ourselves bathed and clean, and sorting out such of our gear as we could to send down to Beirut ahead of us.

The problem of the disposal of the donkeys was now beginning to arise, and we were tempted by an offer we had for Big Stick from a peasant at Ain Zahalta. We decided to hold on to him to the end, for we had no fears of being unable to dispose of him, and to sell all the donkeys from Elias' home at Broumana, not very far from where we had originally started. This agreed, we set off early on the morning of the 25th, seen off by our friends and, crossing the main Beirut–Damascus road at Mdeireidj, pushed on to Falougha that afternoon. Although the heat in the day was still fierce, the weather was breaking up, and clouds had begun to form on the horizon. At night the sheet-lightning played erratically about the sky to the north, and a feeling of finality pervaded the air. We were all a little oppressed by the feeling that our carefree life was ending, and it was an effort to turn our minds to the arrangements necessary for our return to Beirut.

We sent Elias off with as much of the gear as we could spare, and waited for his return in the shelter of a pine-covered spur of the hillside, surprisingly secluded in an area mostly given over to small villas and the summer trade. It was even more surprising to wake early in the morning to find a large jackal standing on a stone ten paces away, watching us with fixed attention, until at our stir he sloped off into the trees. This camp at Falougha was also distinguished by being the only place at which we saw a scorpion, one so tiny that it was less than a finger in length, whose appearance aroused an excitement out of all proportion to its size and capacity for mischief.

Elias returned, and we set out on a grey, overcast morning on the last stage of our journey to Broumana. The weather was distinctly cooler, and a thick, misty drizzle was never far away.

There was something almost Japanese in the aspect of the spurs and knolls of the hillside, each crowned and rounded by clumps of pines, with the mist wrapping dankly around the cliffs, and the ranges of hills succeeding each other mysteriously in the background. Only occasionally did the cloud lift, and the sun shine brilliantly forth, flashing on the distant villages crowning the cliff-tops, and sharply defining the chasms that split the green, pine-clad slopes of the mountain. We were now in the Metn, on Elias' native heath, and our way was enlivened by constant encounters with relations or friends of his family. The weather was against us, and by afternoon it was obvious we should have to seek shelter soon from the storm building up in forbidding clouds, whose misty tentacles were even now swirling up through the still dank woods around us.

The rain came down with a vengeance just as we were entering the village of Qortada, and we were glad to take shelter in the house of some friends of Elias.

The village straggled on the edge of a cliff, above the gorge of the river Djamini, which we would cross the next day, and looking over one could see the long ridge with its thatch of umbrella pines on which Broumana and Beit Meri stood, thrusting out to the narrow coastal plain like an aggressive pointed finger.

It was a dank, cold night, but we slept comfortably enough, for our hostess turned out of the family bed for us – a splendid brass-knobbed affair piled high with quilts and bolsters – and the children were laid out on spare mattresses on the floor.

Next day the storm had washed itself away, and we arose to a sparkling fresh morning, every outline sharp and clear, the roses in the garden still hanging their heads, heavy with the rainfall of the night. We had to descend right down to the river babbling among its rocks and cataracts in the ferny recesses of the glen, then slowly traverse up the face of the cliff under the convent of Deir el Kalaa, built on the site of a Roman temple. The road was good, and deserted, and we walked on cheerfully through the bright sunlit morning, the shaggy hillside and cliffs towering above us as we descended into the narrow gorge, then gradually falling back into proportion as we gained height on the other side. The higher we rose, the wider grew the view in front of us, until at last, looking around the corner of the spur, we saw Beirut lying white and sparkling on its promontory in the sea which filled the whole wider sweep of the horizon. The excitement engendered by this view was only exceeded by the discovery by Anthea of another small tortoise, and so, exclaiming alternately over the tortoise and the sight of Beirut, we emerged on to the road to Beit Meri.

One last steep leg up the donkey track to the village, safe from the hurtling traffic of the main road which had nearly killed Sabrina as we came out on to it, and we stood exhausted and sweating, on the driveway of a friend's villa, ten weeks after our start from Faraya.

* * *

Now that our walk was finished, we were curiously without emotion. We unloaded the gear, the children embraced the donkeys, and we watched Elias riding off with them to his family homestead, with little or no feeling of elation or regret, suspended in a sort of emotional void.

Back in Beirut it was the same. Our beautiful cool house welcomed us back, and our books and pictures and possessions were all about us. It was pleasant to bath, and wear clean clothes, and to have a bed to oneself again, but the feeling of detachment and unreality persisted. We were all affected, and were unable to apply ourselves convincingly to the numerous problems confronting us. Some veil of unreality seemed to hang between us and our old life and our old amusements. We felt no actual regrets for the hardships we had endured, but occasionally a pang of disquiet would pass through our consciousness at the sight of a black-clad peasant standing bewildered in the rush of the city traffic, or waiting patiently for the bus to take him back to his distant village. Then a realisation would steal over us of how far we had come from the primitive simplicity of the life we had been living, of how immutably enclosed we were once again in the compartments of civilised life. For a while we had sunk our identity, and had existed contented, carefree, unconcerned, on the very ground floor of life itself. This was the regret that was lying in wait to seize us, and at last we could bear it no longer.

Not far from Beirut, beyond the Damour river, is a beach to which one descends by a stony, cactus-scored track. Once on the sand, the beach stretches away up the curve of its bay for a mile or so and more. It is deserted, for only the village boys come down to bathe in the clear green water, or to run and wrestle on the white sand. Here we all came with blankets and pillows and slept the night on the beach, and swam and played and idled in the glassy green water, and dived from the sharp-edged reefs, and pottered among the seashells and the seawrack of the long, diminishing perspective of the bay. For two days we abandoned ourselves again entirely to the pleasures of the moment, and then, drowned in sun and sea and sand, and purged of all feeling and emotion, we returned to Beirut and addressed ourselves to the business of leaving the Lebanon.

Books referred to in preparing this account of our journey

Lebanon in History, Philip K Hitti (1957)

Syria, the Desert and the Sown, Gertrude Bell (1907)

Crusader's Coast, Edward Thompson (1929)

Three Years in the Levant, Richard Pearse (1949)

Syria, Robin Fedden (1955)

Crusader Castles, Robin Fedden (1957)

Syria and the Holy Land, Ed. W K Kelly (1867)

Early Travels in Palestine, Ed. Thomas Wright (1848)

The Golden Bough, Sir James Frazer (1956)

Le Guide Bleu du Liban (1956)

Lebanon, Land of the Cedars, Marie Karam Khazat and M C Keatinge (1956)

AFTERWORD

The Izzards: a family biography

J AN MORRIS described Ralph Izzard as 'the beau ideal of the old-school foreign correspondent ... not only brave and resourceful, but also gentlemanly, widely read, kind, a bit raffish, excellent to drink with, fun to travel with, handsome but louche, honourable but thoroughly disrespectful. He was old Fleet Street personified. Not only did everyone in the business know him, but they had also known his father, Percy Izzard, the *Mail*'s highly respected gardening correspondent who was the inspiration behind William Boot in Evelyn Waugh's novel *Scoop*.'

Ralph himself was one of three role models from which Ian Fleming created the fictional James Bond. If you have ever wondered what James Bond, having settled down with Miss Moneypenny, might have been like as a father, then you need look no further.

Ralph William Burdick Izzard was born in Billericay on 27 August 1910, educated at Caldicott Prep and The Leys School, where he played water polo, and went on to Queens' College, Cambridge (1928–31).

Over the long, summer holidays he worked as a steward on Atlantic liners, alongside his chum from school and university, Malcolm Lowry. After graduation he was employed by the *Daily Mail* which sent him to Germany where he rose to become Berlin bureau chief. He was tall, handsome and energetic, spoke very good German, loved to swim and to ride through the forests and delighted in the company of women. In 1931 he married Ellen Schmidt-Klewitz, the daughter of a German general, with whom he had a daughter, Christina, and amicably divorced in 1946. He also fathered a son, Benedict, with Marianna Hoppe, one of the great film stars of her generation. Her role in *Der Schimmelreiter* (*The Rider of the White Horse* (1934)) made her famous overnight and gave her access to the top brass of the Nazi regime.

Ralph reported on the Spanish Civil War, Italy's Abyssinia campaign, the 1936 Munich Olympics and other international stories from Berlin, but returned to England via Denmark and Holland once war broke out, where he joined the Royal Naval Volunteer Reserve. He chose to serve as an ordinary seaman and rose to the rank of gunner on ships protecting the Atlantic convoys, but his linguistic skills soon caught up with him and he was transferred to Naval Intelligence. By the end of the war, he had been mentioned in despatches, awarded an OBE and had risen to the rank of Lieutenant-Commander. Ralph worked alongside Ian Fleming and the future journalist Charles Wheeler in the assessment and acquisition of German technical equipment, especially to do with code-encryption and deciphering. They were affiliated with 30 Commando whose task was to capture scientific equipment and scoop up useful-looking German scientists, using HMS *Ferret* in Derry as their shore base. There were all sorts of covert operations, decoys and risky landings on the occupied coast, such as the Dieppe Raid and Walcheren landings which, although disasters, were all designed with some intelligence gathering in mind. After D-Day they specialised in battlefield intelligence, raiding field-headquarters, securing prisoners and picking up dossiers.

Ralph's other wartime skill was as an interrogator of German prisoners of war. He worked in MI9's 'London Cage' at 6, 7 and 8 Kensington Palace Gardens. While other interrogators made use of sleep deprivation, and maybe towels and water buckets, Ralph was the 'good cop', using his infectious delight in life and his knowledge of German dialects, nightlife and restaurants to build up a conversational relationship with the prisoners. They were often impressed when they discovered that despite the war, the charming British naval officer had not become anti-German, and indeed refused to divorce his German wife. One of his German prisoners, Baron Burkard von Müllenheim-Rechberg, became a lifelong friend.

From these interrogations, Ralph was able to build a detailed picture of morale across the German armed forces and in the bombed-out cities, as well as catching hold of the current German slang, derogatory nicknames, popular songs and films, and the current favourite drinks and cigarette brands. This information was used to brief the British propaganda radio broadcasts that were beamed into Europe and became ever more trusted as they revealed such a finely tuned awareness of their listeners' real lives. Ralph was such a master of the art of subtle interrogation that he was seconded to the United States Navy, helping establish systems that were both humane and efficient. Some of his work also touched on immediate tactical targets, such as the hunt for the *Bismark* and locating V1 and V2 missile bases. His last task in the navy, after victory, was identifying and interviewing German naval officers in prison camps before they were moved to the British zone and released. For at the end of the war, the Royal Navy took an almost fraternal interest in the fate of their old adversaries, which was not the case with the Russian army, then in triumphant occupation of Berlin.

The moment he was demobbed, the *Daily Mail* packed Ralph off as their India correspondent. Here, the run-up to independence and the partition of India was his main story. Molly, who knew India as a child, joined him and they were married in Delhi in January 1947. Over the next twenty years he reported from most of the hotspots of the Cold War: Korea, Suez, Algeria, Aden, Lebanon, Malaysia and Kenya. He was never part of the brat pack of journalists living together in an international hotel, but preferred to base himself in an ordinary house, be it an old Arab house in the centre of Beirut, a fisherman's cottage in the walls of Famagusta or an old courtyard house with a wind-tower in the Manama quarter of Bahrain. In London he stayed in the raffish old Cavendish Hotel.

Ralph always balanced the serious salaried work of a foreign correspondent with quixotic scientific expeditions. He was a recognised authority on lichens, and by nature an observer, an expert witness, not a political analyst. In 1945 he and the naturalist C. R. Stoner went off in search of a lost, dinosaur-like lizard that had reportedly been seen in a remote highland valley of Assam. Izzard's subsequent account, *The Hunt for the Buru*, concluded that the last of these four-metre lizards had died in 1940, though others continued to think they had been extinct for 66 million years. Another madcap exploit was pursuing John Hunt's 1953 Everest expedition all the way to base camp at 18,000 feet, without compass or map and wearing a pair of gym shoes. His book *The Innocent on Everest* was translated into nine different languages. The following year he set off to find the Yeti in the remote valleys of the Himalaya. Recounted in *The Abominable Snowman Adventure*, the story was worthy of Hergé's *Tintin*.

Such was the unusual stamp of the man who took his four young children off to walk the spine of the Lebanese mountains in 1957. Although his name is on the cover of *Smelling the Breezes*, it is mostly written by his wife, whose literary ambitions Ralph always supported and encouraged. *Smelling the Breezes* was Molly's first book and was published in 1959.

Molly Crutchleigh-Fitzpatrick had first met Ralph at Bletchley Park during the war. She had joined the FANY in 1939 and worked as a driver, at one point chauffeuring Duff Cooper, who introduced her to Sefton Delmer, who recruited her to the nascent Political Warfare Executive, a clandestine body set up to produce and disseminate both 'white' and 'black' propaganda. The propaganda staff were a talented lot, many seconded from the SOE, the BBC and

the Ministry of Information. Molly learned script writing, music recording, interrogation techniques and how to analyse reconnaissance photography. She thrived in this environment, which was, in effect, her university and quickly rose through the ranks to become a major. After the propaganda radio stations were closed in April 1945, their bilingual staff were retrained to interview and categorise prisoners of war.

Outwardly Major Molly Patricia Crutchleigh-Fitzpatrick must have appeared a very respectable figure at the end of the war, with her double-barrelled surname and her rank. Five generations of Molly's paternal family had lived in India, working as tea planters in the highlands of Assam and indigo planters in Bengal. Exotic when viewed at a distance, and shot through with Irish spirit, the immediate emotional details of her childhood were in fact not quite so secure.

Molly's father, Vere Fitzpatrick, had volunteered from India to serve in the First World War. He fought in the East African Rifles, was disabled by blackwater fever and was sent 'home' to England to recuperate. There he met Alice, with whom he had two children, Denis (1916) and Molly, born in St Ives in 1919. As a young man he tried a lot of different jobs while travelling the world, including a stint at the Ford factory in Chicago, studying modern mass production. He was a competent manager with a good grasp of accounts and labour relations. After his marriage and the birth of Denis, he took a job as manager of a sugarcane plantation in British Guyana and the young family settled near Georgetown. The heat and humidity of the country did not agree with Alice, and she returned to England for the birth of Molly. After Guyana he moved the family to India, where the children spent their early years. Their early childhood was spent surrounded by dogs, ponies and their father teaching them fishing and hunting. Molly shot her first and only crocodile under her father's guidance. It was subsequently made into a small attaché case and given to her on her eighth birthday. First Denis and then Molly were sent back to boarding schools in the United Kingdom. Molly found the transition to British school life difficult, and her parents eventually sent her to join Denis in Scotland at the Dollar Academy. Alice made regular trips back to England and Vere less frequently.

The marriage broke up in the 1930s, with Molly sent out to live with her father. Following his death in a car accident in 1937, she returned to England and was promptly sent to colleges in France (Cherbourg) and in Italy (Genoa) and then to friends in Hungary by her mother. This must have been a very difficult period, but it did equip her with languages.

The war had been a liberation for both Molly and her elder brother, Denis. It gave them both a sense of purpose that the confusing emotional environment of their childhood had failed to deliver. After the war, Denis worked in the Middle East for Shell. He did well for himself and generously provided for his mother financially, sending her hampers from Fortnum & Mason to mark all the important holidays. He was able to afford a flat in London and later acquired a house in Dorset where he spent his holidays fishing.

From Germany, as we have already heard, Ralph had exchanged his naval uniform for the linen suit of a foreign correspondent. His initial posting was to India, where Molly gave birth to Miles in September 1947. Ralph was always supportive of Molly's work and helped her first break into print journalism with a scoop reporting the funeral of Gandhi. Anthea was born during their next posting in Washington DC in March 1949. Their third child, Sabrina, was born in Cairo in September 1950, though her father was away at the Korean War at the time. Sebastian was born in Nicosia, Cyprus in October 1952. Earlier in 1952 on 'Black Saturday', the Egyptians had decided to burn out the hated British colonial presence from the city of Cairo and the Izzard family chose to rent a home in peaceful Cyprus to use over the long summers.

This was a halcyon time for Molly, surrounded by an intelligent group of expatriates in Cyprus including the historian Rupert Gunnis and the writer Lawrence Durrell. Her paternal cousin, Alan Ross (born in Calcutta 1922), was also making a name for himself as a writer at this time. The children played in the old harbour of Famagusta, swam off the empty sandy beaches or joined in the games of their boisterous Turkish-Cypriot neighbours. The house provided continuity, until they moved with their father to Beirut. Here they made friends with John Carswell (the art historian) and his American Peace Corps wife Peggy with her three children. There were also Kathleen Kenyon digging at Jericho, and a cheerful, life-enhancing colleague of Ralph's, Kim Philby, who made everyone laugh, and who kept in touch with his distinguished old father, the Hadji, St John Philby. St John had explored Arabia, served as an adviser to the Saudi kings, converted to Islam and written half a dozen books. Just then he was in retirement, living in the hills above Beirut with his young Palestinian wife and their two young boys. It was a complex world with many loyalties, but life in Beirut was very

good. The family swam in the sea-pool beside the St George's hotel and the children went to a little convent school, from which Miles moved at nine to be taught by the Jesuits.

This was the mood, the very full life, that Molly and Ralph wished to celebrate on their final exploration of Lebanon, walking the spine of the mountains with their four children. But *Smelling the Breezes* was a watershed moment. After the book was

published, life was never quite so carefree and easy again. Traumatic political events in the Middle East encouraged the *Daily Mail* to cut down its permanent overseas staff, sending them out instead from London when needed to the current crisis zone. The Izzard family, used to the physical and emotional warmth of the Levant, were sent home. They endured a series of freezing farmhouses, lent to them by concerned friends, including Kim Philby, who sent them to stay with his aunt in Crowborough. Eventually, much more out of accident than design, they settled in Tunbridge Wells in Kent. Ralph reluctantly cut his ties with the *Daily Mail*, immersed himself in making adventure travel films with Tom Stobart and David Attenborough for the BBC and then established himself as a freelancer for Reuters, living in an old courtyard house in Bahrain. The life was good, but his earnings were erratic. He was always back home for the summer holidays, but in terms of family life his wife Molly upheld the show. In the words of her daughter, she was 'strong' and a 'survivor'. But she was also talented. She wrote an evocative memoir, *A Private Life* (1963), a biography of Dame Helen Gywnn-Vaughn of the ATS, a history of the mercantile culture of the Gulf, *The Gulf: Arabian Western Approaches* (1979) and a controversial biography of Freya Stark, published in 1993.

Her four children all went off in their own directions, like the four points of the compass.

Miles was nicknamed 'Bo' (shortened from 'Bebop') by his nanny in Washington. He grew up recklessly handsome, with an imaginative sense of style and great elan. Although 'perfectly bright and intelligent', the constant movements of his childhood – 'off every three years' – meant that in later life he never settled nor found his way. He tried his hand at journalism, but it did not take, and his enigmatic, aloof nature made it difficult for him to form lasting relationships. He was never short of company, however, and as many of his friends remarked, he was well-read, had interesting views, a sardonic wit and a sharp repartee; it made him an endearing and amusing companion, much beloved by the women who nurtured and surrounded him.

Anthea (nicknamed Pampi) was another beauty but a restless spirit, by turns an actress, a hippy, a traveller, a radical protester, a searcher after enlightenment and a mother of two daughters. Anthea lived at various times of her life in a squat on Eel Pie Island, on a farm in Wales, in an ashram in India and then followed her guru to Texas. But her interest in the Kabbalah finally led her towards California and conversion to Judaism.

Sabrina, the third child, did not much care for any of her schools, but was always passionate about books. She made her own way

through life, working for the World of Islam Festival Trust, and then for ten years in the antiquarian book trade before becoming the owner of Hall's bookshop in Tunbridge Wells – one of England's most revered antiquarian bookshops. This also allowed Sabrina to keep an eye on her parents, to help them through their last years and to become the stable rock for the family. Ralph died in 1992 and Molly in 2004.

Sebastian, the youngest, 'was different from all the others' and made himself self-reliant from an early age, earning his own pocket money from a paper round (aged 12), and holiday jobs as a hotel

bell hop (aged 13). Bored by the lack of intellectual structure at his Steiner school in Forest Row, Sussex, he left to go to art school, graduating with a degree in Graphic Design from Chelsea School of Art. Here he developed a passionate interest in Japanese prints, and went on to study them at SOAS, successfully emerging with a Phd dissertation on the work of the print artist Utagawa Kunisada in 1980. From there he joined Christie's, who posted him to New York, where he remains. Leaving the auction world in 1997, he set up his own gallery specialising in Japanese art. He is a recognised authority on Ukiyo-e, 'the art of the floating world'.

Barnaby Rogerson
London 2022

ELAND

61 Exmouth Market, London EC1R 4QL
Email: info@travelbooks.co.uk

Eland was started in 1982 to revive great travel books which had fallen out of print. Although the list soon diversified into biography and fiction, all the titles are chosen for their interest in spirit of place. One of our readers explained that for him reading an Eland is like listening to an experienced anthropologist at the bar – she's let her hair down and is telling all the stories that were just too good to go into the textbook.

Eland books are for travellers, and for those who are content to travel in their own minds. We can never quite define what we are looking for, but they need to be observant of others, to catch the moment and place on the wing and to have a page-turning gift for storytelling. And they might do that while being, by turns, funny, wry, intelligent, humane, universal, self-deprecating and idiosyncratic. We take immense trouble to select only the most readable books and therefore many people collect the entire series.

Extracts from each and every one of our books can be read on our website, at www.travelbooks.co.uk. If you would like a free copy of our catalogue, please order it from the website, email us or send a postcard.